LABOUR AND
SCOTTISH
NATIONALISM

Michael Keating
and
David Bleiman

First published 1979 by
THE MACMILLAN PRESS LTD
London and Basingstoke
Associated companies in Delhi
Dublin Hong Kong Johannesburg Lagos
Melbourne New York Singapore Tokyo

British Library Cataloguing in Publication Data

Keating, Michael J
  Labour and Scottish nationalism.
  1. Nationalism – Scotland – History – 20th century
  2. Labor and laboring classes – Scotland – History
  – 20th century   3. Scotland – Politics and
  government – 20th century
  I. Title   II. Bleiman, David
  322′4′2′09411   DA826

ISBN 978-1-349-04680-5   ISBN 978-1-349-04678-2 (eBook)
DOI 10.1007/978-1-349-04678-2

LABOUR AND SCOTTISH NATIONALISM

To the many kind people in Scotland who
extended such a warm welcome to the authors

Contents

Acknowledgements

Many people have helped the authors in their work. Valuable advice, criticism and assistance were given by Chris Allen, John Barber, Jack Brand, Henry Drucker, Judith Ennew, Christopher Harvie, David Heald, Barry Jones, Gareth Stedman Jones, Ann Keating, James Kirkwood, the late George Lawson, Ian McAllister, Ian MacDougal, Ian Maclean, Don MacIver, James Milne, Henry Pelling, Richard Rose, Brian Wilson, the late Arthur Woodburn and Alf Young.

Welcome and hospitality were given by Mr and Mrs Chalmers Geoffrey and Marjorie Gowlett, Martin Hilland, Paddy and Peggy McCusker, everyone at the Labour Party Scottish Council and the Scottish Trade Union Congress, and the staff and students at Reith Hall of Residence, University of Strathclyde.

Thanks are further due to the Social Science Research Council for grants to David Bleiman and to the Nuffield Foundation for grants to Michael Keating; to Pauline Kelly, who typed the manuscript; to colleagues, especially library staffs, at North Staffordshire Polytechnic and Cambridge; and to the Mitchell Library, Glasgow and the National Library of Scotland.

Naturally, any errors of fact or of judgement remain the sole responsibility of the authors.

Preface

This book is derived from two research projects undertaken by the authors, at North Staffordshire Polytechnic and King's College, Cambridge, between 1975 and 1978. Inevitably, our work is influenced by our own political views and values and it is as well to state these at the outset. We are both active members of the Labour Party but are divided in our attitude to devolution. Michael Keating is a supporter of devolution to Scotland and, while critical of the performance of the Labour Government on the issue between 1974 and 1979, believes that the proposals of the Scotland Act 1978 provide a useful beginning for a general programme of devolution. David Bleiman, on the other hand, is an opponent of devolution.

However, we consider that our different views on the merits of the policy of devolution serve to strengthen rather than to weaken our analysis of the history of the issue. We believe that a careful historical analysis of the development of the labour movement in Scotland is essential to an understanding of its present position and that previous accounts have suffered from their attempts to combine such analysis with partisan polemic.

We start with a consideration of the relationship between nationalist and socialist movements, examining the philosophical rationale and basis of support of each. Then we describe the place of Home Rule in the origins of the Scottish labour movement. Chapter 3 examines the upsurge of nationalism in the movement around the time of the First World War and its subsidence as Scottish Labour became firmly committed to the United Kingdom. We then look at Labour's attitude to the Scottish question in the 1930s, finding that, contrary to the view of many writers, this was not a fruitful period for Scottish nationalism. In the same chapter, Labour's reactions to the Scottish National Party's successes in wartime by-elections and to the Covenant movement of the 1940s is examined. Chapter 5 takes us up to the present day, covering Labour and trade-union attitudes to the revival of nationalism since the late 1960s and the controversial decision of 1974 to adopt the policy of devolution. In the conclusion, we examine the options open to the movement at the present time. Here we depart from our agreed analysis to present the pro- and anti-devolution views as currently expressed within the labour movement.

We offer no blueprint for the constitutional future of the United Kingdom, but we do hope that, in addition to providing a historical analysis of a neglected area, our work will make some small contribution to public debate about the issues raised.

December 1978   *Michael Keating*
                                                  David Bleiman

1 Introduction

I. THE WORKING CLASS AND THE NATION

'The working men have no country.'
(Karl Marx and Friedrich Engels, *The Communist Manifesto*)

'The difference between inbred oppression and that which is foreign is *essential*.'
(Mazzini, *The Convention of Cintra*[1])

Nationalism and socialism stand out as the two great mass movements of the modern era, each with sweeping claims about the right way to organise human affairs. Their development and relationship to each other are a central part of modern politics. Yet politicians and scholars alike have continued to disagree on the extent to which they can make common cause or must necessarily conflict. It is to this question that we first turn.

At one level, nationalism and socialism have little in common. We are comparing cabbages and kings, two movements each with a distinctive rationale which ignores the claims of the other. A nationalist movement, viewed from the standpoint of its own rationale, is organised around the existence and development of a nation, a process which spans the centuries and the changing material organisation of society. Its interests thus appear to be 'above' all class interests, which merely express the interests of particular sections of society, interests which come and go as society develops, while the national identity is timeless. Starting from the ideal of national independence, a nationalist movement seeks support in all sections of society where it can be found. But, as Anthony Smith notes, 'the very classlessness of nationalist ideology facilitates its acceptance by different strata with conflicting aims. The result is several competing nationalisms within one movement.'[2] In Scotland, the Union of 1707 has come easily as a scapegoat for a variety of ills to many different people. Thus, what appears entirely principled in terms of its own ideology has led outsiders to see Scottish nationalism as 'the chameleon on the tartan rug', adopting, in turn, all colours of the social fabric on which it rests.

Labour and socialist movements, on the other hand, have developed from the interests of a social class whose interests are both wider and narrower than that of the nation. Within the nation, the working class need not share the interests and values of other classes, while it may have a common cause with the working class in other nations. The claims of class thus cut across and are superior to those of nation.

It is not surprising, then, that, in the age of mass politics, nationalism and socialism, with their rival views of how people are divided, should have come into conflict. The conflict can be traced back to the origins of modern nationalism in the French Revolution. The *Declaration des droits de l'homme et du citoyen* ('Declaration of the Rights of Man and Citizens') of 1789 laid down that 'The source of all sovereignty resides essentially in the nation'.[3] Thus, the conception of the state as the personal domain of the monarch, the doctrine of the *ancien regime*, was challenged by the assertion that sovereignty rested with the general will of 'the people', which was in turn identified as 'the French nation'. Thus the French revolution spawned a nationalist doctrine which was part of the revolutionary assault upon absolutism.

However, very early on, the generality of the ideology came under challenge. Babeuf, leader of the first communist revolt, in 1796, complained that the multitude 'sees in society only an enemy and loses even the possibility of having a country'.[4] As Hobsbawm has pointed out, 'on the whole the classical liberal bourgeois of 1789 (and the liberal of 1789–1848) was not a democrat but a believer in constitutionalism, a secular state with civil liberties and guarantees for private enterprise, and government by taxpayers and property-owners'.[5] Weitling identified property ownership as the key to participation in the nation: 'He alone has a country who is a property owner or at any rate has the liberty and the means to become one. He who has not that, has no country.'[6] This was the ancestry of Marx's famous dictum in the *Communist Manifesto* of 1848 that the worker has no country. Marx went on to claim that the rule of the bourgeoisie in all the advanced countries had reduced all the proletariat to the same condition – lacking property, dependent for their means of life on wage labour. For Marx, therefore, the struggle of the proletariat with the bourgeoisie was the same in content in all these countries, though he saw this struggle as taking a national form: 'Since the proletariat must first of all acquire political supremacy, must rise to be the leading class of the nation, must constitute itself as the nation, it is, so far, itself national, though not in the bourgeois sense of the word.'[7] Thus, the confident assumption of the French bourgeoisie that their interests amounted to the will of the sovereign nation was challenged by the socialist theory that the capitalist nation-state was only the nation of the propertied classes, and that a common international interest could be put forward as the true national interest by the working class.

Indeed, nationalism is itself a disruptive as well as a uniting force, because its very generality makes it susceptible to employment by contradictory interests. For example, nationalism could be used as an argument for creating a powerful nation-state (such as France) or for achieving independence for a small nationality within such a state (the Bretons, for example). Nationalism came to imply, in the nineteenth century, that every people with a collective identity should form a separate state. For example, Mill argued that 'Free institutions are next to impossible in a country made up of different nationalities' and that, therefore, 'the boundaries of governments should coincide in the main with those of nationalities'.[8] Mill clearly regarded Britain as now a uni-national state, but there was nothing to stop Britons on the Celtic fringe from using the same argument to justify the creation of governments based on their nationalities. Although a variety of criteria – common history, culture, ethnic composition and language, for example – were put forward as the constituents of nationality, the question of who is to arbitrate as to whether these differences are sufficient in population x to make x a nation with a right to independent statehood was not given a uniform answer by nationalist ideologues. Thus, the only thing which might be generally agreed is the answer given by Renan to his question 'What is a nation?', that a nation is a 'spiritual principle'.[9] And, if nationhood is a matter of the spirit, then nationalism may be used by any group wishing to assert, for a particular population, the right to statehood. Equally, it may be used to deny this right, by asserting that the population in question is in fact part of another nation.

Thus, even within the established nation-state, movements have emerged to challenge the organisation of politics on the basis of class and to assert the primacy of other divisions – whether cultural, religious or territorial.[10] Competition amongst these movements for the allegiance of the population has often produced severe tensions in the development of the modern state, particularly during extensions of the franchise and the entry of the working class into the political system. Until the recent re-emergence of ethnic and territorial conflict in Western societies,[11] the usual view among political scientists was that these tensions would ultimately be resolved by the organisation of politics on the basis of class.[12] Socialists and nationalists, too, have each made confident assertions about the outcome of these tensions, but both have tended too often to confuse prediction with prescription and to assume that their own preferred alignment is the inevitable outcome of the process of political development.

The nationalist answer to the dilemma is that territorial or cultural interests will come first, with class differences being settled within the framework of the essential unity of the nation. To this end, national traditions will often be presented as embodying an absence of class conflict and stressing consensus and the democratic resolution of differences. In some cases, a myth of a golden age, before the nation was riven with alien ideas of class strife, will be used to strengthen this image. Even on the left, the view that nationalism is the inevitable form of historical development has appeared. It is a major element in the thinking of Tom Nairn,[13] who believes that, far from denying the importance of modern nationalism, socialists should seek to lead it. More reluctantly, the Irish Labour movement earlier this century decided that the national question was primary and withdrew from the crucial 1918 election.[14]

However, nationalism in itself has rarely been enough to form a successful mass movement and has usually felt the need to compromise with class-based movements, adopting elements of their programmes in order to broaden its basis of support. Thus, in Ireland, Parnell was forced to take up the cause of agrarian radicalism,[15] while later on Sinn Fein adopted, without much conviction, a large part of Labour's social programme.[16] Of course, such concessions may further enhance nationalism's claims to embody within itself all such particularistic demands and to provide the means for their satisfaction, but to the outside observer they provide evidence of the weakness of nationalism alone as a mobilising force.

The socialist answer to the dilemma of political development has usually been that, because workers will fail to respond to cross-class nationalist appeals, class-based politics will inevitably characterise the modern age. Often this has taken the form of slogans such as Marx's 'The working men have no country', which are not so much descriptions of reality as calls to action, but a more sophisticated analysis is put forward by the Austrian socialist Otto Bauer, writing before the First World War. Bauer's work on the nationalities question stands apart from other writings of socialist theorists on the question because it attempts to show how the policy of the labour movement actually derives from its organisation and interests, rather than merely putting forward programmatic proposals for party policy. It is worth looking at in some detail because (a) the Austrian Social Democratic Party (like the British Labour Party) was based on the support of a strong trade union movement, and (b) for this reason, Bauer pays more attention to problems of national division and unity within the trade union movement, and their relation to nationality conflicts within the state, than other theorists in the socialist debate on the national question. Bauer also puts forward his analysis in a general manner, referring to principles of trade union organisation which the Webbs had derived from the British experience. Although his work is best known for the programme of national autonomy which was the subject of Lenin's polemical criticism, it is the underlying analysis of the development of working-class policy on nationalism which is most relevant to our study.

Bauer believed that the attitude of the young working class to the nation was determined by its instinctively revolutionary drive, generated in the aspirations of downtrodden humanity. Thus the worker is national, wherever the nation turns against its oppressors.[17] This attitude he characterised as one of 'naïve nationalism.' But, where nationalism is the policy of the classes which the proletariat hates as its exploiters, as in Germany, it is anti-nationalist, and its attitude one of 'naïve cosmopolitanism'. The naïve nationalism of some and the naïve cosmopolitanism of other national working classes gradually gives way to an international policy of the proletariat of all nations, based on a clear consciousness of class interests. This is because the workers of different parts of the same economic area (*Wirtschaftsgebiet*) have a common interest in the wages and conditions of labour which each enjoys. Taking the example of the German and Czech parts of Bohemia, Bauer claims

that the German workers (who were more strongly organised in
trade unions and had better conditions) have an interest in

(a) higher wages in Czech Bohemia, to prevent a flow of immigrant
    labour into German Bohemia, depressing wages there;
(b) higher wages in Czech Bohemia, to prevent the flow of capital
    there, which would cause unemployment in German Bohemia;
(c) the extension of trade-union organisation, unemployment
    insurance (a trade-union benefit) and of trade-union con-
    sciousness to the Czech workers, to prevent their use as a reserve
    army of labour to depress wages;
(d) development of an independent working-class party for the
    Czechs, to develop the Czech worker's sense of equal rights and
    dignity, in order that he refuse to be used as a cowering scab.

Thus, in place of the former naïve cosmopolitanism of the working
class, grounded simply in feelings of humanity, there develops the
internationalism of the mature working class, based on the
recognition of the need for the international solidarity of the class.
From this follows, first, the demand for the unity of workers of all
nations (within the common economic area) against their direct
class enemy; that the trade unions embrace the workers of all
nations; and that, within the unions, the workers of each nation
further the interests of the workers of all other nations as their own
interests. Secondly, because the working-class struggle is also
directed against the state, and for particular economic and other
policies which further the trade union struggle, it also follows that
here again, in political organisation, a common international policy
is demanded. 'Just as the position of the workers in the process of
production demands the international trade union movement, so
the position of the workers in the class state requires international
political class struggle.'[18] However, given the failure of workers in
the Austrian Empire to conform to this theory and to develop the
postulated degree of international solidarity, Bauer was driven to
explain this as a conflict between the 'logic' of identity of interest
and the 'psychology' of the workers, who perceived local interests as
contradictory. The latter were not their true interests but reflected
national conflicts imported into the labour movement from outside.
Thus Bauer too introduces value judgements into his analysis and
fails adequately to account for the emergence of the perceived
conflict of local interests amongst the workers.

In reality, the common interests of the working class only arose by a process of gradual historical development and organisation. Indeed, as Pelling points out,[19] for the first part of the nineteenth century 'to speak of a homogeneous "working class" in Britain' would be anachronistic; in reality there were, and people spoke of, different working classes, each with its own interests. Marx was able as early as 1848 to put forward the argument 'Workers of the world unite! You have nothing to lose but your chains!', but this was a political manifesto. The analysis upon which it was based was that the working class came into existence initially only as a 'class-in-itself' – that is to say, it could be defined as a class by reference to a common relationship, as wage labourers, to capitalist industry. At this stage, workers were divided by competition for employment, which could gradually be overcome by the process of combination in trade unions. Ultimately, it was envisaged that combination and formation of the workers into a united political party would create a 'class-for-itself' – that is, a class organised to promote its own common interests.

That local conflicts between groups of workers existed, recurred in different forms throughout the history of trade unionism, and could be associated with division of the movement on national lines was shown by the Webbs in their painstaking studies of British trade unionism, though the Webbs themselves often failed to realise the significance of their findings. The early trade clubs were typically composed of an isolated group of highly skilled journeymen, who were even more decisively marked off from the mass of the manual workers than from the small class of capitalist employers.[20] The Webbs found

little trace among such trade clubs of that sense of solidarity between the manual workers of different trades which afterwards became so marked a feature of the Trade Union Movement. . . . They exhibit more tendency to 'stand in' with their masters against the community, or to back them against rivals or interlopers, than to join their fellow-workers of other trades in an attack upon the capitalist class. In short, we have industrial society still divided vertically trade by trade instead of horizontally between employers and wage-earners. This latter cleavage it is which has transformed the Trade Unionism of petty groups of skilled workmen into the modern Trade Union Movement.[21]

Unlike the mediaeval craft guilds, the trade clubs did not remain confined to their local origins. The Webbs pointed out that this was because the localism of the trade union member, as distinct from that of the shopkeeper or small manufacturer, was not mainly based on local protectionism.

> What the urban Trade Unionist actually resists is not any loss of work to a particular locality, but the incessant attempt of contractors to evade the Trade Union regulations, by getting the work done in districts in which the workmen are either not organised at all, or in which they are working at a low Standard Rate.[22]

Thus, the attempt to stop work going out of a particular town gradually gave way to the attempt to ensure that, wherever work was done, minimum trade union rates were enforced.

> . . . the whole tendency of Trade Union history has been towards the solidarity of each trade as a whole. The natural selfishness of the local branches is accordingly always being combated by the central executives and national delegate meetings, in the wider interests of the whole body of the members wherever they may be working. Just in proportion as Trade Unionism is strong and well established we find the old customary favouritism of locality replaced by the impartial enforcement of uniform conditions upon all districts alike.[23]

However, the Webbs pointed out that the progress towards national union had been 'much hampered by differences of racial sentiment and divergent views of social expediency'.[24] They gave as an example of different views on social expediency the criticism by English tradesmen of the willingness of their Scottish counterparts to accept competitive piecework and habitual overtime, thus 'nibbling at the Standard Rate'. On the other hand, Scottish workmen criticised the extravagance of trade union expenditure in England and unduly restrictive regulations and methods. However, the Webbs attributed the resistance to the tendency towards complete national amalgamation to 'the sturdy Scotch determination – due partly to differences of administration but *mainly to racial sentiment* – not to be "governed from England" '[25] (emphasis added).

In this case the Webbs contradict their own previous argument, which discloses an underlying trade union impulse in the localism of the trade clubs. It is more consistent to argue that separate organisation of trade unions in Scotland and England was based on real differences of interests. For example, a class of workers enjoying better conditions and stronger union organisation in Scotland than their fellows in the same trade in England would have, other things being equal, an interest in maintaining separate union organisation on a Scottish basis. They would be reluctant to see the funds of their union used merely to help the English bring themselves up to the level already enjoyed in Scotland. Of course, it might be foreseen that, sooner or later, the Scottish workers would suffer from the competition of English labour at lower rates. Bauer's arguments about the interest of German workers in bringing up the level of the Czech workers to prevent undercutting of their own conditions are thus pertinent. However, this process might take some time, and it would normally only be when they found their own conditions under assault by the employers that the Scottish workers would recognise an interest in banding together irrespective of district of nationality with other workers in the same trade, in order to seek the enforcement of a common minimum standard within the industry. Thus, the conflict between local and common interests, even when it takes the form of a conflict between Scottish and common British interests, should not be seen as a conflict between 'illusory' interests or 'racial sentiment' and 'true' interests. It is a genuine conflict of material interests, which is only resolved to the extent that industrial development (combined with the effects of trade union organisation) causes a gradual equalisation of conditions within the same economic area.

Given that real differences of economic interest can separate the working classes of different areas, what are the implications for political nationalism? In describing the relation of the interests and organisation of the labour movement to the national conflicts in the society as a whole, Bauer sees the causal relation as flowing almost entirely from the society to the labour movement. National conflicts within the Empire gradually embroil the Austrian Social Democratic Party in conflicts between its nationally-based sections, which tend to become separate and conflicting parties. The division of the party, as the political form of the working-class movement, creates pressure on the trade unions, as the mass material basis of the movement, which in turn begin to be split on national lines. Within the trade unions, local conflicts which in reality have nothing to do with nationality take on the form of national conflicts and feed the growth of nationalist divisiveness within the movement. Thus, nationalism is seen as working its divisive way from the society, through the party, to the trade unions.

It may well be that this analysis was perfectly appropriate to Bauer's subject of study – the relation of the Austrian Social Democractic Party to the nationalities problem in the Austro-Hungarian Empire – but, as a general analysis, and especially in the British context, it is inadequate. It fails to consider the extent to which the working class itself, through the expression of its economic interests by means of trade union and political organisation, determines the content or even the outcome of national conflicts within the overall society, rather than simply being acted upon by them.

The way in which national interests arise directly out of local or common trade union economic interests can be shown by developing our example of the class of Scottish workers enjoying superior conditions and organisation to English workers in the same trade or industry. Their interest in industrial exclusiveness will carry over into the politics of the union. For example, a Scottish-based union will find it very expensive to make representations to government bodies located in England, and to send delegations to offices or to a parliament in London. More fundamentally, it will desire that any government agencies responsible for regulating or investigating any aspect of conditions of employment be based on Scotland, rather than on Britain as a whole, in order to avoid any tendency to bring down conditions enjoyed in Scotland to the English level. Home Rule for Scotland, at least in the sense of separate government agencies based in Scotland (for instance, a separate labour department of the Board of Trade, a separate wages board, and so forth) is therefore likely to appeal to such a union. To a greater or lesser extent, therefore, the overall movement for Home Rule or national independence may reflect the interests of such a union.

By way of contrast, if the conditions of the Scottish workers in the industry come under assault and they seek, jointly with other British workers, to enforce a common minimum throughout Britain, they are likely to do so in both their industrial and their political organisation. They will seek amalgamation or federation on an all-

British basis, centralise their funds for strike support and other benefits, and seek to bargain collectively at national level within the industry. But they will also be likely to centralise their bureaucracy for the purpose of lobbying government agencies, obtaining representation on relevant bodies, and seeking legislative action. Home Rule is therefore likely to be seen as something of a threat to the solidarity of the union, certainly if it is understood to mean that Government intervention affecting conditions of employment will be applied separately in Scotland. The political activity of the unions will be directed towards common objectives shared by its members throughout Britain.

Why should differences of interest between sections of the working class in different regions be expressed in specifically nationalist terms? Where class and nationality are perceived as being the same, nationalism can enter the labour movement as a reinforcement of the basic class divide. In colonial territories, racial discrimination often produces a cultural division of labour in which high status and highly rewarded occupations are reserved for expatriates from the colonising nation, while the natives are restricted to complementary manual labour. For example, in South Africa this is formalised in a system of job reservation. In such a situation, nationalist and working-class politics can go hand in hand. Hechter's 'internal colonialist' thesis[26] attempts to apply this model to *national* development and specifically to the development of the United Kingdom, where the persistence of nationalism in the 'Celtic fringe' is explained by reference to a cultural division of labour. As we shall show, the development of capitalist industry and of an industrial working class on *both* sides of the border makes this type of analysis inapplicable in the case of Scottish nationalism. However, class and nationalist politics may still go together where the working class is numerically larger and/or politically more advanced and cohesive in one part of the state. The class enemy may then appear to be primarily foreign, and class and national boundaries may be confused by political rhetoric. National independence or a measure of autonomy may even be a tactical necessity for the advance of the working class.

Finally, just as a movement based primarily on territorial claims may find it necessary to compromise with movements organised on other bases, so a labour movement, based on the organised working class, may at various stages of development be forced to take on board other demands. It will face the need to determine the interests of the movement on a whole range of outside issues which have not arisen directly from trade union experience but from the society at large. For example, in pressing for favourable legislation from the Liberal Party, trade unionists not only formed a political lobby within that party, but also became associated with the broader politics of the party, and with other interests which the party represented. This problem by no means disappeared with the formation of an independent Labour Party. For the new party was not established overnight, nor was it purely and simply a trade union party. While trade union and working-class interests were placed in the forefront, and were the motive for the formation of the party, the Labour Party also had to concern itself with the problems affecting other sections of society on which it had to draw for electoral and political support. It also represented the worker in his role not merely as a trade unionist, but also as a member of society with interests other than those represented through the unions. Hence, the party tended to become committed to alliance with a variety of popular causes, and where nationalism was popular we should naturally expect this to be taken up. Thus, nationalism could find its way into the politics of the movement from outside as well as directly arising from local trade union interests.

In general, the stronger the working class and the more powerful its weight in the society, both as an industrial and as an electoral force, the more a working-class party can base its policy on the interests of the class, and the less it is necessary to temper and compromise this policy by means of alliances for the purpose of building up a viable electoral alternative to the established parties. To the extent that elections can be fought and won on the basis of policies appealing simply to the common interests of the working class in Britain as a whole, nationalist movements may be virtually ignored and consigned to the fringes of political life. This is an extreme case, but another possibility is that the party, though taking up a nationalist cause for its popular electoral value, may give it an altogether new content within the context of its overall programme. Superficially this will look similar to the adoption of a nationalist policy as a compromise with a powerful nationalist movement which is a significant electoral threat. Therefore, it is the historical circumstances and context, and not merely the programmatic commitment, which we must look at to decide what was really happening when Keir Hardie, Tom Johnston or Willie Ross espoused the cause of Scottish Home Rule.

Thus, neither the nationalist nor the usual socialist account is able satisfactorily to explain the relationship between the organised working class and nationalism. History has shown neither international working-class solidarity nor cross-class nationalism to be inevitable. The pattern of development must depend on the way a working-class movement develops, how it formulates its goals and its strategy, the changing economic relationships between territories, and the presence or absence of competing political movements. It is these which must be considered when examining the attitude of the labour movement in Scotland to the national question.

II. THE PEASANT'S STOCKPOT: POLITICAL THOUGHT AND POLICY IN THE LABOUR PARTY

Our second great difficulty in relating the debate on nationalism to developments in the British labour movement is the nature of the ideology and thought of the British Labour Party. We must therefore briefly consider the nature of Labour's political thought and the way in which it formulates its policy. The British Labour Party has developed primarily on the basis of the organised working class but has never been an exclusively class-based party. Nor has it drawn its political thought from a single, coherent ideology. Instead, developing as a federal party, an alliance of trade unionists, socialists, co-operators and a diversity of other radicals, it has drawn its thought from all the elements in its make-up and from the groups with which it has made common cause. Labour's political thought has been described as a 'peasant's stockpot', a mixture of relics to which new ingredients are intermittently added.[27] Nothing is removed, but old ingredients are gradually diluted by the addition of new ones. There is no clear ideological framework to which ideas can be related and by which they can be tested for consistency; so, within the movement and even within individuals, inconsistencies and contradictions are common. This has led more cynical commentators to the conclusion that the Labour Party has no ideology, that the movement is infinitely adaptable to the needs of electoral expediency. Such a view is too simple. The tradition does set limits to what is acceptable, and new ideas which cannot be supported by reference to one of the elements in the tradition will not usually be adopted.

Some of the trends within the Labour Party are directly contradictory. Where these are matters of abstract principle or when the party is remote from power, this does not matter. As the party has approached office, however, one trend has usually prevailed. Two sets of opposing trends particularly interest us here: those relating to Labour's view of the state and those relating to centralisation. The anti-state tradition derives partly from nonconformist values of self-help and independence, and partly from the influence, on the left, of non-statist varieties of socialism. The debt of many of the early leaders to nonconformity has frequently been commented upon. Particularly in the early days of the movement, it led to an emphasis on individual self-improvement and the solidarity of the community rather than reliance on a remote and impersonal state. On the left, the anti-state tradition has not completely died, but it has never been as strong as in the years before the First World War, when varieties of syndicalism gained their widest appeal. On the other hand, we have the statist tradition, based on a belief that the state is itself politically neutral and can be captured by workers and socialists and used to advance the cause. It has been pointed out[28] that there has been a tendency in times of prosperity for the unions to espouse self-help or anti-state socialism, while in depression they have looked to the state for help. Thus, Bealey has detected a resurgence of anti-state socialism in the boom following the First World War. Statist ideas became more generally accepted with the onset of the Depression, which coincided with the advance of the Labour Party following the extension of the franchise in 1918. Then, the possibility of Labour's gaining control of the state became real; and, as the party neared power, it concerned itself increasingly with practical policies and less with general visions of the future. The statist tradition finally triumphed with the adoption of the policies of planning and nationalisation in the late 1920s and 1930s, following the Soviet Five Year Plans, and examples of public ownership in the Commonwealth.[29] Another change of emphasis apparent once Labour had established itself as one of the major parties in the state and as a party of government, was a diminishing concern with the apparatus of government or the constitution and an increasing emphasis on what was to be done by government once Labour was in possession. This change of emphasis can be traced to the advent of universal franchise, but it perhaps owes more to the arrival of more immediate and pressing items on the political agenda. When

Labour at last arrived in government, constitutional issues receded into the background. From our point of view, the significance of the growth of statism in the labour movement is that it is much easier to conceive of Home Rule for Scotland in a state performing a minimal role than in a complex and bureaucratic regime. Indeed, where values of local and community solidarity are at a premium, Home Rule is likely to be a general demand. Once the state assumes major responsibilities for the distribution of resources, a degree of centralisation becomes inevitable.

On the issue of the centralisation of the state itself, Labour has inherited contradictory traditions. On the one hand, there is belief in the virtues of local self-government as a democratic form of organisation. In the early days of the movement, practical intervention to improve the lot of working people was largely the province of progressive local authorities, and thinkers such as the Webbs were impressed with the potentialities of the 'gas and water socialism' practised in cities such as Birmingham and Glasgow. In Glasgow the achievements of the City Corporation[30] were a source of inspiration to many of the early leaders of the Independent Labour Party.[31] Some of the early Fabians had made proposals for decentralising government with proposals such as that of the 'new heptarchy',[32] but their advocacy of devolution soon came into conflict with their collectivism. The Webbs' attempt to solve the problem by means of functional as opposed to territorial devolution never gained wide acceptance, and with them serious consideration of the problem by the Labour intelligentsia practically came to an end. In the modern era, some thought has again been given to the question as socialists have grappled with the problems of democratising the massive state apparatus which they have largely been responsible for creating. They have encountered two major obstacles: the difficulties of promoting local autonomy in a state where key decisions on resource allocation must, in the interests of equity, be taken centrally; and the problem of controlling and counterbalancing a private sector which in modern times has become increasingly centralised and, indeed, multinational. In addition, the debates on how to democratise the increasingly technical decision-making process have had a territorial dimension.

Within the Labour tradition, then, there has always been room for decentralist ideas and, despite the frequent characterisation of Labour as a centralist party – which, on the basis of its action, is an apt one – decentralist views are regarded as ideologically respect-

able and can boast a good pedigree. This is as well for the fortunes of
the party, which has often had to incorporate territorial demands
into its policy programme, demands which have arisen both within
and outside the movement itself. Labour's ability to respond to these
demands has also been eased by the failure of the issue of
centralisation to fall into the left–right mould which shapes most
other divisions within the party. The left–right cleavage, a division
of philosophy, politics and personality which has produced what
could almost be described as two cultures within the Labour Party,
is fundamental to any understanding of the way in which it responds
to new issues and demands. Most contentious issues within the
movement, although they may not initially be presented in left–
right terms, soon fall into the mould. A recent example is that of the
EEC, which at first divided both right and left. Gradually, however,
right-wingers graduated to the pro camp and left-wingers to the
antis, so that the final confrontation, in the 1975 referendum,
assumed the character of a set-piece battle between right and left,
each side deploying arguments going well beyond the immediate
issue of Common Market membership. Where a confrontation
assumes a left–right form, the outcome will be determined by the
balance of forces within the party and not by the issue itself.
Decentralisation, however, has attracted advocates of both right
and left, both finding ideological justification in the traditions of the
movement. Opponents, too, have come from both camps, those on
the left preaching the necessity for international solidarity of the
workers and those on the right arguing the need for building up the
apparatus of the centralised state.

Labour's often pragmatic attitude to questions of peripheral
nationalism may owe something to its failure to develop a coherent
ideology of the British state. It has been argued that one of the
consequences of the expansion of Empire so soon after the creation
of the United Kingdom was that no specifically British or UK
nationalism developed. Instead, loyalty was given to the wider
Empire, the decline of which revealed the absence of a sense of UK
identity. Nevertheless, it does appear that the Conservative Party
has developed a set of beliefs in which the Union has an independent
value. Its attitude in the past to Ireland and, more recently, to
Scotland, is evidence of this. On the Labour side, however, the
Union is defended in the case of Northern Ireland not at all and in
the case of Scotland by reference to the need for unity of the
movement and the working class or by a series of pragmatic

calculations. The former, if stated so bluntly, is really an argument
for internationalism, while the latter expresses only a contingent
support for the maintenance of the state. Labour politicians and
their supporters do have some emotional attachment to the UK, or
at least Britain, and a revulsion for the idea of separatism, but what
is lacking is a coherent means of defending and articulating this in
political debate, and an understanding of what support for the UK
should mean in practice. The national symbols – the monarchy, the
flag, patriotism, the race – are the possession of the Conservatives
and Labour lacks anything to match them. Most of the time this
does not matter, but, when faced with challenges to the state,
whether from peripheral nationalisms or from the supranationality
of the EEC, the Labour response is confused and uncertain.

Of course, the actual process of policy-making in the Labour
Party is complex, involving the interaction of the leadership, the
rank and file and the unions, each with its own objectives and
priorities. The aim of the party leadership has generally been to
attain and retain power and to make Labour a 'natural' governing
party. This has involved a 'national' approach, seeing virtually the
whole population as its potential constituency and being prepared
to make compromises between various divergent interests in order
to build the widest possible coalition. Survival in power may dictate
to the leadership compromises with forces which have no place in
the Labour coalition – as the 1968 Commonwealth Immigration
Act (the 'Kenyan Asians Act') shows. Its ability to compromise with
populist causes, however, is limited by the necessity to hold together
the Labour coalition itself. This is not always easy. Gaitskell was
unable to carry the rank and file behind him on unilateralism or
Clause Four, while Wilson in government failed to carry the party
or the unions over *In Place of Strife.*

The party rank and file are a very heterogeneous group. They
include loyalists, for whom 'socialism is what a Labour government
does' and also people whose counter-establishment tendencies are so
well developed that they feel profoundly uneasy when the party is in
office and are much happier in opposition. In many ways, the rank
and file, whose stake in governmental office is less than that of the
other two groups, are the conscience of the party and the least easy
to swing behind any change of policy. Because the leadership
depends on these voluntary activists to keep alive party organisation
in the country, it cannot afford constantly to alienate them on those
matters which arouse the strongest feeling, where ideological beliefs

are most deeply held – though, in government, their tolerance can be pushed a long way.

The trade unions' interest in general policy matters is patchy and sporadic and largely confined to the leadership. Union activists at shop-steward or branch level tend to be more interested in day-to-day collective bargaining issues. Very often, then, union policy on political matters is made by the leadership and then endorsed by the membership, either by a resolution at the union's conference or simply through being incorporated in the executive's annual report, which is, in turn, accepted by the conference. Traditionally, union influence at the Labour Party conference has been used to support the leadership, except on matters of direct trade-union interest, such as wages policy. An exception to this occurred in the 1960s, when, for a time, the big unions, under left-wing leadership, took an independent line, but by the early 1970s the mutual interest of party and union leadership was so strong that the unions were again prepared to support the party on most issues in order to secure the return of a Labour government which could provide them with the concessions they wanted in their own sphere. As we shall see, the issue of devolution was, at one time, considered vital for union interests in Scotland, but it has usually been considered as a political (as opposed to industrial) matter which was not at the forefront of their concerns. Thus, the union leadership has, in recent years, had a fairly free hand on the devolution question and has used it to support the Labour Party leadership. One must not, of course, oversimplify the unions' position. The Labour Party is only a small part of their concerns and, arguably, no longer their main channel of influence. In any case, not all trade unionists are members of the Labour Party. In Scotland, particularly, there is a strong Communist element, which has tended to see the industrial and political struggle as one and has often flirted with Scottish nationalism. On the other hand, amongst Labour trade unionists, there are many with a broad political outlook, and in Scotland these have often given serious consideration to the devolution issue. So the union leadership, like the Labour Party leadership, has at times found itself faced with conflicting demands.

Despite appearances, sections of the labour movement to the left of the Labour Party have been no more consistent in their policy and have tended to be equally pragmatic. The Communist Party, unlike Labour, interprets its policy in terms of a definite ideology. Its attitude towards nationalism is inevitably justified by reference to principles laid down by Lenin in his polemics on the national question. The party was founded as an explicitly British party and the Scottish socialist republicanism of John Maclean was rejected. This was consistent with Lenin's doctrine of the right of self-determination of nations. Lenin had argued for total centralisation of the working-class movement. He opposed political decentralisation, but argued that in certain cases the working-class party should recognise that a nation had the right of self-determination to the point of secession. He argued that this right applied to countries where a 'bourgeois-democratic' national revolution had not been completed:

> The epoch of bourgeois-democratic revolutions in Western continental Europe embraces a fairly definite period, approximately between 1789 and 1871. This was precisely the period of national movements and the creation of national states. When this period drew to a close, Western Europe had been transformed into a settled system of bourgeois states, which, as a general rule, were nationally uniform states. Therefore, to seek the right to self-determination in the programmes of West-European socialists at this time of day is to betray one's ignorance of the ABC of Marxism.[33]

Lenin examined the reasons why Marx had made an exception in the case of Ireland: 'In England the bourgeois revolution had been consummated long ago. But it had not yet been consummated in Ireland . . . .'[34] Therefore, in the absence of a socialist revolution in England, which he had expected would liberate Ireland, Marx had supported the bourgeois-democratic national movement which had arisen there. Lenin never sought to extend this exception to include Scotland, and the Communist Party of Great Britain did not in its early years accord the right of secession to Scotland. Nor was the party noticeably active in the labour movement's campaign for Home Rule, adopting at times a highly centralist stance.

However, in later years the party found that Lenin's doctrine could be interpreted more flexibly, so as to allow adaptation to an environment in which nationalism has become a potent force. The right of self-determination has been taken as applying to *all* nations, so that the party has been able to gesture benevolently in the direction of Scotland's nationhood and national rights. Simultaneously, the unity of the working-class movement has been asserted as a fundamental principle. The apparent contradiction between these two principles has been overcome by the argument that the labour movement, rather than leaving the national aspirations of the working class in the hands of reactionary petty-bourgeois elements, should place itself at their head and give them a socialist and democratic character. By these means the Communist Party has been able to adopt as pragmatic an approach to devolution as the Labour Party. Indeed, the distance of the Communist Party from the problems of political power and the role of the leadership in deciding the 'line' has enabled it frequently to outbid the Labour Party by adopting a more radical devolution policy. Because of the strength of the Communist Party in the Scottish trade union movement, particularly in the Scottish Trades Union Congress, this has been a further source of pressure upon Labour Party policy.

Home Rule for Scotland has been on the political agenda for a very long time. It predated the emergence of an independent labour movement and was one of the issues which the emergent movement had to confront. Therefore, to understand the relation of the Scottish working class to early movements for independence or Home Rule, and the place of these themes in the movement's ideological background, we must now turn to the origins of independent Labour in Scotland and to the emergence of Home Rule as an issue, in the nineteenth century.

2 Home Rule and the Origins of the Scottish Labour Movement

I. SCOTLAND AND THE UNION

The Union of England and Scotland in 1707, concluded amid bitter controversy, has seldom been free from challenge. It has been central to Scotland's political and economic development at every turn, while the tradition of independent statehood prior to 1707 has always pointed to an alternative line of advance. The Union has always been open to attack by any group finding itself politically excluded; and, as the benefits of union were not, and rarely have been, equally distributed among all classes and at different periods benefited different groups, Scottish nationalism has historically been able to find a diverse range of advocates, from the most extreme conservatives to the most advanced radicals.

The Treaty of Union itself was the immediate product of the exclusion of developing Scottish mercantile interests from England's expanding imperial trade, together with worries on the part of English Whigs of a Jacobite restoration; during the eighteenth century, challenges to it came mainly from the old clan society in the Highlands. The defeat of the Jacobites in 1745 and the harrying of the clans were firmly backed by the Lowland middle classes, and for the next hundred years Scottish nationalism was largely confined to Tory romantics of vaguely Jacobite sympathies, while commercial interests in Glasgow and Edinburgh concentrated on exploiting the opportunities which union had opened up. These were certainly plentiful. The woollen trade may have suffered, but trade in cattle and linen and, particularly, Glasgow's tobacco trade expanded rapidly. Capital accumulated in the tobacco trade and, later, in the sugar and cotton trades flowed into mining, transport improvements, textile production and, later, iron production and railway building. In the period 1880–1914 the Scottish economy expanded dramatically in those sectors of heavy industry most associated with Britain's predominance as an imperial and exporting power. In 1885 ten firms in Scotland produced 20 per cent of Britain's steel output. After 1870 Clydeside replaced the Thames as the main centre of British shipbuilding, and, associated with this and with the railways, heavy engineering also expanded.

While Scotland's specialisation in heavy industry was to its eventual disadvantage, to argue, as Michael Hechter has recently done, that this proves that 'development occurred in a largely dependent mode' and that 'England alone developed a diversified industrial economy'[1] is to attribute malicious powers of clairvoyance to the process of historical development. Far from being exploited as a colony by English capital, Scotland by 1880 was a part of the advanced capitalist economy of 'the workshop of the world', based largely on capital accumulated from its own colonial trade, commercial agriculture and from the new industries themselves as they developed. The process of industrialisation did, however, produce a new force, the industrial working class, which in due course had to decide its attitude to the Union.

As for the Highlands, after 1745 the clan chieftains lost interest in nationalism. Englishmen and Lowland Scots alike were convinced that the Highlands must be 'civilised'. The Jacobite clans were disarmed and the wearing of the kilt was forbidden. Jacobite estates were confiscated (although restored in 1784). But the most permanent change was the destruction of the clan system of land tenure in 1747, when Highland land law was made the same as Lowland: hereditary jurisdictions were abolished, and the chiefs converted into landlords with a right of private property in the clan lands.

Having failed to preserve their old way of life as leaders of fighting clans, the chiefs now used their new property rights to turn their land over to commercial agriculture, irrespective of the old obligations to the clansmen who farmed it.

In the period 1800–20, the landlords introduced sheep farming, mainly for wool. This enabled them to obtain high rents from commercial farmers, but required large farms to support the flocks and necessitated the 'clearance' of the original landholders. The clansmen were retained as small tenants, raising cattle and growing crops on smallholdings. Their rents were raised to a level which forced them to work as wage labourers for their landlord, collecting kelp – a seaweed used to provide fertiliser – during the kelping season, or as fishermen. Thus originated the crofting system, a system which enabled the tenant to obtain part of his sustenance from the land, while forcing him to obtain the remainder by seasonal or casual wage labour. Invariably the clansmen were removed from the best land, which was enclosed for sheep farming, while they were resettled as crofters on worse land, usually near the coast, where they could fish and collect kelp. The response of the clansmen – emigration – was virtually eliminated by the 1803 Passenger Vessels Act, introduced because the crofters were of vital economic importance as wage labourers to their landlords. Population expanded, encouraged by the demand for labour and the introduction of the potato as the staple crop, which made subsistence possible on a potato diet.

In the 1820s substitutes for kelp became available, and from 1827 kelping declined drastically. The crofters now became a redundant population, unable to pay the rents demanded; and the landlords began to evict them, to encourage them to emigrate, or to resettle them on worse land still. The land was then let for more commercial sheep farms. Thus, by the 1840s the crofters were completely dependent on potato farming on their smallholdings. In consequence, the potato famine was, in the words of the historian of the crofting community, 'an economic rather than a biological catastrophe'.[2] The famine accelerated the conversion of land to sheep farming, the clearances, and emigration. As a result the population declined drastically.

The 1860s and 1870s were a period of stability, during which the position of those crofters who had escaped eviction after the famine became more secure, although the land they rented was inferior, insufficient and exhausted. They benefited from the rising price of cattle in the 1860s, which provided them with greater cash income, while in the 1870s the severe depression of Highland sheep farming brought an end to the practice of adding crofters' common grazings to sheep farms. The crofters were still dependent on wage labour to supplement their income, the main activities being seasonal harvesting in the Lowlands, seasonal work on the sheep farms, and domestic service for their daughters. By the 1870s the expansion of the fishing industry brought improved wages for fishermen and herring girls.

Nevertheless, at the start of the 1880s, as Hunter says,

crofters had little cause to be satisfied with the conditions in which they lived. Their houses were little more than hovels. They had no security of tenure. On being deprived of their holdings they received no compensation. They depended for their livelihood on wages earned far from home. Above all, they did not have enough land. In the 1880s, when crofters at last launched a concerted attack on Highland landlordism, all these grievances came very strongly to the fore. And all of them, especially the lack of land, stemmed ultimately from the agrarian system which commercial landlordism had itself created.[3]

The relationship of this system to the Union soon came into question. Thus arose challenges to the Union from radical forces which we examine in section IV below.

However, early Scottish radicalism had little connection with nationalism. The French Revolution was warmly supported by radicals and reformers in Scotland, from the Reform Burgesses of Aberdeen, who pledged the Estates General at their annual dinner in June 1789, to Robert Burns, who as exciseman despatched to the Constituent Assembly four carronades taken from a captured smuggler; but the movement in Scotland was linked to that in England. In 1792 came the formation of the Society of the Friends of the People, which was in touch with the London Corresponding Society (founded by Thomas Hardy, a native of Falkirk) and shared the aim of obtaining Parliamentary reform. In October 1793 the third General Convention of the Scottish Friends of the People was joined by a few delegates from England and declared itself the British Convention of Delegates Associated to Obtain Universal Suffrage and Annual Parliaments, indicating that Scottish national objectives were not part of this democratic movement.

In the years of economic dislocation following the end of the Napoleonic Wars in 1815, there was a fresh wave of unrest, in particular amongst the distressed handloom weavers. Once again popular movements for political reform were forcibly suppressed. The Radical Rising (or 'War') in Scotland in 1820 was part and parcel of the movement which had produced Peterloo (where eleven members of a peaceful political demonstration were massacred) a year earlier. A Committee of Organisation for forming a Provisional Government called a general strike, in which 60,000 men participated. The ensuing riots were quelled by the yeomanry, and a special commission sentenced twenty-four to death, although ultimately only three men were hanged.

The interpretation of the Radical Rising given by modern nationalists, with the benefit of hindsight, is exemplified by Billy Wolfe: 'Looking back, one can clearly identify the source of the oppression against which they fought as English imperialism, aided and abetted by the Scottish land-owning and capitalist classes which, in the main, were subservient to English domination.'[4]

A recent account portrays the agitation for reform of the Westminster Parliament as tripartite nationalism, alleging that there were plans for separate Scottish, English and Irish assemblies.[5] But, as a reviewer commented, 'the rebels of Glasgow and the West were orientated towards England, shared the problems of the Northern English industrial population and shared the hopes of the English radical reformers.'[6]

The next wave of popular pressure for Parliamentary reform was in 1831–2. In 1831 there were election riots in Scottish and English cities alike. In July 1832 the Scottish Bill for Parliamentary Reform received the royal assent and a jubilant procession marched through Edinburgh.

Throughout the reforming agitation, links can thus be traced between the Scottish and English movements, based on common interests in overthrowing the rotten boroughs and the power of landlordism. After 1832, the elections on the reformed franchise established Liberal supremacy in Scotland, which was unchecked until the split over Irish Home Rule in the 1880s. In the period of the reform agitation it was the Tory landed gentry and nobility who fostered the Scottish national spirit. Aristocratic nationalism found its literary expression in Sir Walter Scott, who enshrined much of the mythology of modern Scottish nationalism in his novels, arranged the royal visit to Edinburgh in 1822 and the associated revival of tartanry, and in 1826 wrote a series of letters under the pseudonym of Malachi Malagrowther which led to the withdrawal of a Bill forbidding the Scottish banks to issue notes. Scott's attitude to the radical democratic movement is indicated by the fact that he was howled down by a radical mob in the course of campaigning against electoral reform.[7]

In the period after 1832 it begins to be possible to trace the support of trade unions for the further reform of the franchise. In the early 1830s the Glasgow United Committee of Trades Delegates, a forerunner of the Trades Council, demonstrated in favour of

Parliamentary reform, and in 1834 the Trades of Glasgow and
Edinburgh protested against the threatened displacement of the
reforming Whig ministry. The Chartist movement was linked with
organised sections of adherents by trades – for instance, the coopers,
masons, shoemakers, coachmakers and tailors – because the trade
unions, weakened by the slump of the late 1830s, were turning to
political reform as an alternative to economic organisation.

Scottish Chartism was independently organised and had its own
'distinctive characteristics, derived from national peculiarities and
traditions, which link it with the covenanters and "Political
Martyrs" of the revolutionary period', according to Marwick.[8] The
1824 Chartist Petition included a request for Home Rule in Ireland,
showing that the movement (in Britain as a whole) was alive to the
special needs of Ireland. It has been said that Scottish Chartism,
with its air of respectability, non-violence and moral idealism based
on Christianity, was less independent of the middle classes than the
movement in England. Alexander Wilson points out that the major
issue of the day was the struggle for the repeal of the Corn Laws, and
that the Chartists were not hostile to middle-class organisations
struggling for the same objectives as themselves. It was the Tories
and aristocracy who were regarded fundamentally as the enemy of
the working classes.[9] Thus, despite the distinctive characteristics of
the movement, there are no grounds for thinking that Scottish
Chartism was in any sense a nationalist movement, since nationalism at this time would imply an alliance with the landlordism,
romantic Toryism and opposition to reform.

When, in the 1860s, Parliamentary-reform agitation was renewed, the trades councils began to take a leading part. Glasgow
Trades Council, established in 1858, gave the lead in an address of
1861 which called upon the trade societies to involve themselves in
politics. Immediately on receipt of the Glasgow address, the
Edinburgh council, reversing an earlier decision that politics was
not a subject it could rightly consider, made contact with the
middle-class reform committees in the city. In 1866 it was the
Edinburgh Trades Council which initiated the local Parliamentary-reform campaign, with a demand for manhood suffrage.[10]

In the early part of the nineteenth century, then, most of the
energies of Scottish radicals went into the struggle for Parliamentary reform, while after 1832 they were directed into
Liberalism, which began a long period of ascendancy. Not until the

slight revival of nationalism in mid-century was any connection between radical and nationalist ideas suggested. According to Hanham, modern Scottish nationalism was first formulated by three groups of people: Glasgow businessmen who felt that the needs of Scotland were neglected and that insufficient Parliamentary time was devoted to Scottish affairs; the Scottish Tory literary establishment in Edinburgh, who were obsessed by the attempt to revive old glories; and a handful of radicals, such as Duncan McLaren and the Revd James Begg. In 1853 McLaren and Begg, along with the Tory romantics, were involved in the National Association for the Vindication of Scottish Rights.[11] While this collapsed with the start of the Crimean War, nationalism was kept alive on the romantic side by the erection of the Wallace Monument and the campaign against the use of the word 'England' for Britain, and on the practical side by the campaign for a Secretary for Scotland, ultimately successful in 1885.

II. RADICALS AND HOME RULE

It was the revival of radical Liberalism following the franchise reforms of 1867 and 1884 which established the link between Scottish nationalism and radicalism. Scottish Liberalism had for most of the nineteenth century been dominated by the Whiggish east, until in 1876 a radical West and South of Scotland Liberal Association was formed. In 1885, following Joseph Chamberlain's example, Scottish radicals formed the National Liberal Federation of Scotland. This put forward a programme based on the current radical agenda, demanding reform of Parliamentary procedure, of the House of Lords, of the land system and of local government, and disestablishment of the Church of Scotland.[12] Around this time, radicals in Scotland and Wales were noting with envy the discipline and success of Parnell's Irish Party and began to see Home Rule as a possible way of advancing causes such as disestablishment, temperance and land reform, while liberating the energies of the Scottish people for further democratic advance.

Disestablishment had been a live issue since the Disruption of 1843, when one-third of the clergy had seceded from the Church of Scotland to form the Free Church. The secession followed an unsuccessful campaign by evangelicals to restore election of ministers, which had been replaced by lay patronage by Parliament in

1712, in clear violation of the Act of Union. James Hunter has shown how the Disruption was crucial in the formation of a crofting community in the Highlands, which began to conceive of its own interests as antagonistic to those of the landlords. 'In the Highlands the Disruption was not just an ecclesiastical dispute. It was a class conflict. Its battle line was the line of class demarcation, the line between the small tenantry on the one hand and sheep farmers, factors and proprietors on the other.'[13] Thus, the Free Church, which Kellas has described as 'the bulwark of the Scottish Liberal Party', carried into the party a tradition of democratic struggle and anti-landlordism, given a nationalist flavour by the association of the introduction of patronage with the Union of 1707. The disestablishment of the Irish Church in 1868 stimulated the demand for Scottish disestablishment, which became official Liberal policy in 1887.[14]

Temperance was a radical theme taken up even more strongly by the early Labour leaders – for example, Keir Hardie was district deputy (organiser) for the Good Templars in Ayrshire by 1885[15] – and focused on the demand for 'local option', the right of each locality to determine whether it would be 'wet' or 'dry'. It was generally felt that this and other measures to control the liquor traffic would be much more successful if Scotland could make its own decisions.

The third item in the radical creed was land reform. Here, too, Scotland's problems were distinctive, particularly in the Highlands. During the 1880s the Highland 'land war' and the election of four 'crofters' MPs following the extension of the franchise in 1885 forced this issue to the forefront. We examine below the way in which the land agitation contributed to the Home Rule agitation and the emergence of independent Labour.

The Scottish radical tradition was further sustained by a number of myths about Scottish social and political culture. There was a firm belief in Scotland as a naturally radical country which, left to itself, would inevitably adopt progressive policies. This reflected the Liberals' electoral dominance since 1832 as well as the tradition of 'Scottish democracy'. 'Scottish democracy' is a set of beliefs in the inherently democratic and egalitarian nature of Scottish society – beliefs which are sometimes seen as derived from the 'democracy' or 'primitive communism' of the Highland clan system, but are usually seen as derived from the organisation of the Presbyterian Church and of Scottish education. The Reformation had introduced the election of ministers to replace the old hierarchy, with a system of democratic assemblies all the way to the General Assembly, the governing body of the Kirk. While in practice the system owed more to theocracy than to democracy, the impact on Scottish society of this assertion of democratic principle was considerable.

Stemming directly from the Reformation was the Scottish system of education. John Knox had decreed a school in every parish and, while the ideal was never achieved, Scottish education, at least until the spread of industrialisation, was certainly more universal and more open than its English counterpart. It was possible for an able working-class boy to proceed to university and the professions, so that, while Scottish society remained as stratified as that of England, for a minority, at least, social mobility was possible. There thus grew up the tradition of the 'lad o' pairts', the working-class son made good. The tradition was meritocratic rather than egalitarian and, as Hanham points out, the schools were too middle-class in tone to make much impact on the new urban masses of the nineteenth century,[16] but it helped to sustain a belief in Scottish democracy well into the twentieth century. (It is reflected, in the Labour Party in Scotland, in the surprising degree of support for selective education surviving into the 1960s and 1970s.)

An important element in the Scots radical tradition was the tradition of revolt, drawing on the struggles against English domination under Wallace and Bruce and on the Covenanters, who had resisted royal authority in the seventeenth century. A tradition could thus develop which was at once radical and nationalist as social struggles merged with the fight against the English. The increasing anglicisation of the Scottish upper classes in the nineteenth century reinforced the identification of national and social revolt, so that Scots radicals often saw them as a single struggle, as, to a much greater extent, they were in Ireland.

The belief in Scottish democracy often found expression in extravagant praise for the old Scots Parliament, praise which that fallen institution scarcely merited. This strand of thinking was well represented by Morrison Davidson, a radical journalist and republican, sympathetic to the labour movement. For example, in his *Leaves from the Book of Scots* he wrote,

at the Treaty of Union, the Edinburgh legislature was, potentially at least, on the high road to Democracy, as compared with the hereditary 'Caput Mortuum' at

Westminster. Nay, restricted as undoubtedly was the Franchise, the Scots single chamber yet developed . . . an even unmistakable *Republican* trend.[17]

A good idea of the radical picture of Scotland is conveyed by the regular contributions of D. N. Mackay, a Young Scot, and also a labour sympathiser, to the *Forward*:

> If you, reader, were a member of an international Congress of Democrats, assembled to select, for a test or experiment in thoroughgoing democratic government, the country that was freest from racial or religious oppression, ripest in progressive ideas, eagerest to realise itself, likeliest to listen to sound reasoning and to translate theory into practice – what country but Scotland would you select?[18]

Of course, Scotland's natural radical tendencies were being suppressed by the dead hand of London government, including the permanent Tory majority in the House of Lords, blocking the way to land reform, disestablishment, temperance and democracy.

Home Rule, then, gradually emerged as an integral part of the radical programme and became identified, along with extensions of the franchise and curtailment of the powers of the House of Lords, as a logical step towards a fourth radical aim, the advance of democracy. This identification persisted at least until the extension of the Parliamentary franchise in 1918. Thus, in 1906, John M. Robertson, a Liberal MP, could write that Home Rule was 'the central problem of constitutional, as distinguished from social reform', and that, 'by solving it, the Liberal Party will begin a new era in democratic reform',[19] while in 1911 a Young Scots' manifesto described devolution as, 'after the abolition of the Lords' veto, the most urgent reform of the time'.[20]

Gladstone had first floated the possibility of Scottish Home Rule as early as 1879, in the context of the congestion of Parliamentary business. In his famous Midlothian campaign he had declared:

> We have got an overweighted Parliament, and, if we can make arrangements under which Ireland, Scotland, Wales and portions of England can deal with questions of local and special interest to themselves more efficiently than Parliament

now can, that, I say, will be the attainment of great national good.[21]

The supremacy of the Imperial Parliament would be maintained, and nothing given to Ireland which was not given equally to Scotland and to other parts of Britain.

However, it was the Grand Old Man's conversion in 1886 to Home Rule for Ireland which crystallised Home Rule sentiment in Scotland. In the same year, a Scottish Home Rule Association was founded by a group of Liberals, and, while its Edinburgh officers were said to be on the right of the party, there was a strong radical influence in the branches. Ramsay MacDonald was secretary of the London branch, in which crofters' MP G. B. Clark, and R. B. Cunninghame Graham, a Scottish laird who had recently been converted to socialism, were also active. Among the vice-presidents were Keir Hardie and Robert Smillie, the miners' leader. From 1888, Scottish Home Rule was the official policy of the Scottish Liberals, though it was usually recognised that settlement for Ireland should have priority. In 1889 G. B. Clark introduced the first Scottish Home Rule motion into the House of Commons. Thereafter, motions and bills were introduced regularly up to the First World War. The first motion to be carried was that of 1894, followed by those of 1895, 1912 and 1919, while first readings of bills were obtained in 1908, 1911, 1912 and 1913. The 1913 bill even received a second reading. From 1900, further impetus was given by the Young Scots, a group on the left of the Liberal Party, firmly committed to Home Rule. They were the element closest to the Labour Party, where most of their leaders were ultimately to find a home for their democratic, pacifist and radical principles after the Liberal Party had failed them during and after the First World War. In 1910 a group of twenty-one MPs, worried lest Scottish Home Rule recede into the background, founded the Scottish National Committee, while in 1913 the Liberal machine founded the Scottish Home Rule Council and supplemented it with the International Scots Home Rule Association, aimed at enlisting North American support.[22]

As Home Rule became identified with the radical cause and with support for the Irish, so Conservative opposition intensified, polarising the issue on right–left lines. In 1889, Balfour unambiguously stated the Unionist case: 'We object to Home Rule

whether it begins with Ireland and ends with Wales or begins with
Wales and ends with Ireland.'[23]
    It was in this atmosphere that the moves to independent Labour
representation in Scotland took place. The main elements in the
early Labour coalition were the trades unions, land reformers and a
variety of socialists and alienated radical Liberals. Initially, it was a
long way from the character which it later assumed, of a trade-
union based movement of the industrial working class. It therefore
had to give much of its attention to issues other than those which
divided the workers from their employers. These included territorial divisions as well as issues derived from the late nineteenth-
century radical agenda. The move to independent Labour representation came because the Liberal Party was not prepared to
adopt Labour men and measures with sufficient enthusiasm. While
the latter mainly involved industrial policies, there was also
dissatisfaction in radical circles with the party's lack of enthusiasm
for their own causes. Labour, of course, re-ordered the radical
priorities. Our task is to show where the issue of Home Rule fitted in.
We shall therefore consider the various elements in the developing
Labour coalition and their attitude to the issue.

III. THE GROWTH OF SCOTTISH TRADE
         UNIONISM, 1880–1914

We argued in Chapter 1 that the differing labour conditions
affecting workers in different parts of a given economic area would
not automatically evoke a response of solidarity but could in fact
become the basis of conflict along national lines. We now consider
the extent to which this was the case in the British trade union
movement from the 1880s to the First World War, and the
implications for the attitude of the Scottish labour movement
towards Home Rule.
    We have shown that industrial Scotland was, by 1880, part of the
heartland of the British Empire. But how far did this mean that
conditions of labour were the same as in other parts of Britain? In
1886 the Board of Trade Labour Department conducted a wage
census which showed wages and earnings of Scottish industrial
workers to be generally lower than the average for the United
Kingdom, though the differences were not very great. The Board of
Trade Earnings Enquiry in 1906 showed that by then the prosperity

of the iron and steel and the shipbuilding industries had brought
men's earnings above the United Kingdom average, while earnings
in engineering were close to the average. In the service industries
earnings were on average still lower.[24]

Looking at the regional differences within Scotland, we find that
farm labourers in south and central Scotland were relatively well
paid, with earnings well above English levels, and rising during this
period. In 1907 there were eight counties in Scotland where farm
labourers' earnings were above 20s. a week, compared with only
five in the whole of England. But in northern Scotland farm
earnings were well below the British average, and in the crofting
counties they were worse than in any other region in Britain. In
central Scotland, with the bulk of Scotland's population and most of
its industrial workers, wages in the heavy industries, with the
exception of mining, were improving in this period, and by the early
twentieth century it was 'one of the four highest-wage regions in
Britain' (of thirteen regions in all).[25]

The improvement in Scotland's relative position was not the
result of a general tendency towards the levelling of regional
differentials in Britain. As E. H. Hunt points out, 'differentials were
considerably greater in 1850 than they were sixty years later, but
until the First World War what was remarkable was how slowly
change occurred.'[26] The main reason for the improvement in
Scotland's position was economic – the industrial expansion, concentrated on the heavy industries of Clydeside, coupled with the
fact that Scottish agriculture adjusted better than British agriculture as a whole to the competition of imported agricultural
commodities (with the exception of the Highlands, where sheep
farming was severely depressed). The role of the trade unions was
not an erosive influence on regional wage differentials until after
1900, and for much of the second half of the nineteenth century their
influence was to *increase* differentials.[27] Why was this the case, and
what were the implications for union conflicts on national lines?

Trade union strength was very limited. In the 1880s only a small
minority of British workers were organised, and the rapid expansion
of membership only really started after 1910. The least industrialised parts of Britain were beyond the reach of trade
unionism, except for short spells such as the 1870s, when farm
labourers were briefly able to organise. The Webbs showed that in
1892 two-thirds of all trade unionists in Scotland worked in the
Glasgow area, and this concentration of trade unionism in the

industrialised and high-wage areas was typical. Furthermore, at times of cyclical depression, numerical contraction was matched by a geographical contraction of the spread of trade unionism to the strongest industrial areas.

Given this distribution of union strength, the effect of unions would be to increase differentials in favour of the high-wage areas, unless a policy of securing equal pay for equal work was to be pursued very vigorously. Before 1890 – indeed, to some extent right up to about 1910 – trade unionism was predominantly craft unionism, based upon the scarcity value of skilled workers. 'Its main concern was to protect this scarcity and it did this by regulating labour supply; therefore it was exclusive and restrictive and neither its structure nor mode of operation was conducive to the erosion of regional differentials.' In most craft unions the central administrations, even in a centralised union such as the Amalgamated Society of Engineers, had very limited influence on wage determination. Collective bargaining, and the regulation of hours and apprenticeships, was left to the district, 'and when head office attempted to circumscribe local power it ran the risk of fomenting considerable opposition, especially in the high-wage branches which had most to lose from centralized policies and their egalitarian tendencies'.[28] Thus, it is not surprising that in 1900 the engineers and the carpenters, the first of the 'new model' unions, still tolerated rates which gave some of their members twice as much as others.

While the establishment of a standard national rate was regarded by most unions as a distant objective, many unions did succeed in overcoming local differences and establishing standard district rates (district varying in size according to the trade). The unions were able to build upon their strength in areas where demand for labour was high – for example, by encouraging emigration and discouraging inward migration from low-wage areas, to restrict the supply of labour. The greater productivity of industry in the high-wage areas gave them considerable scope to raise wages without fear or precipitating the emigration of capital. But any attempt to make district rates achieved in such areas the basis for a standard national rate foundered inevitably on the willingness of the vast majority of workers in the low-wage areas to work below the union rate rather than join the union and face unemployment.

This was the economic background for the extent of division which existed in the trade union movement in this period. District parochialism was a feature of the centralised British unions, but it was naturally even more marked in the case of unions which had not yet amalgamated on an all-British basis but were divided by geographical area. This might take the form of conflict between a Manchester-based society and one of the same trade based in London; but, inevitably, when a Scottish and an English society were in conflict national antagonism inflamed the differences based on contrasting district conditions.

We may briefly survey the extent of such conflict at the outset of our period.[29] On the Scottish coalfields, the attempts by Alexander McDonald to achieve co-ordination at Scottish regional level had virtually come to nothing by the end of the 1870s, and the real strength still lay in the local associations. The building trades provided some of the worst examples of conflicts between English and Scottish Unions. The Scottish-based Associated and London-based Amalgamated Society of Carpenters and Joiners established branches on each other's territory from the 1870s. The United Operative Plumbers' Association, a national union established in 1865 and based in Liverpool, suffered two Scottish breakaways: in 1872 a Glasgow breakaway took place on the grounds that 'more money went out of Scotland than came into it', and the Operative Plumbers' Association of Scotland was founded, which in 1893 absorbed two lodges which had broken away two years earlier. The basis for the conflict appears to have been the more conservative nature of the trade in Scotland, which was more purely based on house-building plumbers. On the railways there was competition between the Amalgamated Society of Railway Servants, which in 1876 established branches in Edinburgh and Glasgow, and the separate Scottish society; however, both societies co-operated in 1881 in starting a campaign for the nine-hour working day. The Scottish National Operative Tailors' and Tailoresses' Association was engaged in chronic disputes with the corresponding English union throughout the late nineteenth century, and in 1900 the Scottish Trades Union Congress (STUC) recommended that the two societies should 'confine themselves to the well-defined boundaries of Scotland and England'. The basis for separate organisation was apparently the fact that the Scottish society had obtained better conditions by eliminating out-work, which remained a trade custom general throughout England and was recognised by the English-based Amalgamated Society of Tailors.[30]

This picture began to alter after about 1890, under the impact of

the 'new unionism'. Increasingly in the years immediately before
the First World War, the industrial and general unions began to
alter the character of the trade union movement, and to transform it
into one of the forces responsible for eroding, rather than bolstering
up, regional wage differentials. The number of trade union
members expanded dramatically, from 750,000 in 1888 to over 4
million in 1914. At the same time trade unionism spread geographi-
cally, so that its influence was felt over far more of Britain. Most
importantly, the expansion after 1888, and especially after 1910,
embraced large numbers of unskilled and semiskilled workers:

> The more egalitarian and centralized character of the new
> unions began with their members' lack of scarcity
> value. . . . The new unionists had few skills to defend and
> were threatened by blacklegs at every turn; in these
> circumstances orthodox unionism offered no solution. The
> remedy lay in the opposite direction – to include within the
> union as many as possible . . . .

As a result the new unions' attitude towards regional differences in
the conditions of labour was entirely different from that of the craft
unions in the earlier period:

> The craftsmen's ability to regulate wages by exercising subtle
> pressure on labour supply had helped to preserve local
> autonomy . . . but these remedies were not open to the
> unskilled. Accordingly, they looked more to their head offices
> and to Westminster, and from head office regional wage
> variations appeared both more obvious and more
> anomalous.[31]

Often pressure was put on the Government, largely because the new
unions were relatively weak in terms of negotiating strength and
thus used their centralised organisation to lobby the Government to
give them by legislation what they could not gain by direct
industrial action. The Fair Wages Resolution of 1891 established
the important principle that government contracts should not be
awarded to firms that paid 'unfair' rates (less than 'good' employers
in the district). Local authorities adopted similar measures under
trade union pressure. The Trade Boards Act established a floor to

wages and conditions in some of the worst organised sweated trades, but first became operative only in 1913.

Other influences making for national wage bargaining and corresponding developments in trade union policy and structure came from outside the movement. The increase in the size of firms, especially after 1890, when concentration of industry proceeded more rapidly, increased pressure on regional differentials, which were seen as more anomalous where different rates for the same job were paid by the same employer. The railway companies, which were substantial employers long before 1890, occasionally met to discuss wage policy, and railway pay varied less than pay in most other occupations. Government and local government inclined in the direction of uniform wage rates, and were of increasing significance in the labour market. Government employees were more sensitive to regional differentials, and tended to organise from the outset on a British, rather than a Scottish–English, basis, with the notable exception of the teaching profession. Postmen were demanding national standard rates in the 1890s, and the Association of Municipal Employees submitted a similar claim in 1905.

The substantial expansion of employers' associations after 1890 helped spread the influence of industrial concentration to the smaller companies. This came partly as a response to trade union growth and the tendency of the new unions to widen the field of disputes, but in some cases it was the employers who set the pace, by imposing centralised bargaining on craft unions whose structure was still geared to local negotiations. This was the case, for example, in the engineering industry, where the employers carried out a general lock-out in 1897 and established an industry-wide organisation. The pace of such developments varied from industry to industry. In the building industry, where the craft unions were strong and employers had little competition from outside their own locality, centralisation proceeded very slowly.

The effect of these changes, especially the growth of unskilled unionism, can be traced in the development of increasing national bargaining and of union amalgamation or federation on an all-British basis.[32] The rise of unionism amongst the unskilled was most marked in the transport sector. On the railways there had been relatively good relations between the English and Scottish railway servants, but in 1892 the Scottish society was so weakened by a strike for shorter hours that it had to accept incorporation into the

English-based Amalgamated Society. The national railway strike of 1911 was followed by the amalgamation of several unions in the National Union of Railwaymen, founded in 1913. At about the same time, the North British Railway Clerks' Association was absorbed by the Railway Clerks' Association. In the summer of 1911 a national strike of seamen and dockers was directed by the newly formed Transport Workers' Federation (TWF), and was followed by local disputes in Dundee and Glasgow. The Scottish Union of Dock Labourers became associated with the TWF in the following year. However, the limitations of the TWF were shown by the lack of support for the national strike it called in support of the London dockers in 1912. Furthermore, in the road-transport sector, the Scottish Horse and Motormen's Association stood apart from the TWF.

Among the old unions, the miners were moving increasingly towards a national union. In 1888 the Miners' Federation of Great Britain (MFGB) was formed, and in 1893 it led a strike involving nearly four in five of all underground workers. The 1912 miners' strike, the largest ever in Britain up to that time, involved 1 million men and concluded after Government intervention and the passing of a Minimum Wage Act. This established district minimum wages and the miners were forced to accept greater regional variations than they would have liked. Thereafter, the Scottish Federation, though active in the MFGB, retained a large measure of autonomy. In 1915 the eight county associations became more closely associated in the National Union of Scottish Mineworkers, with 100,000 members. Thus, paradoxically, the most powerful example of an independent Scottish union at the end of our period owed its strength in large measure to the solidarity of the MFGB, and its continuing independence to the inability of the miners as yet to secure a national minimum wage.

The advance of trade unionism into unorganised sectors included the establishment of a strong new Scottish Farm Servants' Union in 1913, based in Aberdeenshire, but soon spreading throughout Scotland. Earnings of farm labourers in lowland Scotland were superior to those in England, and this, as well as the local origin of the union, accounts for its organisation on a separate Scottish basis.

Other unions retaining their independence were older unions, chiefly in the consumer-goods industries, where the old craft traditions still mainly prevailed – the bakers, boot- and shoemakers, tailors and printers. The same was true of the building trades, where masons, plumbers, plasterers, painters and slaters all retained their independence, while the two rival carpenters' and joiners' societies finally united in 1911, and the Scottish Electrical Union merged in the national union in 1913.

Distributive and white-collar unions – for example, the National Union of Clerks and the shop assistants – had from the outset been constituted on a British basis. In the textile industries a mass of minute local unions of specialised workers still existed, although the Yorkshire-based National Union of Dyers was able to organise workers in the dyeworks in the Vale of Leven in 1911.

Thus, the trade union movement in 1880 was still very much divided on a district or regional basis, and, although the underlying tendency was towards greater centralisation, especially after the development of general and industrial trade unionism embracing the unskilled, great differences in conditions of labour and conflicts of interests between and within unions on a geographical basis were still to be found even at the end of our period, in 1914. How far these provided the basis for a separate Scottish trade union movement, with its own interests and an interest in political Home Rule, can best be considered by looking at the formation of the STUC and its role in this period.

Why a separate Scottish Trades Union Congress? According to the STUC's evidence to the Kilbrandon Commission, the STUC was formed in circumstances which

reflected the uneasiness in Scottish trade union circles about the 'remoteness' of London, the inability of people there, including trade union people, to understand or be interested in the Scottish scene, especially with regard to the unfair interpretation by the Sheriff Courts of the law as it affected workpeople and their dependents.[33]

However, the current research officer of the STUC has stated that

The founding of the STUC had absolutely nothing whatever to do with national feeling amongst Scottish trade unionists. . . . [It] was in large part political reaction initiated by the Scottish Trades Councils to the decision of the General Council of the British Trades Union Congress to debar Trades Councils from participation in Congress decisions.[34]

In fact the truth is probably a mixture of the two. By excluding the trades councils from the TUC in 1895, the leaders of the TUC had been able to stave off for a few years the defeat of their policies by the proponents of independent Labour representation. However, they had also excluded, by the same stroke, a large section of the Scottish trade union movement from representation.

The trades councils played a larger part in the Scottish than in the English trade union movement, perhaps because of the geographical isolation of the centres of the industrial population around Glasgow, Edinburgh, Dundee and Aberdeen. The president in his address to the first congress of the STUC, in 1897, referred to the fact that many of the smaller trades that were unable to afford to send their own delegates to the TUC had raised the matters which concerned them through the trades councils. Thus there was a coalescence of the interests of independent Labour representation, which could be more rapidly furthered in a separate Scottish TUC, and the interest of the trades councils and the small Scottish unions. Socialism marched hand in hand with parochialism in the founding of the STUC.

Politically the STUC was markedly more advanced than the TUC. Because it represented the trades councils and did not introduce the card vote, it gave the advantage to the activists who attended as delegates, rather than to the leaders of the large unions (such as those of the mining and textiles industries), who wielded the block votes at the TUC. The STUC took the lead in supporting independent Labour representation, and a resolution in favour of the 'working class Socialist parties already in existence' was carried at the second congress, in 1898.

At the same time, the STUC furthered the particular interests of the Scottish trade unions. For example, at the first congress a resolution was carried unanimously which stated that the existing Labour Department of the Board of Trade needed to be greatly extended and,

> Further, that, in view of the differences that exist between the industrial conditions in England and those in Scotland, and the critical phases through which the textile and other industries in the latter are now passing . . . this Congress urges on the Government the necessity for establishing a branch of the Labour Department of the Board of Trade for Scotch [sic] affairs . . . .

The Secretary for Scotland told a deputation that he thought divisions of the Board of Trade should remain on trade and not geographical lines, and in the course of discussions the STUC deputation explained that 'what was required . . . was permanent officials with a thorough knowledge of local labour conditions to be on the spot and always accessible' and that this was a principle 'capable of application to the big industrial centres in England as well'.[35]

Thus, the demand was not in essence a nationalist one, but reflected the desire of some of the Scottish unions for greater access to government, in view of their separate organisation, or the prevalence of wage determination at district rather than national level. In 1900 the miners, in a similar resolution, unsuccessfully tried to have the word 'Scottish' deleted from the clause 'and in particular that Scottish labour affairs should receive more attention', and in 1903, when the 'hardy annual' came up again, the whole clause was deleted. In 1904 the controversial clause was reinstated, but in 1909 was again omitted.

The STUC regarded itself, and not the TUC, as the voice of organised labour in Scotland, at least with regard to matters on which it felt that conditions were different. Therefore, in an age when trade union leaders still relied heavily on the deputation, a recurring issue was the right to be received by Ministers. In 1898 the Second Congress protested against the refusal of the Home Secretary to meet a deputation of their Parliamentary Committee, the seconder of the motion stating, 'They must give their Ministers to understand that in Scotland they held distinct opinions on certain questions and that they must get a fair hearing. The Congress would be shorn of its usefulness if a Cabinet Minister were allowed to refuse to hear them.'

Home Secretaries continued on occasions to refuse to meet deputations from the STUC's Parliamentary Committee, and Winston Churchill caused a storm of protest when in 1911 he informed a deputation that he understood 'that all the principal Unions comprising the Scottish Congress are affiliated to the TUC, and that the latter body represents the whole of the United Kingdom, and not merely England and Wales'. The debate at Congress consisted of a mixture of political criticism of Churchill and defence of the role of the STUC. The delegates of the Scottish Miners' Federation dismissed the political side of the argument, and took the view that, since the questions that Congress wished to raise

with Churchill had been discussed at the British TUC, and the
Home Secretary was prepared to meet a deputation from that body,
'there was no necessity to meet a deputation from them.' But this
was a long dissentient view. More typical was the statement of A. R.
Turner of Glasgow Trades Council, who

> said he understood Mr. Churchill made loud professions of
> being a democrat, and had received valuable support from
> the Young Scots' Society, which had for one of its planks
> Home Rule for Scotland, and yet championed the cause of
> one who refused the principle of Home Rule to Scottish
> Trade Unionists.

In 1912 the new Home Secretary, McKenna, refused, on the usual
grounds, to meet an STUC deputation, but, following representations from a group of Scottish MPs, ultimately changed his
mind.[36]
    Another longstanding claim was for separate representation of
Scottish labour interests on Government committees and commissions. In 1906 the STUC urged representation of the Poor Law
Commission, because of the different systems of poor relief in
Scotland, but this claim was rejected by John Burns, President of the
Local Government Board and Lib–Lab MP. Representations were
made to the Secretary for Scotland 'that on all future Commissions
and Inquiry Committees appointed to deal with working-class
affairs the Scottish workers should have their full and proper
measure of representation'.[37] Some success appeared to have been
achieved when Robert Smillie was appointed a member of the
Royal Commission on Mining Accidents and John T. Howden was
appointed to the Houseletting (Scotland) Inquiry Committee.
However, dissatisfaction with representation of Scottish labour
interests was to resurface in the wartime atmosphere of increased
government intervention and consultation, as we shall see in
Chapter 3.
    A Scottish section of the Board of Trade's Labour Department, a
right for the Scottish TUC to be received by Ministers and for
Scottish trade unionists to be appointed to commissions and
committees of inquiry – these and similar demands show the way in
which the differences in the conditions of labour, including social
conditions, in Scotland, and the associated separateness of organisation, led naturally to demands for specific and limited measures

of Home Rule or devolution, although without any specifically nationalist flavour. We have seen that by the end of our period the trade-union movement was increasingly oriented towards lobbying for legislative change at national level, and securing standard national rates. In certain industries amalgamation and federation were proceeding apace. How were these changes reflected in the composition and role of the STUC?

At first the affiliation of the STUC was very largely from the independent Scottish unions and the local trades councils. However, this was beginning to change towards the end of the period, as the following comparison shows:

	1898	*1911*[38]
Membership	76,274	140,705
Affiliated unions	45	44
Scottish unions	30	22
Trades councils	8	6

The changing composition of the STUC, and the increasing centralisation of the labour movement in general – including, as we shall see, the organisation of the new Labour Party on an all-British basis – led some in the STUC to regard the independence of the STUC from the TUC as a divisive, or, at best, superfluous, survival. In the years 1908–10 these views were expressed in a serious attempt to reorganise the STUC as a subordinate body.

The first resolution on reorganisation, carried at the 1908 congress by the narrow margin of 58 to 50 (after a recount), was an attempt to overcome the overlapping in the forces of labour. It was proposed that the Parliamentary Committee (PC) should submit its decisions directly to the Executive of the Labour Party and no longer send deputations to lobby MPs. The mover, David Palmer of Aberdeen Trades Council, who was a member of the PC, said that he 'believed in the principle of centralisation, but . . . also accepted the principle of devolution. He believed there ought to be a central organisation, giving local autonomy and powers to each particular district.'

How could the PC put this resolution into effect? Palmer was invited to submit a statement explaining what the resolution meant, and how it could be implemented. He explained that the idea was

that there should be a closer union between the various
Trades Congresses in England, Ireland and Scotland and the
Labour [Party]. They were of opinion that there was really
no need for these various existing bodies that the Labour
Party and the General Federation of Trades Unions were
quite sufficient and they believed the results would be much
better and suggested that a Conference of all these bodies
should be held with a view to this being brought
about . . . .[39]

The PC eventually decided to report to the 1909 congress that to
give effect to the terms of the resolution would mean the extinction
of the STUC. The report stated that the PC had decided to take no
action on the matter 'in view of the fact that the Congress had
during its existence rendered real and valuable service to the Trade
Union and Labour movement in Scotland'.

Nevertheless, at the 1910 congress another attempt was made to
dissolve the STUC. The Postmen's Federation moved 'That it be an
instruction to the PC of the STUC to confer with the PC of the
TUC, with a view towards amalgamation of the aforesaid TUC
under the title of Trades Union Congress of Great Britain and
Ireland.' This time the resolution was defeated by a large majority.

Thus, the STUC survived the pressures towards amalgamation
with its independence and structure intact. It continued to be a
pressure group for the separate interests of the Scottish unions and,
more generally, of working people in Scotland. As a body which had
struggled to establish its own right to exist, and to speak for Scottish
labour, it was naturally willing to embrace the principle of Home
Rule in politics, although this was quite distinct from separatism.
The way in which this distinction was felt by the leaders of the
movement was brought out very clearly by Robert Smillie in his
presidential address to the Hawick congress of 1905:

I think that I am voicing the opinion of my colleagues on the
P. C., and also of the rank and file of the organised workers
of Scotland, when I again repeat that this Congress does not
exist as a rival to any other similar body, but is rather an
attempt to concentrate the energies of the workers of Scotland
in the direction of dealing with some of the many grievances
and injustices which affect them locally, which would not be
touched by the British Congress, while at the same time

joining with the British and Irish Congresses in advancing by every means in our power any movement which has for its object the improvement of the condition of the workers of the country as a whole.

It is in this context that the STUC was willing unanimously to endorse the principle of Scottish Home Rule, when it was first moved by Glasgow Trades Council at the 1914 congress. The resolution was merely an affirmation of belief in the principle, requiring no action from Congress. Perhaps this was because Emmanuel Shinwell, who drafted the motion for the Parliamentary Bills Committee of Glasgow Trades Council, had initially opposed submitting a resolution on the subject at all.[40]

Although it proved acceptable to the STUC, the principle of Home Rule had come into the movement from outside, and in particular through the association of the early movement for independent Labour representation with the crofters' movement, and other radical forces in Scottish society. To trace this process, we must examine the 'land and labour' campaigns and the emergence of independent Labour representation.

IV.   LAND, LABOUR AND HOME RULE

The most important element in the Labour coalition was the leadership of the crofters' movement, which in 1885 had broken the hold of the Tory and Whig lairds on the crofting constituencies. Their victory was the result of the effectiveness of the Highland Land Law Reform Association (HLLRA), which, established in 1883 and with a branch structure based in the crofting townships, has some claim to the title of the first mass political party in Britain.[41]

Although the driving force in the crofters' movement was the struggle for more land, in conditions of extreme agricultural depression in the Highlands in the 1880s, the effectiveness of the movement depended also on the emergence of a powerful pro-crofter coalition in the Lowlands. For years, John Murdoch, as editor of the *Highlander* (1873–81), had campaigned to force the middle-class Gaelic revivalists of the southern Gaelic societies to support the struggle of the crofting community for a fairer agrarian order in the Highlands. Murdoch had been involved in Irish nationalist and land-reform politics in the 1850s, and for him it was the plight of the Irish peasantry which was the greatest condemnation of the Anglo-Irish Union. He saw the condition of the Highland crofters as being analogous, strove for solidarity of the Celtic peoples, and as early as 1876, in the *Highlander*, canvassed the idea of Scottish Home Rule.[42] In 1882, following the intervention of the Glasgow Constabulary against Skye crofters on rent strike for the restoration of common grazings, and the ensuing 'Battle of the Braes', the plight of the crofters made national headlines, and Murdoch's campaign began to bear fruit.

The Highland 'land war' was, from the start, heavily influenced by the example of Michael Davitt's Irish Land League, whose tactics of rent strike and other direct action had, in Gladstone's Irish Land Act of 1881, elicited the concession of security of tenure and judicially determined rents. In the Highlands these tactics and land-raiding (the direct settlement by crofters of the land they claimed) were used primarily in a struggle for more land, rather than lower rents. The Crofters Act of June 1886, which provided security of tenure, compensation for improvements carried out, and set up a Crofters' Commission empowered to fix fair rents, did not appease the hunger for land and was condemned by HLLRA meetings throughout the Highlands. The HLLRA reconstituted itself as the Highland Land League and land-raiding intensified. It was at this time, and in the context of the electoral victories of their candidates and of Gladstone's commitment to Irish Home Rule, that crofters' meetings began to call for Home Rule for Scotland.[43] Support for Irish Home Rule was already widespread among the crofting community and flowed from their sympathy with the Irish Land League, while, as in Ireland, a nationalist tinge was given to land agitation by the anglicisation and, often, English domicile of the absentee landlords.

After the fall of Gladstone's Liberal government on the Irish Home Rule issue, the new Tory Government immediately resolved on the use of troops to support the Highland landlords against the intensified land-raiding which followed the 1886 Act. By 1887, this coercive policy had convinced many crofters that 'the only sure mode of obtaining their rights was by Home Rule for Scotland'.[44]

The Lowland supporters of the crofters included, apart from the Gaelic revivalist element, a contingent of land reformers and socialists who sought to extend the movement to the Lowlands, partly as a means of broadening its support, and partly because they hoped to arouse a mass response for some version of land-reform demands in the Lowlands. There was a tradition of working-class support for land-law reform going back to the Chartists, and Henry George's lecture tours helped to coalesce a grouping of radical and socialist forces in the Lowlands who supported the crofters and some of whom went on to support an independent Labour Party. In 1884, during George's second visit to Britain to popularise his proposal of an abolition of all taxes save the 'single tax' on land values, the Scottish Land Restoration League was founded. The league put up five unsuccessful candidates in the Clyde area in the 1885 elections, simultaneously with the HLLRA candidatures in the crofting counties. Dr G. B. Clark, formerly a member of the General Council of Marx's International Working Men's Association, later recalled the campaign:

Land Law Reform candidates were run for several other seats in Scotland. Two of our active members secured seats – Dr W. A. Hunter for Aberdeen, and Professor Robertson, now Lord Robertson of Lochee, for Dundee. We had no success in Glasgow, although we expected to gain the Bridgeton and Hutchesontown divisions, where Forsyth and Shaw Maxwell stood, but they were defeated, as was also Bennet Burleigh in Govan, and John Murdoch and Morrison Davidson in Partick and Greenock.[45]

The Scottish Land Restoration League backed Hardie and affiliated to the Scottish Labour Party in 1888.

Another body founded in the same year, the Scottish Land and Labour League (SLLL), had a more socialist objective. It was founded by Andreas Scheu, a Viennese expatriate who was a member of Hyndman's Social Democratic Federation (SDF), but 'argued that it had failed in Scotland because it had neglected local sympathy for crofter agitation and the Irish Land League'.

When the Socialist League split away from the SDF in 1884, it took the SLLL with it, as an affiliated body. J. L. Mahon, a young engineering worker, became the paid organiser of the Socialist League in the provinces, and led the 'Parliamentary faction' within it which wanted to stand Parliamentary candidates.[46] The SLLL provided a direct link with the west-of-Scotland miners, through William Small, who set up a branch based on a political organisation of Lanarkshire miners committed to his campaign for the nationalisation of mining royalties. From the middle of 1885 he was urging the Lanarkshire miners to imitate Highland crofters and run their own candidate at the forthcoming general election, and this may have influenced Keir Hardie to consider the project when he lost faith in the Liberal Party.[47] Certainly, the SLLL affiliated to Hardie's Scottish Labour Party in 1888, and it was then (with half a dozen branches) the largest socialist organisation in Scotland.

The trades councils supported the crofters' movement, and supported one or other programme of land reform. For example, Aberdeen Trades Council in 1884 suggested that the land laws be reformed so as to make it compulsory for the landlords to cultivate the land, and urged the removal of all obstacles in the way of extending peasant proprietorship. In 1886 they favoured the extension of Highland crofting legislation to all of Scotland, and in 1889 actively supported a campaign by squatters protesting against the appropriation by a number of lairds of the hill of Bennachie in Aberdeenshire.[48] There were solid economic reasons for the Lowland trade unionist to support the Highland crofter. Kellas has pointed out that Lowland workers – for example, the Glasgow Liberal Workmen's Electoral Union – wanted land reform in order to keep the crofter at home and out of the Glasgow labour market.[49] In Aberdeen, which was the centre of a vast agricultural district, there was a similar problem of rural depopulation and an influx of labour depressing the local labour market.

At the same time that they canvassed support for the crofters, their Lowland supporters popularised the idea of Scottish Home Rule. The Scottish Home Rule Association of 1886 included both the advanced radical and Gaelic nationalist wings of the coalition which supported the crofters, with many of the branches in the hands of radicals who had already – in the case of the HLLRA leaders – shown their willingness to fight the official Liberal Party on the crofters' behalf. As we have seen, G. B. Clark, Cunninghame Graham and Ramsay MacDonald were all prominent in the Home Rule Association.

There was thus a substantial body of advanced radical opinion in Lowland Scotland by the late 1880s, which was keen to extend the crofters' Parliamentary breakthrough to the Lowlands – if necessary, by supporting independent candiates against official Liberalism. Given the weakness of the miners' unions in the West of Scotland, Keir Hardie was more than willing to co-operate with these groups, who, after all, emerged out of a radical tradition shared by him.

V. THE EMERGENCE OF INDEPENDENT LABOUR

The formation of the British Labour Party was a long and uneven process. The initial moves to found a party or stand a candidate were usually local, and therefore largely the result of local events and pressures. As Howkins states in a study of the decline of working-class allegiance to Liberalism, 'the working class was forming itself politically as a class at local level, at different rates, and in different ways.'[50] A strong desire for representation of working people by men of their own class and with their own policies had led to increasing dissatisfaction with the Liberal caucuses, and the 1880s saw a growing movement for independent working-class representation on town councils, school boards and boards of poor law guardians, but, as John Saville points out, 'what must be emphasised is the native growth of these ideas of independent representation within the radical lib–lab tradition, which remains allied to the Liberal Party and which has no wish to separate itself off from the G. O. M. [Grand Old Man] and the Party of Progress.'[51]

According to W. H. Fraser, 1885 was the key date for the Scottish trades councils' break with Liberalism. The assumption that, following the franchise extension, the Liberal Party would provide the openings for working-class representation was disappointed in Glasgow, Edinburgh and Aberdeen alike.[52] In the case of Aberdeen, the way in which radical Liberals, many of them actively associated with the Trades Council, initially attempted to push the Liberal Association forward by establishing active parallel organisations, has been well documented by K. D. Buckley.[53] They were successful in promoting the radical candidature of W. Hunter in 1885, but the resistance of the local Liberal Association to the policies of Trades Council nominees in local elections led many of the prominent leaders of the Aberdeen Junior Liberal Association and Radical Association onto the road away from the Liberal Party. However, the break was not a clean one – for example, until 1896 Aberdeen Trades Council continued to support Hunter, the radical Liberal MP for Aberdeen North, because he was responsive to their interests.

A similar development from radical Liberalism can be seen in the case of the Scottish miners. Keir Hardie had helped in 1884 to form a Junior Liberal Association in Cumnock, and, when he first became committed to the idea of a legislative eight-hour day for underground miners, he saw no reason why this could not be furthered through the Liberal Party:

As Hardie saw the politics of the early 1880s, the demand for many forms of State intervention was growing within the Liberal Party. Besides prohibition of the liquor traffic and free education, nationalisation of the land was being canvassed by 1885 in those Scottish Liberal circles described at the time as 'advanced'. The best interests of the miners, Hardie believed, lay in co-operating closely with the advocates of such proposals to form a Radical wing that could push the Liberal Party's leadership forward along the road of State intervention.[54]

It was the failure of west-of-Scotland Liberal newspapers to protest against the police suppression of the Lanarkshire miners' strike in 1887, and the neglect, by the Lib–Lab MPs Burt and Broadhurst, of the Scottish miners' interest in the legal limitation of working hours, that convinced Hardie by April 1887 that 'working men should be taught to be members of a Labour Party first, and Whigs or Tories, after. . . . We want a new Party, a Labour Party pure and simple, and trades unions have the power to create this.'[55]

In 1888 Hardie finally challenged official Liberalism and stood as an independent Labour candidate in the Mid-Lanark by-election. However, he was still reluctant to break completely with the Liberals, and, apart from the call for the statutory eight-hour day and nationalisation of mining royalties, his programme was more of an advanced radical package than a blueprint for socialism. He even ended his election handbills with the solgan, 'A vote for Hardie is a vote for Gladstone'.[56] His supporters included Michael Davitt, the militant Irish land campaigner, who in 1887 had toured the Highlands arousing support for land reform and Home Rule, and he sought and received the endorsement of the Glasgow branch of the United Irish League, pledging support to the Irish cause.[57] Further support came from Ramsay MacDonald, then London secretary of the Scottish Home Rule Association, who wrote to Hardie:

I cannot refrain from wishing you God-Speed in your election contest. . . . The powers of darkness – Scottish newspapers with English editors (as the *Leader*), partisan wire-pullers, and the other etceteras of political squabbles – are leagued against us.

But let the consequences be what they may, do not withdraw. The cause of Labour in Scotland and of Scottish Nationality will suffer much thereby. Your defeat will awaken Scotland and your victory will re-construct Scottish Liberalism. All success be yours, and the National cause you champion. There is no miner – and no other one for that matter – who is a Scotsman and not ashamed of it, who will vote against you in favour of an English barrister, absolutely ignorant of Scotland and of Scottish affairs, and who only wants to get into Parliament in order that he may have the tail of MP to his name in the law courts.[58]

After polling a respectable 617 votes out of 7381, Hardie called together his sympathisers in May 1888 to arrange a founding conference for a new Scottish Labour Party. The new party embraced all those elements who had supported his candidature, and amongst those who took a prominent part were John Murdoch, veteran land-reformer and Home Ruler; Cunninghame Graham; Dr G. B. Clark; John Ferguson, a supporter of Davitt's from Glasgow; and Shaw Maxwell, one of the former candidates of the Scottish Land Restoration League. J. L. Mahon and John Bruce Glasier brought in the SLLL, which provided much of the membership. Glasgow Trades Council recommended that its affiliated trade union branches affiliate to the party, and its secretary, George Carson, was actively involved. The new party was thus a motley collection, perhaps better understood as 'a land, labour and Home Rule party' than as a modern trade-union based labour party. Hardie made clear that, 'if anyone, peasant or peer, is willing to accept the programme, and work with it and for the party, his help will be gladly accepted.'[59] The programme of the party reflected its origins. Of the eighteen points, the first seven dealt with constitutional matters. These were adult suffrage, triennial Parliaments, reform of the registration laws, payment of MPs, Home Rule for each separate nationality in the British Empire with an Imperial Parliament for imperial affairs, abolition of the House of Lords, and the second ballot.[60]

Thus, support for Home Rule in the early days was an integral part of the character of the Scottish Labour Party, part of its shared background with radicalism. Looking back on the nature of the Home Rule commitment of the Independent Labour Party leaders in the mid-1920s, John MacCormick (founder of the Scottish National Party) referred to this earlier heritage:

I think that most of them had a special sentimental compartment in their minds and it was there that they cherished as a somewhat distant dream the idea of Scotland governing herself. Many of them had begun their political life as Liberals in the Gladstonian tradition and Home Rule was inherited along with other items of the Radical faith . . . .[61]

Buckley has described the continuing appeal of the radical tradition to the working class in Aberdeen:

The Radical tradition of sturdy individualism and suspicion of government and imperialism, of independence and assertion of civil liberties, of hostility to landowners, and belief in the benefits of popular education, was deep-rooted and made a strong appeal. These various strands were often entwined with one another, as in the case of Irish and Scottish Home Rule . . . .[62]

McLean has described Keir Hardie's early socialisation in similar terms:

The ballads and folk tales of the Borders and the south-west of Scotland introduced Hardie to the traditional values of rural Scotland; puritanism, respect for education, scorn for distinctions between man and man based merely on social status. The most enduring influences were the Covenanters, Burns and Carlyle.[63]

Of course, the spirit of Scottish legend did not make all the early Labour leaders political nationalists, but, until they had learned to distinguish political from cultural nationalism, it provided a strong emotional tug in that direction and, indeed, for some figures, such as Tom Johnston and the Clydesider Davie Kirkwood, continued to do so until the 1930s and 1940s. Home Rule was so strongly

identified with the cause of progress and democracy that few
questioned its desirability. Even Herbert Morrison, later the great
centraliser, felt obliged to declare, on a visit to Scotland in 1911, 'I
have become convinced that Scotland should have Home Rule no
less than Ireland.'⁶⁴ However, as the labour movement began to
change in character and the emerging party based itself increasingly
on the trade unions, the nature of the commitment to Home Rule
underwent a subtle change.

The trades councils had begun to stand candidates for local office
in the late 1880s – for example, in 1888 Glasgow Trades Council ran
four candidates for the Town Council to which one was returned.
By 1891 feeling for independent Labour representation was running
so high in the Scottish trades councils that a conference called by
Aberdeen Trades Council resolved to secure support for 'direct
representation of labour in Parliament and on local administrative
boards', and in 1892 a second conference founded the Scottish
United Trades Council's Labour Party (SUTCLP).⁶⁵ The Executive Committee represented all but a few of the Scottish trades
councils. George Carson attended as a representative of Hardie's
Scottish Labour Party. The SUTCLP, although short-lived, was
undoubtedly more representative of the trade union movement
than was the Scottish Labour Party. As Marwick has pointed out,
the latter body, 'though supported by some active trade unionists . . . had no direct connection with union organisation'. It was
soon excluded by the SUTCLP, which based its local organisation
on the trades councils. The programme, adopted in 1892, included
the eight-hour day, adult suffrage, 'local option', and the nationalisation of the land, the mines and the railways, but not, apparently,
Home Rule.⁶⁶

Keir Hardie welcomed the establishment of the SUTCLP. His
own efforts were now directed towards the formation of a British
Independent Labour Party (ILP), which, on its formation in 1893,
made both the SLP and the SUTCLP redundant. Both decided, by
the end of 1894, to merge their branches into the ILP. Hardie was
chairman of the new party, and other leading Scotsmen were on its
National Administrative Council.

The greater involvement in the ILP of trade union activists,
especially from the trades councils, is reflected by a different
attitude to Home Rule. Buckley has described the divisions within
the ILP in Aberdeen on the question of Scottish Home Rule:

In their revulsion against Liberal concentration on political
reforms, many independent Labour men in the city were
inclined to deride political reforms which had little social
content in them. This attitude, though not by any means
common to all members of the ILP, was made sharply
apparent in the Trades Council when A. Catto, himself a
leading advocate of independent Labour, proposed that the
government be petitioned in support of the proposal of
Dr Hunter, Radical MP, that after their first reading all
Scottish Bills should be remitted for consideration by Scottish
MPs: in effect, Hunter was suggesting a concession to the
sentiment in favour of Home Rule in Scotland. Catto then
accepted a suggestion from Leatham [of the Aberdeen
Socialist Society, which advocated 'Home Rule to all sections
of the Empire'] that the words 'While believing that only a
Parliament sitting in Edinburgh can effectively deal with
Scotch business' be added to his motion, but W. Clark
Mitchell, who was a joint-secretary of the Aberdeen ILP,
opposed the motion and put an amendment: 'That this
Council believing that social legislation is of more importance
than mere political changes respectfully declines to petition'.

Although on this occasion the motion in favour of Home Rule was
carried by a large majority which must have included many ILP
members, the *Aberdeen Labour Elector* was scathing in its criticism of
ILP men who had joined with the 'Socialist contingent' in carrying
the resolution.

A few months later, when a proposal that the Trades Council
petition in favour of Gladstone's second Irish Home Rule Bill was
moved on the grounds that 'it was a measure not only necessary for
Ireland but also for Scotland', an amendment reaffirming the
council's neutrality in the matter was carried. 'In effect,' Buckley
concludes, 'most members of the Council were expressing their
conviction that social legislation was more important than 'political' measures.'[67]

The main efforts of the ILP were now directed at getting the
support of the trade unions at national level for independent Labour
representation. As we have seen, this received a setback when the
TUC excluded the trades councils from representation in 1895. As a
result, the independent Labour men allied themselves with the
small Scottish trade unions excluded from the TUC by virtue of the

same measure and pursued their aim of establishing a Labour party through the STUC. The STUC authorised, on the proposal of the ILP, the summoning of a conference on Parliamentary representation, which took place in Ebinburgh on 6 January 1900, preceding by seven weeks the inaugural conference of the Labour Representation Committee (LRC) established by the British TUC. The main basis of the Scottish Workers' Parliamentary Elections Committee (SWPEC; soon to be renamed the Scottish Workers' Representation Committee), founded at this conference, was affiliation by trade unions, trades councils, co-operative societies and socialist societies, including of course the ILP, and its role was to co-ordinate the candidatures of its affiliated bodies. The programme of the party included, in 1901, the nationalisation of the land, railways and the mines, and the taxation of land values and other forms of unearned investment, but there was no specific mention of Home Rule for Scotland.[68]

At first, there was some friction between the LRC and the SWPEC over their respective territories. The Scottish executive wrote to the LRC asking it not to receive affiliation fees for the Scottish membership of its affiliated unions. Significantly, the LRC executive which discussed this in March 1901 included Ramsay MacDonald, Keir Hardie and Alexander Wilkie. Having succeeded in establishing a British trade-union based labour party, these Scottish labour leaders were not concerned to limit its coverage to England. Thus, a tussle went on over the affiliation fees to be paid to each body by various trade unions, which was only partly resolved by the agreement of the two executives to establish a common Parliamentary fund.

By 1904 Ramsay MacDonald had become convinced of 'the deadness of the Scottish Committee' and 'the imminent necessity of our taking over the whole country'. The biggest problem faced by the Scottish Workers' Representation Committee (SWRC) was that its affiliation fees were purely voluntary; as a result its electoral activity after 1900 was virtually confined to seats where the Scottish miners were prepared to sponsor a candidate, and no seats were won. In 1906 the LRC also put up candidates in Scotland, and managed to win two seats. This difference in performance was a further blow to the SWRC, which gradually became redundant.

In 1909 the miners effectively dealt it its death blow by affiliating to the Labour Party, as the LRC had been known since 1906.[69] It was now no longer financially viable, and so, despite the protests of members who pointed out that Scotland had distinct problems, and the claim by Shinwell that its programme was 'in advance of the English section',[70] it was wound up. Labour organisation continued to be weak in Scotland. Because the MacDonald–Gladstone electoral pact had not extended to Scotland, the party had won only two Scottish seats in 1906 and failed to make any advance on this until 1918. As a result of these weaknesses, it was felt necessary to revive a distinct Scottish organisation, within the national Labour Party. In 1912, the Parliamentary Committee of the STUC expressed the 'opinion that the state of the Party in Scotland demands the immediate formation of a Scottish Committee with a view to securing cohesion among the various forces in the movement'.[71]

In 1915, therefore, the Scottish Advisory Council was founded, its title clearly indicating its subordinate role. While its formation owed less to nationalism than to a desire to improve organisation in Scotland, it did nevertheless provide a platform for Home Rulers, who were not slow to exploit it. At its inaugural meeting, Ramsay MacDonald rhetorically asked why the labour movement in Scotland was weak, and answered: 'First of all, it had not been Scotch enough.' Thus, when Home Rule feeling began to mount in the Labour Party during the First World War, there was an organisation ready to direct it.

In the early years of the century, however, the overriding trend within the labour movement was towards integration with England and a downgrading of the Home Rule cause. The cause was further weakened by the accommodation of the main demands of the crofting community within the politics of the two major parties, particularly the Liberal Party.

By 1888, renewed prosperity had combined with repressive sentences on some of the Lewis land-raiders to bring the land war to an end. The cessation of crofting violence was also accompanied by a rapid decline in the political campaign. From the late 1880s wages were rising for work in the fishing industry, while the fall in the price of meal more than made up for poor cattle prices. The 1886 Act, for all its deficiencies, had enabled the crofters to carry out major improvements in cultivation and in their houses, without having to fear arbitrary eviction without compensation. At the same time the leadership of the Highland Land League had lost support through its political manoeuvrings, which had converted the League from a mass social movement to what one local crofters' leader referred to

as 'a mere political association'.[72] It had firmly identified with
the Liberal Party and with its policy of Irish Home Rule, and in
1897 suffered, along with the Liberal Party, from the weakness of
Rosebery's further land reform proposals. The Conservatives had
based their demolition of the Liberal and Land League candidates
in the Highlands on a programme of government purchase of land
to enable crofters to become peasant proprietors. Land settlement
was slow and expensive, and, as a result, further rounds of land
seizures took place in the 1900s. However – in contrast to the 1880s –
it was now generally accepted that the solution was purchase of land
to resettle landless families, and this was a policy which was fought
out between the Liberal and Tory parties, with a resurgence of
crofter support for the Liberals as a result of their commitment to
sweeping land reform in the 1906 election.

Thus, by the turn of the century the crofting community was no
longer a source of strength for independent Labour representation
in Scotland. Many of its former Lowland leaders and supporters
continued to be active in the Labour cause, but, shorn of the mass
support they had wielded in the early days of the Land League, they
were now forced to attune their programme far more to the interests
of a predominantly trade-union based party. This does not mean
that the commitment to Home Rule and land reform was
abandoned, but only that its nature underwent a change. It ceased
to be an integral part of the party's character, and became more of a
programmatic tactic, a means of seeking to enlarge the party's
support in areas where trade unionism was weak.

The first attempt of this kind followed on the revived land-raids,
which coincided with the Liberal Party's attempts, following their
1906 victory, to introduce further land reform. In 1909 a new
Highland Land League was formed in Glasgow; it was essentially
the creation of Tom Johnston, editor of the *Forward*, a paper aligned
with the ILP, and was designed, as Johnston put it, to be 'absolutely
free from the coat-tails of the Liberal Party'. Land League
candidates were to be asked to adhere to the constitution of the
Labour Party! G. B. Clark was persuaded to become president of the
new organisation. The crofters were not to be prised away from their
support of the Liberal Party, which was making efforts – against
opposition from the Tory majority in the Lords – to introduce
further land reform, and the new League did not gain enough
support in the Highlands to contest any constituency in either of the
1910 elections.[73] Nevertheless, the attempt to win support for

Labour on this basis inevitably revived the old alliance with Home Rulers and Gaelic enthusiasts, who were also seeking a basis for their politics in the discontents of the crofters.

By the end of our period, then, Home Rule was no longer as important and 'live' a demand as in the 1880s, and remained part of the policy of Labour in Scotland mainly because of the radical heritage, and the fact that Labour tended to follow Liberal Party policy on the issue. Nevertheless, apart from a feeling in some quarters that political issues tended to be a distraction from the more important social needs of the working class, there was no outright hostility to Scottish Home Rule, and it remained an acceptable and traditional part of the programme.

Thus, in its regular series of 'Black Lists' of reactionary MPs, Tom Johnston's *Forward* included a list of Members who had opposed Home Rule.[74] However, even *Forward*'s interest was sporadic and largely prompted by the interest of Roland Muirhead, a wealthy nationalist and ILP member who was a shareholder; of G. B. Clark, who wrote for it as well as being a sponsor; and of the radical Liberals, who continued to have the hospitality of its columns, in accordance with Johnston's policy of encouraging dialogue between the various sections of the Scottish left. Indeed, Johnston later admitted that a friend had remarked in jest that it was always possible to know 'when the *Forward* was in exceptionally deep water; it would then come out with a specially strong Home Rule issue: that would be preparatory to "touching" Mr Muirhead for a loan'.[75] When given prominence it was usually for tactical reasons, as part of an attempt to revive the alliance with the crofters and win their support for Labour, but this was never successful. Finally, expressions in general terms of support for the principle of Scottish Home Rule accorded well with the sentiments of a large part of the Scottish trade union movement, which still felt itself to have interests separate from those of the English working class, without apparently hampering in any way the rapidly developing integration of the labour movement on a British basis.

3 The Nationalist Phase: Rise and Decline, 1914–31

I. THE RISE OF THE HOME RULE CAMPAIGN

The period from the beginning of the First World War to the mid 1920s marks a crucial phase in the development of the Scottish labour movement. It saw the movement first veer in a nationalist direction as the leading element in a new Home Rule coalition, but then settle decisively for a strategy of UK political advance and a permanent split with the forces of Scottish nationalism. A general disposition to nationalism was, as we have seen, part of Labour's heritage, but the appearance of the issue in the forefront of Labour's concerns is attributable to the conjuncture of a number of key factors in the 1914–22 period. In the longer term, the significance of the period lies in the failure to set the movement on a separatist road and the consequent decisive choice of the UK strategy.

The First World War and its aftermath provided a favourable climate for European nationalist movements, as the Allies' rhetoric about the rights of small nations, though perhaps not intended for consumption within the British Empire, put the question of self-determination on the political agenda. Within the Empire, the role of the Dominions in the war and their separate representation at the Peace Conference pointed, as did the events in Ireland, to fundamental changes in its structure and operation. In the new imperial order, many people thought that Scotland's position must be given consideration, in the form of Home Rule or even Dominion self-government – the general understanding, which underlay many of the arguments over Ireland, being that 'Dominion status' was a long way short of separation and implied a continuation of the British Empire as an actor in world politics. Scottish Home Rule had already been mooted before the war, with the series of bills culminating in Sir Henry Cowan's measure which received a second reading in 1913. After the war, an inconclusive Speaker's

Conference on devolution was held and Home Rule Bills were moved by Liberals in 1920 and 1922. As an emerging force in Scottish politics, the labour movement needed to define its position on the national question in the light of its own interests and priorities.

The rise and strength of Home Rule agitation in the labour movement can be documented from three principal sources: the records of the Scottish Council of the Labour Party, the records of the STUC and the activities of the Scottish Home Rule Association. The Scottish Council, after its formation in 1915, passed resolutions in favour of Home Rule at every annual conference until 1923. By 1918 a distinctively nationalistic tone had crept into the debates, as comparisons were made between the position of Scotland and that of the Dominions, and the issue began to occupy a great deal of conference time. In 1919 a draft Bill was presented to conference by the Executive. After recounting how Scotland's reconstruction problems 'require the concentration of Scottish brains and machinery upon their solution', this went on,

> Whereas, Scotland, though temporarily deprived, without the consent of her people, and by corrupt means in 1707, of the exercise of her right to self-determination, is at present, as anciently, entitled to legislate for the governance of her national affairs in a Parliament of her own, the full exercise of that right is hereby restored.[1]

It then proceeded to list in some detail the method of electing a new Scottish Parliament. The provisions of this Bill betray the party's continuing concern with political, as opposed to economic and industrial, questions, the somewhat vague conception of Home Rule held by Labour at this time, and the identification of it with an extension of democracy. Nine clauses dealt with procedures for the democratic election of the Parliament, but its functions were covered in a single clause, excluding from its jurisdiction 'Army, Navy, Civil, Diplomatic, Colonial and other Imperial Services.' In 1918, the Dominion comparison led to a call for separate Scottish representation at the Peace Conference, though, as a compromise between national and class consciousness, the demand was limited to representation for the Scottish labour movement. In 1920, the Scottish Executive announced a committee to work with the Parliamentary Party and the National Executive to draft a Home

Rule Bill. Although the committee's work was delayed by the Irish problem, it eventually bore fruit in George Buchanan's Bill of 1924. Within the Scottish Division of the ILP, Home Rule sentiment rapidly built up after the war, though from an early date ideological misgivings were heard. In 1919 its conference passed a resolution calling for a Scottish Parliament but defeated an amendment calling for 'a Scottish Socialist Government in Scotland', after an Irish delegate had declared that the only freedom which mattered was economic freedom. In 1922 the conference went a great deal further and demanded a constituent assembly so that the Scottish nation could determine its own form of government. In January 1924 the chairman of Conference (seemingly ignoring the fact that the United Kingdom was by then enjoying Labour government, albeit precariously) declared that, as Labour was now the biggest party in Scotland, if they had Home Rule they would have a Labour government. The following year, more opposition was heard, with one delegate asking who had given the Scottish members of the ILP in Parliament permission to bring forward a Scottish Home Rule Bill. The ILP thus reflected both extremes, of support for and opposition to Home Rule, and, while a solid majority were in the former camp, the ground was laid for the later ideological wrangles on the correct socialist attitude to the question.

Trade union enthusiasm for Home Rule was even more intense, though shorter-lived than that on the political side of the movement. In the STUC, Home Rule resolutions were carried unanimously or with large majorities every year from 1914 to 1923, and at meetings with the Prime Minister and Secretary for Scotland in 1918 and 1919 Home Rule was at the top of the agenda. The STUC also demanded Scottish representation at the Peace Conference and in 1923 voted for 'Dominion Self-Government'.[2] This was to remain official policy for eight years, though even by 1923 sporadic opposition had begun to appear, with one or two speakers deploring the pursuit of Home Rule as likely to divide the working class. As in the Labour Party, support for Home Rule was general, but the leading role of the Glasgow Trades Council is noteworthy.

In 1918 Roland Muirhead, the wealthy owner of a tannery and at that time secretary of Lochwinnoch ILP, formed a new Scottish Home Rule Association (SHRA).[3] Although officially a non-party body, this was increasingly dominated by Labour politicians, to such an extent that it was regarded in some right-wing circles as little more than a Labour 'front'. Several major Scottish unions, such as the miners', as well as the STUC, were early affiliates, and prominent in its early days were James Maxton, then a rising ILP firebrand with a record of opposition to the war; Robert Smillie, the miners' leader; and Tom Johnston, then editor of the radical paper *Forward* and scourge of the landed classes. William Gallacher of the Scottish Co-operative Wholesale Society was president, and the chairman was James Barr, a radical clergyman who had been in trouble with his presbytery for his wartime activities in the Union for Democratic Control and had joined the Labour Party from the Liberals. Also represented were the Highland Land League, several Liberals and a very few Unionists, such as the Marquis of Graham and the ex-Provost of Hamilton, though the Unionists soon dropped out as the left-wing basis of the Association became clear. Graham withdrew his support in 1922 after confusing the Co-operator W. Gallacher with his Communist namesake, and, though he later admitted his mistake, ceased to take an active part in the campaign. As Home Rule became more strongly identified with the emerging left, a widespread right-wing attitude was to identify it with Communism, Papism or even both! Thus in 1922 a correspondent in the *Glasgow Evening Citizen* declared, 'Those who advocate Home Rule are principally Socialists, Communists and Irish, whose aim is to establish Russian rule in Scotland',[4] while the *John o'Groats Journal* thundered:

> Behind this propaganda for Home Rule for Scotland lurks a real danger which is apt to be lost sight of. We cannot shut our eyes to the fact there is in the mining and industrial parts of the country a strong anti-British element, aided and abetted by a powerful section out for Romish domination. . . . If a separate Parliament were set up in Scotland, there is a grave danger that many seats in the areas referred to would be captured by extremists and Romanists, who would use the power thus obtained for their own ends.[5]

The Scottish Council of the Labour Party, however, did not see things in such simple terms. For it, the fact that the SHRA contained non-Labour members presented a serious problem. It did not approve of co-operation with members of other political parties, which could prejudice its central objective of securing greater independent Labour representation, yet it supported Home Rule and did not want to appear antagonistic to it. It therefore ruled that, as Labour was committed to Home Rule, support for the party was the best way to secure this objective, and that Labour Party members should not join the Association. Maxton and Smillie, who were members of the Executive of the Scottish Council, were criticised and asked to withdraw.[6] Such admonitions were of little avail. The SHRA went from strength to strength, increasing its affiliations from trade unions, co-operative societies and ILP branches. As these, rather than local Labour parties, constituted the basis of Labour organisation in Scotland, there was little the Scottish Council could do. Between 1918 and 1928, at least twenty-nine Labour MPs were active in the SHRA,[7] which carried on a vigorous campaign of rallies and demonstrations as well as lobbying politicians and writing to the press. In 1919, it even secured the services of Mrs Annie Besant for a demonstration. Parliamentary by-election candidates were vetted for their views on Home Rule and a recommendation made against any who were not sound on the issue. In practice, it was mainly Unionists who were condemned, and the only Labour candidate who failed to receive an unqualified clean bill of health was Patrick Dollan, later Lord Provost of Glasgow and determined opponent of devolution, who in 1924 received only qualified endorsement at Ayr, on the ground that, while he supported Home Rule, he did not feel able to put it first on his programme.

While, on the surface, the Scottish labour movement in the post-war period appeared set on a determinedly nationalist course, the great upsurge in support for Home Rule must, if the campaign is to be properly explained and evaluated, be seen in the context of Scotland's economic and industrial position and Labour's position within a changing Scottish political structure.

Wartime demands produced a tremendous boom in Scotland's traditional heavy industries. Shipyards were almost overwhelmed with orders and the textile industries were kept busy with orders of all kinds, from sandbags to uniforms, while Clydeside became the most important single munitions centre in Britain.[8] Even the Highland railways, many of which had never really been viable, were now put to intensive use. Wartime expansion was followed by a post-war boom and, although in Scotland this proved even shorter-lived than in the rest of the country, it appeared real enough while it lasted. One result of the boom, with its accompanying high wages and full employment, was a sense of confidence in the Scottish labour movement, in its own strength and in that of the Scottish economy. While the strength of the Scottish economy was never cited as a positive reason for supporting Home Rule, there is no doubt that it was a vital factor in making self-government a viable proposition, and, in contrast to later periods, there were no misgivings felt about the ability of Scottish workers to look after their own interests.

Wartime conditions also saw the emergence of the militant shop stewards' movement and the outbreak of industrial unrest which laid the basis of the myth of 'Red Clydeside'. During the war the heavy industry and engineering skills of Clydeside made it a crucial centre for the munitions industry. The refusal of a wage increase in engineering for which a demand had been pending at the outbreak of the war led to an overtime ban in January 1915, followed by strike, led – against the wishes of trade union officials in the major national unions – by a Central Withdrawal of Labour Committee (composed of shop stewards), which later evolved into the Clyde Workers' Committee. At the same time, pressure for the wartime regulation of trade practices under the Munitions Act, and in particular the dilution of skilled work by the introduction of female and unskilled labour, aided the development of a powerful shop stewards' movement, which sought to oppose the terms of dilution and ultimately achieved a measure of control in its implementation. The shop stewards' movement, co-ordinated in the munitions and engineering district of Clydeside by the Clyde Workers' Committee, was a new and – for a time – rebelliously independent part of the trade union movement. As against the earlier predominance of centralised trade union negotiation, it represented an element of local autonomy which could easily become associated with specifically Clydeside-based political movements.

In January 1919 the official and unofficial Scottish trade union movements joined together in the Forty Hour strike movement – an attempt to secure some protection against expected post-war unemployment by an improvement in working hours. However, 'the Unions in the engineering and shipbuilding industries declined to countenance the Strike or pay Strike Benefit', having balloted their members on the basis of a forty-seven hour week.[9] Dissatisfaction with the damper put on the Scottish movement by national unions was one reason for a desire, under the industrial conditions in the wake of this strike, for Home Rule.

Much of the antagonism in the wartime disputes was directed at government, and, in the absence of strong Scottish Labour representation at Westminster, it was common to blame any shortcomings on the 'English' Government. While it would be mistaken to portray the whole Labour and trade-union movement in Scotland as being in the grip of revolutionary militancy, there was a great deal of sympathy expressed in the STUC with the victims of Government policy and much resentment against government, this resentment often assuming a nationalist form. Much of the impetus for Home Rule within the STUC came from Glasgow Trades Council, which had been much involved in, and occasionally taken the lead in, the Clydeside protests of 1914–19. While it is not possible, except in the case of a few individuals, to establish a direct link between industrial militancy and nationalism, it does appear that the grievances which fed militancy also fed nationalism, which was thus, for a time, able to add to its traditional 'radical' basis of support. This was also made possible by the absence of elements inimical to nationalism in the politics of the Clydeside militants. The two main ingredients of these politics were a traditional defensive craft unionism, manifested in the dilution crisis and revolutionary socialism. The latter tended to be of a syndicalist or anti-state nature and some elements within the movement could even envisage that the Workers' Committee might form the basis of local organs of state power on the soviet model. Indeed, a would-be Glasgow soviet was briefly established. In the event, the turmoil on the Clyde proved short-lived and largely devoid of revolutionary content, but as late as 1921 the continuing belief in the greater strength and militancy of the Scottish movement is reflected in a claim by a delegate to the STUC that there would have been no Triple Alliance failure north of the Tweed if Scottish workers had acted alone.

On the formation of the Communist Party of Great Britain (CPGB), in 1920, the Scottish elements of the Socialist Labour Party, originally founded on Clydeside, and the Scottish Workers' Committee, successor to the Clyde Workers' Committee, tended to stay aloof. After Willie Gallacher, on Lenin's advice, had, in 1921, persuaded the majority of them to join the CPGB, a minority, under the leadership of John Maclean, remained outside, demanding a separate Scottish party. This deprived the Communist Party of its most nationalist elements and for a long time it showed no interest in the national issue. Maclean, a figure of legendary stature in Scottish socialist folklore, had gained considerable support for his stand against the war, which had cost him his job as a school-teacher and several spells in prison. He now moved in an increasingly nationalist direction and, impressed by the example of Sinn Fein and the Celtic nationalism of Erskine of Marr, saw the ferment on the Clyde, the land agitation in the Highlands and the clamour for Home Rule as creating the conditions for the declaration of a Scottish Workers' Republic. In 1918, he received the endorsement of the local Labour Party for his candidature in the Gorbals division of Glasgow after the sitting member, George Barnes, had declined to leave the coalition. In 1923, having refused to join the Communist Party, he stood in the same constituency as a Scottish Workers' Republican candidate, but died before the end of the campaign. An increasingly isolated figure in the left, Maclean in his later career is of interest for his distinctive, though mistaken, interpretation of Scottish politics. His nationalism was partly tactical, based on the belief that Scotland was ripe for a socialist revolution which must be postponed for many years if it had to wait upon England; but it also stemmed from his Celtic roots and his belief in the essential communism of the old Highland clan system.[10] In fact, modern interpretations[11] have discounted the revolutionary significance of the short-lived turmoil on the Clyde, which died down soon after the war. The land agitation, too, was short-lived, never attained Irish levels and was largely stilled by the Land Settlement (Scotland) Act 1919. Thus, while conditions were present to give a temporary boost to the Home Rule movement, Scotland did not possess the wherewithal for a nationalist–socialist revolution.

For the solid centre of the Scottish trade-union movement, a major source of grievance was dissatisfaction with the arrangements for bringing Scottish matters to the attention of the Government. As early as 1905, the STUC had complained, relative to the Unemployed Workmen (Compensation) Act, at the lack of consideration of Scottish conditions.[12] With the growth of Government intervention and bureaucracy in wartime, the problem was much exacerbated. During the war the STUC was directly represented by its chairman on the Workers' National War Emergency Committee, and, in addition, Robert Smillie became chairman of this committee. However, the STUC still pressed for adequate representation on the various Government national and local committees set up in the course of wartime, and claimed the right to nominate their representatives directly. The Home Secretary took the view that this was a 'domestic matter which they ought to arrange with their own Parliamentary representatives who were generally consulted upon matters of that kind',[13] and a meeting was held to impress on the officials of the Parliamentary Labour Party that the Scottish Congress should always be considered in the selection of national committees to deal with public questions. Nevertheless, in 1918 the STUC still found it necessary to pass a resolution of protest at the treatment of Scottish trade union interests by the Government, and to affirm that 'no National Committee can be considered as complete unless Scottish Trade Unionism is officially represented'.

While the focus of protest was the Government, an ambiguous remark by Hugh Lyon of the Scottish Horse and Motormen's Association, in his presidential address to Congress, indicates that English trade union leadership was equally the object of resentment: 'The Scottish Trade Unionists and Co-operators have been badly treated by the predominant partner in the past, but more so since the war began. We have simply been ignored . . . .' It was in this context that Lyon advocated Home Rule:

> We have simply been ignored, and personally I can see that if any reconstruction is to take place in Scotland after the war, then we should not be humbugged by writing and sending deputations to people in London who know absolutely nothing of our wants. A Parliament should be set up in Scotland, thus saving time and expense and giving the people of Scotland a fair opportunity of working out their salvation.[14]

Although Scottish trade-union and labour leaders had played a leading part in committees, this had apparently been in their capacity as national figures. Meanwhile, important sections of the Scottish labour movement – the independent Scottish unions, such as Lyon's Horse and Motormen's Association; the bakers, who proposed the resolution referred to; and the powerful Glasgow Trades Council, which played a leading policy-making role in the STUC – felt themselves completely unrepresented in any official capacity. This was clearly a most important motive for the demand, at the 1918 congress of the STUC, for Home Rule.

The issue remained a live one, and after the war the Minister of Labour was asked to keep in closer touch with the STUC on matters relating to reconstruction and demobilisation. However, in 1921 the demand for separate representation on committees dealing with

industrial questions introduced the proviso that the trade unions
in the industries concerned should directly appoint their representatives. This resolution was supported by the Amalgamated
Engineering Union, on only the second occasion that the engineers
were represented at Congress, and was a concession to the national
trade unions, since previously it had been maintained that nomi-
nations should be made by the Parliamentary Committee of the
STUC itself. Thereafter, the issue of Scottish labour representation
on Government committees seems to have dropped from the
forefront of STUC concern, following the dismantling of wartime
controls and the advance of Labour Parliamentary representation,
which provided an alternative channel of representation for
Scottish labour.

On the political, as on the industrial, front, the period following
the war was one of optimism. Because of this, it has often been
suggested that Labour's support for Home Rule was tactical. By this
is meant either that Labour adopted a nationalist posture as part of
its electoral strategy, to tap nationalist feelings among the electorate,[15] or that Labour, being stronger in Scotland than in
England, thought that socialism would be delayed by seeking
advance on a UK front.[16] These two theories are not strictly
compatible. The former implies that a commitment to socialist and
Labour goals was not sufficient to rally mass support in Scotland
and that nationalism needed to be added; the latter, that the
Scottish working class had been converted to socialism. In fact, as
we have noted, nationalism was widely perceived in this period as
an integral part of radical, liberal and socialist philosophies and not
as a competing ideology with which compromises must be made,
though in later times it did indeed assume such a role. Despite
Ramsay MacDonald's remarks in 1915, it is fairly clear that Labour
failed to make a major electoral breakthrough before1918–22 not
because of a lack of commitment to Scottish nationalism but
because of the reluctance of the Irish, both Catholic and Protestant,
to support it. Difficulties with the Catholic vote persisted at least up
to the Irish treaty of 1921 and with the Protestant vote for much
longer. In the Highlands, Home Rule propaganda accompanied
land-reform propaganda, but, in the Lowlands, Labour leaders, far
from having to compromise with nationalism, seemed, at this time,
actively to encourage it.

The argument that Labour saw Home Rule as providing the
opportunity for a more rapid advance, on the basis of Labour's

greater strength in Scotland, has greater force. Whereas, before 1918, Labour's position had been weaker in Scotland than in England, the advance of 1918 was greater in Scotland. From 1918 to 1929, its position was much stronger in Scotland than in England, particularly in terms of Parliamentary seats. While, as we have seen, the Home Rule agitation started before 1918 in the industrial wing of the movement, partly in response to Government industrial policy, after 1918 it was taken up with even greater vigour than before by the political wing. The great Labour advance of 1922 gave further support to those who argued against waiting for England to catch up. By 1923, the Scottish Labour conference was being told by its chairman that, if Scotland had had Home Rule, she would now have a Labour government. As we show below, Labour's very strength could serve to undermine the case for Home Rule, but the immediate effect was to give it added force. A British Labour government seemed a remote prospect in the immediate aftermath of the war, and to aim first for power at a Scottish level seemed a sounder policy. Before 1922, Scottish Labour lacked an effective political platform. After 1922, the platform was there; but real power, or even the prospect of it, was not.

One area in which Labour did consciously seek to broaden its electoral base was the Highlands, and the party's efforts to capitalise electorally on the renewed land agitation in the post-war period constitute another of the forces making for the Home Rule commitment. In order to win support in the Highlands and Islands, where trade unionism was much weaker than in the Lowland industrial belt, the Labour Party had to come to terms with the problems in these areas and in particular the land question, a focus of radical agitation in Scotland since the 1880s. Inevitably, the socialists, having once gained impetus from the crofters' movement at the germinal stage of the Labour Party in Scotland, were reluctant to concede the political leadership of the crofters to the Liberal Party. The question thus arose of what political and organisational strategy to adopt.

In 1915 Joseph Duncan proposed to the inaugural conference of the Labour Party's Scottish Advisory Council that, with the help of trade unions, such as the branches of the newly-founded Scottish Farm Servants' Union (SFSU), local organisations should be established to 'rope in rural Radical opinion'. The formation of the SFSU, organising the farm wage workers, provided a suitable basis for a strategy of building a trade-union based Labour Party in the rural areas – at least, those in which the union had a basis. In practice this may have been largely confined to the east of Scotland, especially Aberdeenshire.

There remained the problem of what to do about the Highlands and Islands, where the trade union movement was weakest and a significant portion of the population were crofters and cottars, who drew part of their living from the land and only part from wage labour – largely seasonal work in the harvests and fishing boats. Land nationalisation was one possibility widely canvassed in the Scottish labour movement. Robert Smillie told the 1917 conference that 'he hoped to see the day when every Highland constituency would assist in the movement to regain common ownership of the land by returning Labour representatives to the House of Commons'. No doubt to this end, a resolution was carried calling for expropriation of the land within thirty years, or two generations, 'paying compensation only for buildings erected thereon', and so on. But Dr G. B. Clark, veteran crofters' MP and delegate from the SFSU, opposed the resolution. Although the SFSU had no objection to nationalisation of the land, and wanted the land used for the benefit of the nation, it could not support the scheme as proposed, because, 'if the landowner was to be compensated for his capital outlay on buildings, then the farmer ought to be compensated for the capital he had invested in farming'. Evidently the interests of the crofter or small farmer could not simply be assimilated with those of the farm labourer in drawing up a land programme for Scotland.

The issue became more acute in 1918, when the party had to face a General Election. A Highland Land League (HLL) had been revived in 1909, by a group of Gaelic enthusiasts and Labour supporters, such as Tom Johnston.[17] This soon re-established the link between Highland land agitation and Scottish Home Rule. In 1916 the council of the HLL reported that 'the question of making autonomy for Scotland a foremost plank of the League's platform [had] been considered by the Council and the necessary alterations to the Constitution and objects to admit this . . . recommended to the General Meeting, as the experience of government by Westminster has been a sad one for the Gaelic race.'[18] In 1918, land agitation and raiding were revived by the return of landless ex-soldiers from the Highland regiments, who had been promised land on their return from the trenches. The HLL conducted a tour of the Highlands and Islands to propagate its programme, namely

'Autonomy for Scotland, the Land for the People, and Native (as opposed to English or Feudal) Culture'.[19] Robert Smillie had promised that the HLL would enjoy the full support of organised labour in Scotland, provided that its policy of these 'Three Essentials' was suitably supported by the people to whom its appeal was principally addressed – i.e. the crofting community.

The HLL's issue of an 'Appeal to the Scottish People' placed the Labour Party in the position of having to decide whether to co-operate with it electorally and support its programme. The Labour Party Scottish Advisory Council informed headquarters that it considered this a matter within its own right to determine, and Henderson agreed to leave the matter in its hands provided that the appeal was in harmony with the land policy of the party. The Executive proposed to the 1918 conference that the party enter into an electoral agreement with the League, involving support of its candidates in five constituencies. This was carried, but aroused some opposition. Joseph Duncan of the SFSU moved reference back of the relevant paragraphs of the Executive's report, on the ground that the party was relying insufficiently on their own efforts, and that trade union and Labour Party branches in the north should be able to select their own candidates just as elsewhere. However, Dr G. B. Clark of the same union supported the alliance.

This strategy represented a defeat for Duncan, who, as we have seen, advocated a trade-union based Labour Party in the Highlands, and a victory for Smillie and Clark. Clark, although, like Duncan, a leader of the SFSU, was of another generation, a veteran Parliamentary supporter of the crofters' movement; Duncan, by contrast, was a modern, practical trade unionist, more concerned to further the interests of the wage labourers in the SFSU than to embark on a risky alliance with a group claiming, with dubious credentials, to represent the crofting community.

The *Scottish Programme* which was used in the 1918 General Election thus included at the head of its list of ten items '(1) COMPLETE RESTORATION OF THE LAND OF SCOTLAND to the Scottish People'. Item (3), 'THE SELF-DETERMINATION OF THE SCOTTISH PEOPLE', was already established policy. A joint committee of the Labour Party Scottish Advisory Council and the HLL was appointed, and a joint national appeal was issued for the election. However, the electoral alliance was a failure, and shortly after the election the Scottish Council broke off its association with the HLL. Difficulties had apparently arisen from the interference of the

London Council of HLL. The Executive reported to the 1919 conference:

> These difficulties have caused your Committee to come to the CONCLUSION that further co-operation with the London Council of the HLL . . . is impracticable. Moreover, we are of opinion that, in any case, the organisation by Londoners of a Scottish movement is alike administratively impracticable and inconsistent with the first principles of the alliance – namely, 'Home Rule for Scotland' . . . although the Highland Land League has in years long past justly earned a great reputation, it is now but the shadow of what it once was, and has little or no prospect of effective revival . . . the total membership is probably not above 500 in Scotland, the majority of whom are not resident in the Highlands. [No doubt this disappointed Labour leaders, who had been impressed by the HLL's ballot of its members throughout Scotland, who voted by 5220 to nil in favour of the electoral arrangement with the Labour Party![20]] On the other hand, we have a list of close upon 100 Branches of Trade Unions, practically all of which are affiliated to the National Labour Party, in the four Highland Divisions alone. . . .
>
> The opinion of your Executive is that the only chance of self-betterment by political means of the conditions of the workers in the Highlands, lies in their organisation on the lines of the Labour Party Constitution . . . .

Thus Duncan's strategy was entirely vindicated. Nevertheless, the Labour Party continued to make special efforts to win support in the Highlands, and, when the Parliamentary Committee of the STUC decided to affiliate to the SHRA, this was one of the arguments used to support the decision when challenged at the STUC's 1919 congress:

> Baillie Robert Climie (Ayrshire Trades Council) said it was true that they had a little trouble with their Home Rule friends at the General Election, but that was not a real obstacle. They had to keep in mind that there were many people in the Highlands who could not affiliate with the Labour Party, and the Home Rule Association was one way

of keeping in touch with them. Their withdrawal would have a bad effect on the Home Rule movement.

A Highland Labour Party based in Glasgow was constituted, to agitate among Highlanders in Glasgow on the conditions of their kith and kin in the Highlands. Joseph Duncan objected on the usual grounds that organisation in the Highlands should not be from outside, but Ben Shaw, the secretary of the Scottish Council, assured him that the Glasgow Committee would mainly be forwarding the development of the orthodox Labour Party organisations in the Highlands on the same lines as elsewhere in Scotland.

Despite the 1919 Land Settlement Act, legal land redistribution still proceeded at a snail's pace, and land raids continued in 1920 and 1921. A resolution at the 1920 Scottish Labour Conference would have committed the party not only to support for the land-raiders on the Isle of Lewis, but also to a general policy of establishing smallholdings. Joe Duncan objected to this part of the resolution, on the grounds that 'small holdings . . . would raise a bulwark of reaction. . . . Lewis could not maintain its population by a system of small holdings . . . .' The Scottish Council agreed to remit the resolution for redrafting on the lines indicated by Duncan. In 1921 the request of the Highland Labour Party (Glasgow section) for representation on the Scottish Council and its Executive, and for a full-time organiser for the Highlands, was sympathetically rejected by the Executive.

Thereafter, the Labour Party seems to have given up any special organisational adaptations to the problems of winning support in the Highlands. By 1924, as Hunter points out, the post-war crisis in the Hebrides was over. Practically all the potentially arable land in areas where the land hunger had been most acute had been resettled under crofting tenure. By the end of the 1920s, therefore, the long struggle for the land was virtually at an end. With the end of the land crisis, the hopes of winning the crofting community's support away from the Liberal Party on the basis of a sort of land-and-labour agitation ended too. If not a bulwark of reaction, the smallholders were henceforth no longer a major radical force in Scottish politics.

As we have seen, Highland land reform and Scottish Home Rule had been linked since the 1880s, as a result of the alliance between Gaelic revivalists and Lowland radicals on the one side and the crofting community on the other. The revival of land-raiding in the

post-war crisis, and the need to broaden the basis of electoral
support in the crofting areas persuaded the Labour Party to renew
the alliance, this time bringing in organised labour as an ally of
Gaelic revivalism. However, as Hunter has shown, 'the established
political parties were able to compromise much more with rural
than with urban unrest'. For example, in the Western Isles
constituency in 1918, the pledges of the Asquithian Liberal and
coalition candidates 'were scarcely less revolutionary than those
made by the Land League–Labour candidate who came a poor
third in the poll'. The most urgent of the crofters' demands could be
settled by the Liberal Party, so that, by the mid 1920s, the land-and-
labour motive for labour-movement support for Scottish Home
Rule – an indirect connection at the best of times – became no more
than a sentimental remnant.

Much of the support for Home Rule after the First World War
came from the third of the three major elements in the labour
movement – the Co-operative movement. The chairman of the
Scottish Co-operative Wholesale Society (SCWS), William
Gallacher, was appointed president of the SHRA at its first annual
meeting, in March 1919, and the first published list of organisation delegates to the SHRA's General Council included eighteen
Co-operative societies (with twenty-eight delegates), eleven Co-
operative women's guilds, and two Co-operative men's guilds. This
compared with only eleven trade unions (mainly local branches)
and five trades councils and only three ILP branches. How can the
high level of Co-operative support for Home Rule be explained?
First, the movement in Scotland was politically in advance of the
English Co-operative movement in seeking independent political
representation, and was indignant at subsequent English attempts
to interfere with its own political autonomy. Linked to this, as an
organisation of consumers based on the locality, the Co-op
movement was more immediately representative of a variety of
Scottish popular interests outside the organised trade union movement than any other part of the labour movement, and it is only to
be expected that it brought such popular causes as Home Rule into
the debates on labour-movement policy. Second, there was the
desire of the movement, and of some of the trade unions representing its employees, to retain machinery for the determination of the
conditions of labour on the existing Scottish basis.

The greater readiness of Scottish Co-operators to commit
themselves to political activity has been attributed to the effects of

the attempt by Glasgow traders to resist the growing influence of the Co-ops by the boycott campaigns of the 1880s and 1890s. The traders had boycotted the Co-ops and sacked employees who were Co-op members. The second of the boycott campaigns, in the late 1890s, and especially the butchers' boycott in Glasgow (when wholesalers refused to deal with the retail Co-ops), was the most important turning point. In the Scottish Section of the Co-operative Union a Defence Committee was formed, with the object of getting elected to town councils, county councils, parish councils and school boards candidates pledged to support Co-operation.[21] Further resentment was aroused during the First World War, when Government control of the food supply was seen as favouring private retailers as against the Co-ops. For instance, the SCWS was prevented from using its links with Canadian producers to secure cheap wheat for Scottish Co-operators.

It is not surprising, therefore, that, before the 1917 Swansea congress of the Co-operative Union decided to establish an independent Co-operative Party on friendly terms with the various sections of the Labour Party, the Scottish movement had already formed a Central Co-operative Parliamentary Committee, representing every conference district in Scotland. In addition to this national committee, the district associations formed local committees to organise the Co-operative vote in the constituencies.

This more rapid political development in Scotland was apparently well understood and welcomed by the Labour Party. In March 1917 Ben Shaw, secretary of the Labour Party Scottish Advisory Council, wrote to Jimmy Middleton, assistant secretary of the Labour Party, shortly before attending the Falkirk conference of the Scottish Co-operative movement:

There is a controversy going on in Scotland as to something like an amalgamation of the two Co-operative Wholesales, but I do not think it will carry. The tendency is to keep the Scottish and English Co-operative Movements separate economically and to introduce an element of separation, even in Educational matters. Should this eventuate in an independent Co-operative Union for Scotland, in place of the 'Section' presently existing, the Co-operative Movement in Scotland will rapidly drift into politics.[22]

Thus, the separatist tendency within the Scottish movement was seen as helping the Labour Party.

However, when the Co-operative Union set up national machinery for securing Parliamentary representation, the already established Scottish organisation was not recognised. This caused indignation in the Scottish movement, and at the Scottish Cooperative conference held in Glasgow in April 1918 the following resolution was carried by a very large majority:

That a separate Committee be instituted for Scotland, consisting of three members of the Scottish Section, two members of the Scottish Co-operative Wholesale Society's Board, one from each of the ten Conference District Committees, one from the Scottish Women's Guild, and one from the Men's Guild. This Committee to exercise all the powers, so far as Scotland is concerned, as the scheme confers on the Central Parliamentary Representation Committee, and to work in close co-operation with the Central Parliamentary Representation Committee in its national policy.

During the debate it was said that the Scottish movement had been dragged at the heels of England ever since the Perth congress (when, in 1897, Sir William Maxwell, Chairman of the SCWS, had addressed delegates in support of direct Parliamentary representation). The *Scottish Co-operator* of the following week remarked in a leader:

There was strong expression of opinion [at the conference] that Scotland must have freedom to work out its own social and political salvation. This does not involve any antipathy to England or any other country, as it ought to be recognised that a confederation of self-governing units was far stronger than any organisation which could be managed from any one centre.

However, the Co-operative congress meeting at Liverpool defeated by a large majority the proposal of the Scottish societies. Erskine of Marr's *Scottish Review* commented: 'The political activities of the Scottish Co-operators will still be controlled by "a Committee sitting in London or Manchester", and the movement in Scotland will be clogged by the deadweight of English conservatism.'[23]

In March 1919 William Gallacher of the SCWS became the

president of the SHRA. The association of the Co-operative and nationalistic movements was welcomed in the *Scottish Review* in an article entitled 'Towards the Commonwealth', which concluded: 'In Scotland the union of Co-operative, Labour, and National Parties is one of the most hopeful developments in our political life.'[24]

Thus, the Co-operative movement seems to have been brought firmly into the Home Rule camp by a combination of resentment at being held back by the politically more backward movement in England, and indignation at the suppression of the autonomy of the Scottish movement in political work. The latter was seen as necessary on the familiar grounds that Scotland was a radical country held back by England from carrying out necessary reforming legislation. This popular view naturally found expression in a large movement based on popular membership in the localities. It was also a traditional view in a movement whose leading members had, 'for the first eighty years of the nineteenth century, belonged generally to the Radical Party'.[25]

The economic divergence of the English and Scottish Co-operative movements was apparent at an early date. The Co-operative movement was necessarily local in its origins, finding the capital for new ventures from the dividend reinvested by members. The success of local Co-ops, the spheres of distributive and productive activity into which they entered and the conditions of labour affecting their employees were all affected by locally differing conditions. On the employment side, the Scottish movement had certain characteristics which may have accounted for a desire to retain autonomy in the settlement of conditions of labour, not just on the part of the societies, but also of some of the unions representing their staff.

One of the features of the movement was the strength of the productive side as against the retail side. The earliest productive ventures were the bakeries, some of which were established as federations of a number of retail societies. The largest of these, the United Co-operative Baking Society of Glasgow, had 1400 employees by 1919. In addition, many local societies had their own bakeries. The SCWS established a shirt factory in 1881, and in 1886 opened the giant Shieldhall industrial estate between Glasgow and Renfrew, which ultimately included the following productive departments: tailoring, boot-making, cabinet-making, hosiery, jam-making, printing, confectionery and tobacco. Elsewhere, the

SCWS was engaged in the manufacture of soap, flour, margarine, wood and jute. The boot and shoe factory was the largest in Scotland, employing about 1000 workers at the turn of the century.[26]

These ventures were not purely intended to cheapen the cost of living. One of the major objects was to secure better conditions of labour, and efforts were made to establish Co-operative factories as showpieces exemplifying that the best trade union rates and hours were compatible with commercial success and a low-priced product. Some of the unions in the productive sectors heavily affected by Co-operative enterprise were old-established Scottish unions – notably the bakers (Operative Bakers and Confectioners) and the boot- and shoemakers. It may be that the good conditions offered in these trades by a leading employer of unionised labour reinforced the satisfaction of these unions with purely Scottish or even district negotiations and made Home Rule an attractive option. However, the large distributive and shop workers' unions were founded from the first on an all-British basis, and their interests might therefore be expected to be different. In the early years of the century, district hours and wages boards had come into being, with a national council as supreme court of appeal. They were intended to standardise local conditions of hours and wages, and to deal with disputes between societies and their employees. The Amalgamated Union of Co-operative Employees (AUCE) was by this time a powerful union, organised on industrial unionist lines (embracing all Co-op employees, without regard to particular skills).

In 1922–3 the issue of national wages machinery was considered by the STUC arising from proposals of the British TUC General Council for the revision of the machinery of the Joint Committee of Trade Unionists and Co-operators. These proposals were intended to supersede the purely Scottish machinery, with eight joint conciliation and arbitration area councils being proposed, presumably to include Scotland, under one national council. The STUC Parliamentary Committee took the view that disputes arising in Scotland 'should continue to be dealt with by machinery created within the Scottish Area', and convened a special conference of the unions concerned.· The National Union of Distributive and Allied Workers (NUDAW), which was a fusion of AUCE with another distributive workers' union, was the largest of the unions representing Co-operative employees. Its delegates stated that 'they were not particularly in favour of Scotland having

Home Rule, as they were out to establish National Rates embracing England and Scotland. Scotland could be represented on the National Joint Council.' Furthermore, 'they believed that the Unions should be directly represented on any machinery'. However, the other, smaller unions disagreed. Councillor W. G. Hunter, of the Operative Bakers and Confectioners, representing a 'purely Scottish Union', stated that 'they had decided against a National Wages Board in Scotland, desiring to revert to district arrangements in the Baking Trade'. The Shop Assistants' Union was not quite so localist, but 'was strongly in favour of the Scottish position being maintained'.[27]

In the event, the NUDAW was outvoted, and the STUC Parliamentary Committee drew up proposals for a new Joint Arbitration Board for Scotland which would be separate from the English machinery, and which would include *indirect* trade union representation, through the STUC General Council, rather than the direct representation sought by NUDAW.

The Co-operative movement's interest in Scottish autonomy, however, did not survive the changing climate of the 1920s, and later events reinforced the interests of the unions in strengthening the national arbitration machinery. By the late 1920s, differences between the English and Scottish movements were no longer fuelling the fires of Home Rule sentiment, and the remaining Home Rulers, such as William Gallacher, were basing their case on more traditional grounds. In a 1927 article, 'Scottish Home Rule: The Case for Self-Government for Scotland', Gallacher does not even refer to divisions within the Co-operative movement and the argument is put forward in general, political terms. The main argument is that, aside from reasons of national sentiment, the practical case for Home Rule rests on the drag placed on social reform in Scotland by the dominance of Conservative England. The issues referred to are familiar in the Home Rule repertory: land reform, housing conditions, infant mortality, unemployment and emigration, education, the expense of local-authority Bills at Westminster, the congestion of the Commons, temperance reform.

II.   CLIMAX AND SLUMP IN THE CAMPAIGN

The Home Rule campaign in the labour movement reached a peak immediately after the electoral breakthrough of 1922 had raised

Scottish Labour confidence to new heights, and it slumped shortly afterwards as the economic recession began to bite. At the 1922 General Election, Labour, while doing slightly better in Scotland than in England in terms of votes, won proportionately twice as many Scottish as English seats. Twenty-nine Scottish socialists were returned, against a mere seven in 1918. This was a crucial election in Scottish political history, fundamentally altering the political balance, but it is generally remembered for the unleashing on Westminster of the famous Clydesiders. The atmosphere of euphoria is vividly recalled by contemporaries and the scenes of enthusiasm surrounding their departure for Westminster are deeply ingrained in the Scottish Labour memory. As staunch supporters of Home Rule, they promised that they would soon be back to sit in a Scottish Parliament. John Wheatley, on arrival at Euston, told reporters: 'There is no subject that arouses such enthusiasm there as the subject of Scottish Home Rule.'[28]

The Scottish Home Rule Association's activities, too, reached a peak around 1922–4. Its individual membership grew steadily until 1926 and corporate members included over a hundred trade-union branches, over sixty Co-operative societies, and fifty 'political organisations' – mainly ILP branches, Labour Party branches not being permitted by the party to affiliate. At least twenty-nine Labour MPs, from all sections of the party, as well as leading trade unionists, were active in the Association in the 1920s. As the main forum for radical agitation for Home Rule in the 1920s, the SHRA held a series of meetings and demonstrations, at which the principal speakers were usually Labour MPs. Following the Irish settlement of 1921–2, efforts were stepped up, with a major demonstration in Glasgow, and by 1923 enthusiasm was still greater. On 25 August, 35,000 people were reported to have gathered on Glasgow Green to hear ten Labour MPs harangue them on the need for Home Rule. James Maxton, working up to a pitch of excitement, declared that experience of Westminster 'had converted him absolutely to the necessity of making a strenuous effort to keep their own Parliament in Scotland',[29] and went so far as to add: 'We mean to tell them they can do what they like about English children but that they are not going to suffer Scottish children to die.'[30]

Such extreme sentiments owed their origin partly to a contrast between a Scotland in which Labour was in the ascendancy and a largely Conservative England, such that the party and class divide seemed to many in the labour movement to coincide with the national boundary. The tactical advantages of Home Rule to Scottish Labour were greatly strengthened by the gains of 1922 and the further advance of 1923, when the party came to within two seats of an overall Scottish majority. The chairman, J. R. Bell of the National Union of Railwaymen, commented at the 1923 conference,[31]

> Had Scotland been in the enjoyment of Home Rule, it is certain that a Labour Government would now have been in power North of the Tweed, and this thought should stimulate to greater efforts the large and growing number of Scotsmen who are bent upon having a Parliament in Edinburgh to manage Scottish domestic affairs.

Members of the National Executive Committee of the party were happy to give their full support to the Scottish Labour Party's demands for Home Rule, although expressing the desire that this should not evolve into a demand for separation. As the fraternal delegate from the NEC remarked to the Scottish Council in 1923:[32] 'National autonomy was not in conflict with international socialism. . . . England was always Conservative. . . . It might, therefore, be that "the Celtic fringe" would save Saxon England from the folly of its own Conservatism.' Reading between the lines, a Labour government in a Home Rule assembly in Scotland would be most welcome, provided Scotland was still sending Labour MPs to swell the socialist presence in an overall Imperial Parliament at Westminster!

Labour demands for Home Rule continued under the Labour Government of 1924, when the bill in preparation by the Scottish Council of the Labour Party and Scottish Labour MPs since 1920 was introduced by George Buchanan. SHRA demonstrations in support of the bill reached a climax with a rally in St Andrews Hall in Glasgow, attended by six MPs, with apologies from several more, at which Maxton again excelled himself, declaring that he would 'ask for no greater job in life (than to make) the English-ridden, capitalist-ridden, landlord-ridden Scotland into a Scottish socialist Commonwealth'.[33] The election of the new Government had raised the hopes of Scottish Home Rulers, as Home Rule all round had been Labour Party policy since 1918 and both the Prime Minister and the Secretary for Scotland were supporters. Buchanan's bill proposed a system of federal Home Rule, with the Scottish MPs remaining at Westminster pending the achievement of Home Rule all round. Claiming the support of all the Scottish Labour MPs, including the Secretary for Scotland, Buchanan asked for, at least, time for the bill or a committee of inquiry. Thomas Johnston, seconding, talked of the different needs of Scotland in areas such as land, education and religious affairs, as well as discoursing on Scotland's national achievement and on Stevenson, Burns and Bannockburn. William Adamson, the Secretary for Scotland, gave the Government's approval in principle to the measure and suggested a committee of inquiry. However, when Buchanan, along with Macpherson, Neil Maclean and Maxton, tried to move the closure, the Speaker, in a highly controversial ruling, refused and the bill was talked out by Conservatives amid typically 'Clydesider' scenes of uproar and disorder.[34]

In view of the pressure from Scottish Labour, the Cabinet was in principle willing to appoint a committee of inquiry and asked the Lord Privy Seal, J. R. Clynes, to draw up terms of reference.[35] Clynes's suggestion of a royal commission was turned down in Cabinet on the grounds that, on such a constitutional matter, the investigation should be undertaken by MPs, but a select committee of MPs was, in turn, ruled out, because of the likely attitude of the Conservatives and because the Government would lack a majority on it. The Prime Minister was thus authorised to inform Labour and Liberal Scottish Home Rulers that, while the Government had the idea of an inquiry under consideration, the practical difficulties made it impossible for the time being.[36] In its precarious position, it is difficult to envisage the Government doing other than stalling on the issue. While Home Rule was indeed Labour policy, it had never featured strongly in Labour propaganda outside Scotland and was too far down the list of national priorities for it to be worth putting the Government's survival at risk for it.

In the 1924 General Election, in both England and Scotland, the vote of both Conservative and Labour parties increased at the expense of the Liberals. In Scotland this left Labour as the most popular party in terms of votes, but second to the Conservatives in terms of seats, having suffered a net loss of eight. Nevertheless, the fall of the Labour Government did not, as might be expected from the 'tactical' hypothesis, lead to a renewal of demands for Home Rule. The focus of attention had shifted decisively to Westminster, and the 1925 Scottish Labour conference was entirely taken up with post mortems on the late Government, with no mention of Home Rule throughout the proceedings.

In retrospect, the climax of the Home Rule campaign in 1924 can be seen to disguise a fatal weakening of it around 1922, as economic recession and political advance pointed the movement towards closer involvement in UK politics. In Scotland, dependent as it was on export-oriented and heavy industries which had been over-expanded to meet wartime demands, economic slump followed the post-war boom even more rapidly than in England. As early as 1921, the bottom had fallen out of the ship-building market, dealing a heavy blow to the industries of the Clyde, whilst on the east coast the jute industry of Dundee suffered a similar fate.[37] Agriculture, too, began a long depression, with prices falling by about half between 1920 and 1922.[38] By 1922 there were over 80,000 unemployed in Glasgow alone,[39] and trade-union membership slumped. This was reflected in affiliations to the STUC, which fell from 560,000 in 1921 to under 227,000 in 1922. The National Union of General and Municipal Workers and the Scottish Farm Servants' Union did not renew their affiliations at all for 1922, while affiliations for the miners and the Iron and Steel Trades Confederation were more than halved.[40] The power of the unofficial Clydeside movement declined.

At the peak of the depression in 1921, unemployment in engineering rose to 27 per cent. As early as 1920, an observer wrote: 'The unofficial shop stewards' movement is at ebb tide, because of the percentage unemployed in the metal trades. The man at the gate determines the status of the man at the bench.'[41]

Not that this was a period of industrial peace. On the contrary, it saw a series of struggles, culminating in the General Strike of 1926, but, instead of the locally based unofficial action which had taken advantage of the labour shortage in wartime, the disputes were characteristically large-scale and protracted *defensive* struggles, often involving whole industries.

Within the STUC, the Home Rule agitation came to a head in 1923 with a successful resolution calling for Dominion status, but even the mover felt obliged to add that 'Scotland could not exist as an economic unit'. The recession and the consequent weakening of organised labour had cut away the foundations of the earlier aggressive optimism and no more was heard at the STUC on the subject of Home Rule until 1931.

On the political side of the movement, the electoral breakthrough of 1922, while giving a temporary boost to the Home Rule cause, can now be seen to have fatally weakened it. As we have noted, before 1922 Scottish Labour had lacked a political platform or an avenue leading to the prospect of governmental power. 1922 gave it a base at Westminster and decisively shifted the focus of attention to London. Nationalists within the Labour camp were now faced with a dilemma. To the extent that support for Home Rule was instrumental or tactical, it was always liable to be superseded by other means of attaining the same ends and could never be placed at the head of the programme. As long as Home Rule was not at the head of the programme, agitation for it would always come second to the use of existing constitutional machinery for attaining its primary aims. One of the 1922 generation of MPs told us that the end of Labour support for Home Rule was marked by the euphoric arrival of the Clydesiders at Westminster. While the process in fact took longer than this, it is certainly true that 1922 and the advent of the Labour Government in 1924 were vital stages in the process by which the Scottish Labour leaders were converted to a strategy of UK-wide advance. The significance of 1922 is that, from this point, Scottish Labour was faced with the choice of continuing to demand Home Rule and, given the indifference of the national Labour Party to the issue and its preoccupation with other matters, sliding into separatism, or of concentrating on those immediate issues on which English and Scottish Labour could unite, while using the UK political machinery to secure their distinctively Scottish demands. Perhaps, in other circumstances, had there been no Labour government in 1924 or had Scotland continued to advance economically and politically ahead of England, Scottish Labour might have moved to a separatist position, but its choice of the UK strategy was to render almost inevitable the break with the nationalists in 1928. Simultaneously to attack Westminster and to attempt to gain power within it was, in the long run, an impossible combination.

Longer-term developments during the 1920s ensured that Labour's Home Rule commitment was progressively downgraded. On the industrial front, the period saw a continuing concentration of industry, a relative decline of the Scottish economy and Scottish wage levels and, consequent upon this, an emphasis on national wage bargaining, organisation of labour by industry and the amalgamation of Scottish with English unions. All these developments pointed away from support for Scottish Home Rule, though in some unions a residual political commitment to some sort of Home Rule in principle survived after the economic and industrial logic had turned against it. To examine the evolution of policy on Home Rule within each union and then trace this back in each case to industrial conditions prevailing would be a long and tedious exercise. We shall therefore take three examples before considering the position of the STUC in the 1920s.

The Scottish Farm Servants' Union is a useful case study, since it was one of the large independent Scottish unions in this period. Before the war, it was a matter of pride to the Scottish farm labourers that their wages were several shillings a week higher than those of the drudges on the land in England. Evidently there would be little advantage to them in throwing in their lot with the English farm workers.

This difference in conditions of employment became a political issue in the First World War. The enormous increase in Government intervention in the wartime economy, including the sphere of wage regulation, tended to bring about an equalisation of wage levels and conditions throughout Britain. National collective-bargaining machinery was established in the form of joint industrial councils; or, where trade unionism was too weak for full collective bargaining, wage boards were established. Towards the end of the war an attempt was made, for example, to regulate the wages of farm servants by the introduction of a minimum wage. The Labour Party put forward the proposal of a 30s. minimum weekly wage, but the Government, with the support of certain Labour ministers in the coalition, established the figure of 25s. This was to be applied to Scotland as well as England. In England wages in 1917 were in some areas still below £1 a week, so that the minimum wage would be of some benefit. But the SFSU protested. Wages in Scotland, inclusive of allowances, were already at least 10s. a week above the proposed minimum. In the most well paid districts farm workers earned as much as £2 a week. After a campaign organised by the SFSU, an amendment it had drafted was put down by Ramsay MacDonald and ultimately accepted by the Government. According to a prominent nationalist and Labour journalist of the time, 'by this amendment agreements arrived at between the Union and the local farmers' societies have virtually the effect of Wage

Board decisions. The result is a notable triumph for Scottish national sentiment . . . .'[42]

Although one might query the enthusiast's evaluation of this outcome as a triumph for Scottish national sentiment, the Scottish farm workers' campaign does show that, in a sector where Scottish workers enjoyed superior conditions of employment, separate legislative provisions would be required in addition to separate union organisation in order to maintain these conditions. Given separate industrial conditions and the need for separate legislation, we can see that the political campaign for a Home Rule parliament to deal with such matters would be attractive to a Scottish union.

It is thus not surprising to find Joseph Duncan, founder of the SFSU, an early advocate of Home Rule. In 1915 he told the Labour Party's Scottish Advisory Council that English habits and conditions had held back the movement in Scotland and that 'the Scottish people had a distinct sentiment, and needed a distinct political programme.'[43] The inter-war period, however, saw a relative decline in the wages of Scottish farm workers and by the mid 1930s they had fallen behind English farm workers, who were protected by statutory regulations.[44] By 1931, Duncan was opposing Home Rule at the STUC on the ground that the interests of Scottish and English workers were identical and in 1933 the SFSU was absorbed by the Transport and General Workers' Union (TGWU).

We have seen that the National Union of Scottish Mineworkers (NUSM) was the largest independent Scottish union on the eve of the war. In addition, this union played a leading role in the Labour Party, with a number of sponsored MPs in Scotland. The industrial conditions affecting mining can therefore be expected to have had some influence on the movement's attitude to Home Rule. During the war the coal industry had benefited from a massive increase in demand and a corresponding increase in price. However, in 1921, with demand slumping and the price of coal falling, the mine-owners wished to force the miners to accept wage cuts in line with the fall in the price of coal, on a district-by-district basis. The mine-owners suddenly rejected the proposal, which they had previously accepted in negotiation, for a national wages board for the whole of the British coal-mining industry. At the STUC's 1921 congress, Peter Chambers of the NUSM put forward his union's demand for a national wages board: 'The real objection of the employers to the

National Board was, he opined, because it would mean that when any district was attacked the whole of the mineworkers in the British Isles would down tools to protect that district.'[45] The effect of the slump and of the owners' lockout on the Scottish miners' attitude towards their English and Welsh brothers was evident from the speeches made in support of a resolution proposed and seconded by the NUSM at the same conference, proposing workers' joint action. Peter Chambers moved that, in view of the consolidation of undertakings into trusts, trade unions should take steps to achieve joint action. He expressed the view that 'Capitalism today did not believe in sectionalism or any other -ism, and to him Capitalism had no nationality. . . . They must look to the day when the workers of all countries would become one great industrial organisation.'[46] The motion was unanimously endorsed by congress.

Although there is no indication that the miners had ceased to support Home Rule, which had been supported by James Brown MP, their delegate to the 1920 STUC, where it had been carried by a great majority, the debate on Home Rule in 1921 was certainly coloured by the experience of the miners' lockout, and a delegate from the theatrical employees contended that 'the Scottish Miners could not act without the miners in Wales and England and were, in fact, locked out because the owners wanted to deal with them sectionally instead of industrially.'[47] He concluded that 'organisation by industry was the policy they should support'. Although an amendment to this effect was heavily defeated on this occasion, the miners' lockout of 1921 was only a foretaste of developments in the industry which were to be crucial for the whole British labour movement. Attempts at co-ordinated trade-union action, culminating in the General Strike in support of the miners' resistance to wage cuts, had an impact not merely on the Scottish miners but on the whole Scottish movement's attitude towards the possibility of sectional organisation.

The Scottish miners themselves had showed an increasing concern with political matters during the First World War,[48] and from 1918 backed Scottish Home Rule, which they supported at the STUC and the conference of the Labour Party's Scottish Council in 1919 and again in 1920. In 1920 they affiliated to the SHRA and shortly afterwards confirmed their political orientation by supporting Home Rule for India and warning against intervention in Russia. Robert Smillie, president of the NUSM until 1918, when he resigned to assume the full-time post of president of the Mineworkers' Federation of Great Britain, which he had held part-time since 1912, was a leading figure in the SHRA in its early days; and, later, following his election to Parliament for an English constituency, was on the committee of the National Convention of the late 1920s. After the early 1920s, however, the Scottish miners, preoccupied with national industrial disputes, ceased actively to press for Scottish Home Rule. In 1926, we find the Scottish *mine-owners* demanding Home Rule, i.e. that wage negotiations should be conducted in Scotland and not be 'upset by people in London'.[49] Nevertheless, the Scottish miners' political commitment remained, and, when in later years the issue of Home Rule was raised, they usually supported it.

The position of the railway workers is more complex, influenced by rivalry with other transport unions as well as the usual suspicions of employers and of government. Scottish railwaymen had ben-efitted greatly from Government control during the war. Between 1913 and 1921, the wages cost of Scottish railways had increased by 300 per cent, as against 200 per cent for those of England, as a result of national wage bargaining.[50]

When railway control came to an end in August 1921, the companies were no longer under an obligation to recognise the wartime agreements made between the unions and the Government. Despite talk of the need for drastic reductions in wages, the miners' dispute of 1921 persuaded the railway directors to agree to the principle of continuing national settlements, and the two tribunals set up by the Government to deal with railway wages and conditions – the National and Central Boards – continued in existence. A sliding-scale agreement provided for reductions in wages in line with the falling cost of living. Following on decontrol the Scottish – but not the English – companies demanded a further drop in wages, but this was resisted. Towards the end of 1921 the demands of the Scottish companies were referred to the National Wages Board. The original demand asked for drastic changes in hours and wages, on the ground that the Scottish companies could not continue on the basis of the existing conditions. Ultimately a compromise award was made, which agreed that the application of the eight-hour day in some rural districts involved the companies in heavy expense, and provided for some variation. The only dissen-tients were two of the Scottish managers, who held that the award did not give the companies sufficient relief. Some time later the

English companies suggested to the unions that they should agree to similar changes in England, and this proposal was accepted.

As part of the rationalisation of railways at the time of decontrol, Sir Eric Geddes, the Minister of Transport, had proposed a Scottish railway company. In view of their professed inability to pay the nationally negotiated wage rates, the Scottish companies protested vigorously. It might have been expected that the railway workers would have supported them in this. However, they seem to have regarded the national wage agreement as won and to have been concerned that the less profitable trading conditions in Scotland would lead companies based in England to trim their Scottish operations, with a consequent loss of jobs. In 1921 Geddes bowed to pressure from the Scottish companies and the Scottish Railways Act provided for the amalgamation of the Scottish railways with two English groups to form the London, Midland and Scottish (LMS) Railway and the London and North-Eastern Railway. Some of the railwaymen's fears were soon borne out, when the new LMS started to centralise the railway workshops. In the summer of 1924 men were dismissed from the former Highland Railway Company's workshops at Inverness, resulting from the takeover of the company by the LMS, and the National Union of Railwaymen (Inverness) expressed its opposition to the feared removal of railway workshops from the town. The Town Council of Inverness held interviews with the railway management, and received assurances that as much work as possible would be sent to the Inverness works, so as to keep the number of workers up to almost the old standard. However, four years later it was clear that the company had gone in for a scheme of standardisation of stock and centralisation of effort, which gradually reduced the status of the smaller workshops. The LMS directors announced that the company's workshops would be centralised in St Rollox (Glasgow). Thus, the Inverness workshops were losing work and the workshops in Kilmarnock were to be virtually closed down, retaining only some men to carry out light repairs. The Kilmarnock No. 2 Branch of the NUR was affiliated to the SHRA.

This explains the view of some of the Scottish railwaymen that amalgamation had not been in the interests of the workers. At the NUR conference of 1924, a Glasgow delegate moved an amendment expressing this opinion, prompting an exasperated fellow delegate, C. T. Cramp, to remark 'that he could not resist a dig at Mr. Tiggins. . . . the Clyde men were said to be strongly in favour of Scottish Home Rule. If that were brought about, the men in

Scotland would have to depend on the Scottish railways. In those circumstances, it would be "Nah Poo" for the Scottish railways'.[51] More antipathy towards the Scots is apparent from the speech of another delegate, who ridiculed the remarks of the Scottish speaker, who had called for nationalisation. He thought they would make a worse muddle of the railways than their employers had done. In the same year, the annual conference of the NUR Scottish National Shopworkers' Council unanimously passed a resolution viewing with gave concern the indications that the grouping of the railways had resulted in worsening the conditions of many of the workers.

This concern seems to have underlain much of the pressure for Home Rule among the railway unions in the post-war period, and the support of both the NUR and the Railway Clerks' Association (RCA) for the Home Rule resolutions at the congresses of the STUC in 1922 and 1923. Personal factors also played a part. In 1921 J. Marchbank, a member of the SHRA, became the new president of the NUR. He was secretary of the Glasgow No. 4 branch, one of the largest in Glasgow, which was affiliated to the SHRA, and he had been president of the Glasgow and West of Scotland District Council of the NUR and a member of the National Executive of the union. The Scottish secretary (1919–40) and later general secretary (1940–47) of the RCA was Charles Gallie, an enthusiastic Home Ruler and a leading figure in the STUC and the Labour Party's Scottish Council. George Mathers of the Edinburgh No. 1 branch, later a Labour MP (Edinburgh West, 1929–31; West Lothian, 1935–51), was very active as president of the Edinburgh branch of the SHRA in the mid 1920s. In 1924 and 1926 he successfully moved resolutions at the Association's Scottish conference calling for Home Rule and citing the closure of the Rosyth Dockyard and the Scottish Pensions Office in Edinburgh as examples of the effects of administration based in London. In 1927 a resolution was carried urging all branches to affiliate to the SHRA, and in the same year it was Mathers who moved the Home Rule resolution at the conference of the Scottish Council of the Labour Party. Patterns of union organisation also played their part. A peculiarity of the RCA's constitution was the very restricted remit of its Scottish Advisory Council, the Association's only representative Scottish body between conferences, which was allowed to consider only non-industrial questions relating to Scotland. It is not surprising, then, that Scottish Home Rule formed a large part of its deliberations or that convinced Home Rulers should have dominated its proceedings.[52]

By the late 1920s Scottish railwaymen were coming to see the identity of interest between themselves and their English colleagues. In 1928 J. H. Thomas scathingly pointed to the essential contradiction in their position; recalling the reorganisation he said: 'The first decision was that Scotland, who wanted Home Rule in all things, should have Home Rule in its railways. But Scotsmen are far-seeing people. They want Home Rule in everything that does not cost anything.'[53] In 1931 the NUR delegate at the STUC opposed Home Rule and deplored any division between Scottish and English workers, though he may have been partly influenced by the fact that the Home Rule resolution was being moved by the Scottish Horse and Motormen's Association (SHMA), at that time in bitter dispute with the railwaymen. Under the influence of Gallie and Mathers, the RCA maintained its Home Rule commitment into the 1940s but ceased to give it prominence after the mid 1920s. At the 1931 STUC, Gallie, that year's president, supported Home Rule but admitted that economic separation was not possible.[54]

By the mid 1920s, then, the interests of the great bulk of Scottish workers lay in national (i.e. British) organisation, and this was reflected in a series of amalgamations of Scottish with English unions. The STUC had for a long time supported union amalgamation on industrial lines and several mergers had taken place before the war. The amalgamation movement of the 1920s also received STUC support, but, the further it proceeded, the more questions it raised about the role of the STUC itself.

Promotion of amalgamation implied close co-operation with the British TUC, a fact recognised by the president in his address to the 1920 congress, when he called for negotiations between the two Parliamentary committees with a view to preparing a scheme for the amalgamation of unions by industry. This would be presented to both congresses and then voted on by the workers in each industry, union by union. This placed Hugh Lyon of the SHMA in a difficult position, as evidenced by a remark of his at the congress that 'there was a great need for Trade Union reconstruction, and he wanted to see all the Scottish Unions in one big federation, with the congress as the governing body'. But, although nothing as grand as the president's amalgamation scheme emerged, Lyon's desire for one big federation of Scottish unions under the STUC was clearly a dream running against the tide of events – for, in so far as amalgamation could be promoted, it was on industrial and British lines.

The SHMA remained the single greatest obstacle to the amalgamation movement in Scotland in the 1920s. In 1920 a joint meeting was held under the auspices of the Parliamentary Committee of the STUC covering the road transport industry. The United Vehicle Workers, claiming 44,000 workers in England, wished to amalgamate with the SHMA, claiming 18,000 members in the same industry in Scotland, in order to form 'a united body of Road Transport Workers' within the TGWU, then being formed. Peter Webster, for the SHMA, said that 'if one Union could be achieved for Scotland, and one for England, that would, in the first place, simplify the problem and lead to the possible amalgamation of all into one, though it would have to be recognised that a strong national feeling existed in Scotland'. However, the SHMA soon hardened its attitude further and informed the Parliamentary Committee:

> The Scottish Horse and Motormen's Association have decided to take no part in any scheme of amalgamation or fusion which involves handing over of their funds and the relinquishing of their independence and individuality as a Scottish Union to any Executive with Headquarters in London or any part of England.[55]

That there were other unions which sympathised with this viewpoint is indicated by the advice of James Dwyer of the Scottish Union of Dock Labourers that the solution to the difficulty of the rival seamen's unions, another area of difficulty in the amalgamation movement, 'was the formation of a Scottish Sailors' and Firemen's Union as a distinct organisation . . . the the rank and file were clamouring to get together against the common enemy which was exploiting them'. This was in 1921, the year in which the National Sailors' and Firemen's Union suffered another breakaway in Scotland – the National Maritime Union, with branches in Glasgow and elsewhere. However, Shinwell's earlier breakaway, the British Seafarers, with its base in Southampton as well as Glasgow, was evidently not interested in specifically Scottish unionism and in 1921 joined with the National Union of Ship Stewards to form the Amalgamated Marine Workers' Union, in close co-operation with the TGWU.

The Parliamentary Committee of the STUC did not always support the centralisation of collective bargaining or arbitration procedures. As we have seen, in 1922 it supported the maintenance of separate bargaining machinery in the Co-operative movement. This, however, was the exception. By 1924 the need for union amalgamation in the face of employers' concerted attempts to reduce wages had produced a general feeling against the retention of local autonomy, against craft unionism, and in favour of amalgamation on industrial lines, which was seen by some as being associated with the need to prepare a basis for ultimate control of industry. These views found expression in the debate on the functions of Congress. Watson, of the Scottish Typographical Association, indicated the roots of this prevailing mood:

> In the printing trades they had a federation second to no federation in the UK. . . . As a Union they had tried to get the others in the federation to amalgamate, but local autonomy always jumped in and cleared the pitch [sic]. . . . There was a different spirit even in the geographical centres in Scotland, the Scottish could not see their way to ally themselves with the English, nor the English with the Scottish. . . . In the last decrease in wages they were rent asunder because some Unions within the federation said they could not be expected as strong Trade Unions to ally themselves with the weaklings, consequently every Union had to do the best it could to get off as cheaply as possible.

The same mood continued in the next two congresses. In 1925 a resolution put forward by the General Council suggesting 'the preparation of a plan for developing and co-ordinating the organisation and activities of the unions with a view to increasing the strength of the Movement' called forth a wide-ranging debate and more demands for industrial unionism.[56] For instance, James Walker, of the Iron and Steel Trades Confederation, pointed out that

> They in Scotland could not create a scientific form of organisation without having some consideration for the British section of the TU movement. When they talked about industrial unions, they must remember that the bulk of British industry was not confined to any one particular geographical

area, but that there were several chief areas in the country, and their future organisation must be one which would embrace all the industries in Great Britain.

The following year a General Council statement advocating industrial unionism as more suited to securing 'control of industry' and as 'the structure essential for the complete development of the trade union movement' was carried unanimously. Joseph Duncan of the Scottish Farm Servants pointed, in his presidential address, to the need for national (i.e. British) organisation of the trade unions, in order to develop national wage bargaining and to deal with the Government – which had intervened in the miners' dispute of 1925 to postpone wage cuts by means of a subsidy. Coming from the leader of one of the remaining Scottish unions and a former supporter of Home Rule, the statement is of particular significance.

By 1925, the amalgamation movement had advanced so far that three out of five Scottish trade unionists were members of British unions and many of the Scottish unions were closely linked with British unions in federations engaged in collective bargaining with employers on a British basis, or perhaps seeking unsuccessfully to do so. However, the amalgamation movement was not maintained in the late 1920s, perhaps because the employers had by then generally the upper hand in enforcing negotiations at the district or local level, which was preferable to them in a depression, and the opportunity of amalgamating to resist this had now passed. The commitment in principle to amalgamation by industry remained, but it was recognised that the opposition to amalgamation was not going to disappear overnight. In a debate on a motion of the TGWU for 'One Union for all the workers', in 1930, Walker of the Iron and Steel Trades Confederation remarked sardonically, 'Every Union had certain vested interests and he was afraid Lyon's £120,000 (the reserves of the SH&MA) had something to do with the failure of the amalgamation negotiations in the transport industry.'[57]

In 1930 the SHMA became involved in a dispute with the NUR, over the alleged poaching of its former members among carters around the railway stations. This dispute continued at the 1931 congress, where, as we have seen, it coloured the debate on Home Rule. The SHMA, which at the outset of our period had been an influential force within the STUC, was now regarded as an organisation with a parish-pump outlook and had especially discredited itself by its breach of strike discipline during the General Strike of 1926.

The STUC's encouragement of union amalgamation on British lines in part reflected its own changing composition. For increasingly the British unions were stealing the show from the purely Scottish ones. But this itself was no accident: rather it was the result of active recruitment by the STUC, which faced a choice of either bringing in the Scottish sections of the large new British unions, or else extinction, as a body whose function had now been superseded.

In 1919 the relationship of the STUC to the TUC had been described by the vice-chairman of the STUC thus:

It would be foolish for us to aspire to be rivals to the British Trades Union Congress; but, if I may use the illustration, I would say that the Scottish Trade Union movement generally exercises the function of a Home Rule body. In political matters, we believe that the time has come when Home Rule for Scotland, Wales, Ireland, and England is necessary, in order to relieve the pressure upon the Imperial Parliament; but that does not imply that there is any desire for separation, or to weaken the Imperial Parliament at Westminster. As a matter of fact, the Imperial Parliament would be enormously strengthened by the establishment of Home Rule in the different countries of the United Kingdom. I would apply that illustration to the Scottish Congress in relation to the parent body. You represent 5,250,000 people this week, at this Congress, and that is an unwieldy membership for one body to control. We believe that the time is not far distant when the question of devolution, industrially as well as politically, will have to be taken up. . . . we sincerely hope that those of you who are entitled to give us your Scottish membership will seriously consider the question . . . .[58]

In 1920 the Parliamentary committees of the two bodies met to discuss a memorandum on their future relationship. This asserted that in the near future some form of Home Rule or Devolution would be enacted and thus make necessary a corresponding relationship between the two congresses. By this time, the decline of independent action by the official and unofficial movement in Scotland and the moves of the national trades unions towards a co-ordinating centre for industrial matters, a 'Labour General Staff',

were already raising questions about the STUC's role in the absence
of Scottish Home Rule.

The TUC itself was changing its role. For most of its first half
century, it was mainly a political as opposed to an industrial body.
That is, it functioned as a co-ordinating body for proposed
legislation in defence of the legal rights of trades unionists and as a
lobby at Westminster, but avoided involvement in industrial
disputes, which were considered the exclusive concern of individual
unions. The title of its central body, the Parliamentary Committee,
indicated the focus of its concern, and its administration by a part-
time secretary the scope of its activities. However, from the latter
half of the First World War, there were important changes as the
Governement, anxious for union co-operation in the war effort – for
example, over the relaxation of restrictive practices – involved TUC
representatives in a wide range of consultative machinery. This
wartime relationship led naturally to the TUC's desire to be
involved in committees dealing with post-war problems and to a
new role as a mediator between individual unions and the
Government in some of the massive post-war industrial disputes. In
1921, following the failure of the Triple Alliance, the General
Council – with the functions of co-ordinating industrial action,
promoting common action by the unions in all industrial affairs,
mediating in inter-union disputes and helping trade-union
organisation – was brought into being. The General Council was
divided into industrial sections to encourage the co-ordination of
union organisation and policy in industry. In 1923 the first full-time
general secretary took office.

In 1922 the STUC followed suit and new rules were introduced,
which, however, preserved the two distinctive features of its
organisation: the representation of trades councils and the absence
of a card vote. The result of this reorganisation was to make the
STUC more representative of the trade union movement in
Scotland and to facilitate co-operation with the TUC. In 1923 the
Organising Campaign of the TUC, intended to reverse the decline
that the slump had brought about in trade union membership, was
to be conducted in Scotland as a joint campaign, under the
administration and supervision of the STUC Parliamentary
Committee. The recognition of the need for co-operation of the two
congresses and the special role of the independent STUC could not
have been more forcefully expressed; at the same time, the STUC
was in effect doing the work of the TUC, fitting into a TUC

campaign and playing its part in Scotland. Further fruit of the reorganisation was the success in persuading national trade unions to affiliate their Scottish membership. In April 1924 the TGWU affiliated, on the basis of 20,000 members in Scotland.

There was also an increasing emphasis on industrial, as opposed to political, matters, an emphasis reflected in the General Council's Report 'Functions of Congress', presented in 1924. This pointed out that the situation of the trade union movement had changed from the days when organised labour was merely seeking political expression and Congress did little more than pass resolutions year after year and demand recognition of the right to be heard by MPs and Ministers of State. The Trade Unions had now obtained recognition, and 'a strong National Labour Party provides a medium for the expression of general social ills and possible political reforms. The Trade Union Movement, emphasising the necessary permanency of its organisation irrespective of the political party in power, demands Control in Industry. It is therefore essential that Congress concentrate on enlarging its functions as a "national organ for the improvement and development of Trade Unionism in its industrial aspect", in order that the objective be made possible of achievement.' It was thus proposed that the General Council be instructed to prepare detailed reports on structural problems of the movement ahead of Congress, and that each congress devote sufficient time to considering these reports. In short, Congress was asked to become more business like, to devote more time to the problems of trade union organisation and structure, and to reduce the amount of time spent on the passing of resolutions and sending of deputations, as it was felt that the Labour Party could now cover the political interests of the movement more adequately. In this business like atmosphere, one would expect that the passing of resolutions of general principle which had become 'hardy annuals', such as that on Home Rule for Scotland, would fall into second place in the proceedings of Congress. Indeed, with the problems of industrial organisation in the forefront, and co-operation with the British TUC the keynote, nothing more was heard on the subject of Home Rule until 1931, when a Home Rule resolution was rejected.

But, as has been mentioned, for some the reorganisation was insufficient. In the debate on the functions of Congress, Carmichael of the Workers' Union, the large general union later to merge into the TGWU, considered that it was wrong for the trades councils to be represented at Congress:

They must either admit that representation should be through localities, as expressed by Trades Councils, or that the Councils have no right to attend Congress. . . . He would go further, and be courageous enough to tell the workers of Scotland that the time was passed [sic] for a Scottish Trades Union Congress. He knew that would not be nice for people who had little craft unions in Scotland, but as far as the big working class movement was concerned they were developing to centralise our Executive power in Great Britain. The Scottish Trades Union Congress had been held for thirty years; it had done useful propaganda work, but nothing else. Because of its mechanism it could do no more.

This was a minority view expressed only by the Workers' Union at the 1924 congress. However, from the mid 1920s an increasing tendency for the left to support centralisation is discernible. In the summer of 1924 the Communist Party established the National Minority Movement (NMM) on the left wing of the trade-union movement, and the NMM's programme included a General Council with full powers to direct the activities of the unions and under an obligation to Congress to use those powers. 'All power to the General Council' became one of the slogans of the party, and this did not leave much room for a specifically Scottish trade union movement. So, at the 1925 congress we find Aitken Ferguson of the Glasgow Trades Council protesting against the 'narrow national-istic viewpoint which had been expressed by one of the delegates'. Thus, although after the 1923 changes the STUC's existence was never seriously threatened, the left was always ready to snipe at it.

The General Strike gave it an opportunity. In 1927 the National Union of Vehicle Builders (NUVB) moved:

That this Congress, having in view the necessity of co-ordination and centralisation of the whole Trade Union Movement of Britain, regards as a danger the existence of two Trades Union Congresses in Great Britain, namely the Scottish Trades Union Congress and the British Trades Union Congress. It consequently instructs the General Council to enter into negotiations with the General Council of the BTUC with a view to establishing the STUC as an Advisory Council of the BTUC on similar lines as those operating in the National Labour Party of Scotland. The practicability and necessity for this step was seen during the recent General Strike when the STUC became the representative of the BTUC in Scotland.[59]

Milne, the NUVB delegate, pointed out that this resolution had only narrowly missed being forwarded from their district committee the previous year, but that the experience of the General Strike had convinced all members of the committee that the time had come when the STUC should become simply an advisory body. The reason was that during the strike the STUC General Council had been unable to act in the crisis, and had simply had to wait for instructions from over the border. Glasgow Trades Council seconded the resolution, pointing out that all the large unions were definitely associated with the TUC, and 'in no circumstances that could possibly arise at any conceivable time could the Scottish Congress act independently'. The council's delegate, Frank Stephenson, cited also the example of the forty-hours strike, when the STUC declared the strike official but the National Executives of the unions concerned refused to do likewise. This 'showed that the National Executives would only tolerate the Scottish Congress so long as it assisted in their organising work. There was not a single thing which it could do as a separate autonomous body which it could not do as an Advisory Council.' He also argued that 'It was ridiculous that they should have two separate Congresses when they had not even two Parliaments' – an argument which neatly turned on its head the view, put forward by an STUC memorandum to the TUC in 1920, that the expected imminence of Home Rule was an argument for Home Rule for the STUC in relation to the larger body. Finally, by blaming the STUC for perpetuating their existence, Stephenson also turned on its head the argument that the STUC was needed to represent the small Scottish unions: if it were not for the STUC, he said, 'many of them would have been forced to amalgamate with the larger Unions'.

Duncan and Gallie, two heavyweights on the General Council, moved the amendment of the General Council calling instead for continued efforts towards better co-ordination of the two congresses. They implicitly admitted that the STUC was no longer as independent as in earlier days, but argued that it would be better to avoid getting into the same relative position as the Scottish Advisory Council of the Labour Party. Aitken Ferguson then spoke in favour of the main motion, for Glasgow Trades Council. However, the

General Council's amendment was carried by a large majority.

While the move to wind up Congress was to a large extent a demonstration against the right-wing leadership, it did indicate continuing left-wing support for centralisation. Hinton and Hyman point out[60] that the NMM did not change its policy fundamentally after the General Strike. The slogan 'all power to the General Council' was retained, but this was explicitly 'not because we believe in the present leaders of the General Council but because we believe that a centralised leadership is a necessity of the movement'. Thus, it was consistent with Communist Party policy for Aitken Ferguson to move a resolution, at the same congress, that the lesson of the General Strike was the traitorous attitude of the leadership and the need to substitute a new militant leadership, while calling for the STUC to become merely advisory to the existing TUC. This is an episode which apparently does not merit mention in Communist Party synopses of the consistent attitude of the party to the national question in Scotland.

The issue of 'one TUC' was the subject of a further resolution the following year, 1928. Interestingly, the Fraternal Delegate from the British TUC expressed support for the need for the STUC to discuss both Scottish questions and 'national questions from a Scottish point of view'. This time the resolution was moved by Einburgh Trades Council, and seconded by the Amalgamated Society of Woodworkers (ASW). The ASW, like the NUVB, was one of the unions in which there had been considerable support for the Red International of Labour Unions. Stephenson of the NUVB and Strain of the ASW were mover and seconder respectively of a motion at the same congress calling for international trade union unity through a conference which the British TUC and the Russian trade union movement were to be asked to convene. Thus, once again, it was the left of the movement, specifically the bodies in which Communist Party influence was strongest, which were campaigning for unification of the STUC with the TUC and accusing those who wished to preserve the autonomy of the former body of being nationalists.

The ASW delegate, Wolstencraft, argued that 'those who would oppose the resolution would be mainly those who were out for Scottish nationalism'. This time, therefore, in moving an amendment to the resolution, Duncan and Gallie took care to avoid 'donning the tartan', of which Aitken Ferguson had accused them the previous year. Duncan opened by claiming that 'they were actuated by no strong national feelings' – something he would hardly have said in 1918, but evidently had to say in 1928. He asked Congress to allow relations between the two bodies to develop naturally, and submitted that, 'on questions involving the whole country, the Scottish Congress did not interfere but left it entirely to the British Congress. On national decisions they followed the lead of the British Congress. . . . They had their own sphere of work and were in the most harmonious relations with the British Congress . . . .' Both Duncan and Gallie hinted at the Communist associations of the ASW movers of the motion. Wolstencraft had complained of the burden of having to pay affiliation fees to two bodies, the British and the Scottish. Gallie drily remarked that 'the ASW probably contributed to some international organisation as well as to the British Congress'.

By the late 1920s the STUC's efforts to carve out a more limited niche for itself and attract support from the British unions had succeeded, despite the difficulties outlined. By 1929 the major British unions had affiliated their Scottish sections to the STUC. The changing balance of British and Scottish unions in Congress was illustrated by the fact that the National Union of Scottish Mineworkers was unable to reaffiliate in the same year, for financial reasons.

Concern with the issue of Home Rule was confined to one or two leading figures, such as Gallie and Lyon, but for the mass of Scottish trades unionists the issue had ceased to be of consequence.

III. PARTING OF THE WAYS

Within the Labour Party, a token support for Home Rule remained general through the 1920s, even as the party moved ever further away from it in practice. In 1927, after concern had been expressed at the centralising effect of proposals to dismantle the Scottish Boards of Health and Agriculture and vest their functions in the Scottish Office, then based in London, the Scottish Council of the Labour Party passed, with only eight dissentient votes, a resolution calling for 'an adequate measure of self-government for Scotland'. There was, however, little enthusiasm expressed for the resolution and none of the nationalist fervour of earlier years. The Communist Party of Great Britain, as we have seen, moved increasingly in a centralist direction. Even the Scottish Division of the ILP lost

interest in the issue. At its 1929 conference there was a division on
the issue, with some speakers attacking Home Rule as contrary to
socialist internationalism, and, while the Home Rulers carried the
day, it was reported that many of the delegates did not bother to
vote.[61]

The Scottish Home Rule Association continued its activities but
with diminishing support from leading Labour figures and a distinct
lessening of the emotional fervour which had characterised its early
demonstrations. In 1924, following the failure of Buchanan's bill, it
sought to broaden its base by summoning a National Convention.[62]
This attracted considerable local-authority support, though dominated by SHRA leaders, and met annually up to 1927. One of its
first acts was to appoint a committee to draft a bill, which, after
several delays, was ready by July 1926. Now that mainstream
Labour figures were ceasing to play such an important part in
SHRA affairs, the drafting committee was dominated by the more
extreme nationalists, though a liaison committee with the Scottish
Labour MPs did exist and a committee appointed to follow the Bill
through included George Mathers, James Barr MP, Neil Maclean
MP, Tom Johnston MP, Peter Webster of the STUC General
Council, and W. Wedgwood Benn, then Liberal MP for Leith and
about to join the Labour Party. Barr, formerly a leading SHRA
member, admitted at the 1926 convention that Parliamentary
duties had prevented him from playing a great part in the work of
the drafting committee.

He defended the Bill on the grounds that Scotland needed Home
Rule to deal with 'matters of temperance, matters of religious
equality and the great principles of moral and social advance'.
These were Barr's own political priorities but reflected the general
tenor of the campaign from the mid 1920s in Labour circles, where it
was increasingly the old-fashioned radicals who were left as the
standard-bearers of Home Rule. A trade union delegate commented that, while his branch supported Home Rule, most union
branches did not discuss the issue until a circular from the SHRA
came round.

The new Bill was a much more radical measure than the 1924
Bill, providing for Dominion status and the withdrawal of Scottish
MPs from Westminster. The latter provision had lost it the support
of many Labour Members and prevented agreement in the liaison
committee. It was introduced in the House in 1927 by James Barr,
seconded by Tom Johnston, but, in the face of Labour apathy, was

talked out, or rather laughed out, by Conservatives.[63] Even Johnston later admitted that he did not approve of the withdrawal provisions, and his comment that the Bill was 'all pretty airy fairy'[64] seems a fair reflection of Labour sentiment.

The STUC was also unhappy with the extreme provisions of the Bill. In January 1927 three representatives of the General Council – Peter Webster, Joe Duncan and William Elger – met representatives of the SHRA to discuss aspects of the Bill which disturbed them, in particular the withdrawal of Scottish members from Westminster and the handing over of all national services and departments to a Scottish Parliament. The General Council then wrote to the SHRA requesting that when a new Government of Scotland Bill was being drafted it should be given an opportunity to consider the draft Bill before it was published. It was informed that the National Convention had already approved the identical Bill. Thus it was too late for the General Council to influence the scheme which Barr was to present to Parliament. Not surprisingly, an SHRA circular calling on affiliates to protest to local MPs about the talking out of the Bill received a cool response from the STUC.[65]

The SHRA was, from the start, an alliance of two very different kinds of Home Ruler: on the one hand, Labour men, trade unionists and Co-operators, for whom Home Rule was part and parcel of Labour's advance; on the other, committed nationalists, for whom the alliance with the Labour movement was useful only to the extent that it served the national cause. The contradiction between these wings remained latent in the early 1920s, when working class and national politics seemed completely harmonious. But the rift began to open as Labour concentrated on the practical measures which might be achieved through Westminster.

As early as 1923 the SHRA *News-Sheet* noted that MacDonald's commitment was to Home Rule for matters of local concern only, leaving the Government at Westminster to deal with national affairs. The editor commented: 'Our own firm conviction is that a Scottish National Party is needed to give driving-power to the movement. All parties concerned primarily with imperial issues tend to lose sight of Scotland's national claims.'[66] Muirhead later stated that his disillusionment with Labour dated from 1924, when the Labour Government had refused to give Scottish MPs a second day to discuss Buchanan's Home Rule Bill, which had been talked out. In October 1925 the *News-Sheet* floated the suggestion that a national party should be formed, 'the idea being that this party should adopt the same attitude towards Scottish Home Rule as the Irish Nationalists did towards Irish Home Rule, namely the subordination of all other political questions to the main issue'.[67] This inagurated a lengthy campaign by Roland Muirhead, his brother (who edited the paper), and others on the nationalist wing of the SHRA to persuade the organisation to inaugurate a new Nationalist Party. However, they failed repeatedly against the opposition of the trade-union and Co-operative affiliates, who provided the bulk of the SHRA's active support in the branches, and whose delegates controlled its General Council and annual general meetings. They were, of course, unwilling to set up a rival to the Labour Party, to which they were affiliated and in most cases individually committed. Resolutions for the formation of a separate Nationalist Party consequently failed at the SHRA's annual general meetings of 1926 and 1927.

The failure of Barr's bill proved to be the last straw for the SHRA. Muirhead, disregarding the views expressed repeatedly by SHRA meetings, now sought closer co-operation with more extreme nationalist organisations, who were moving towards the formation of a separate party. For the Scotland's Day demonstration of 1927 he formed a joint committee of the SHRA with Erskine of Marr's Scots National League. In contrast to previous rallies, where Labour MPs such as Tom Johnston, Duncan Graham, James Maxton and Davie Kirkwood had spoken, the main speakers were to be Erskine of Marr and Cunninghame Graham. Both were nationalist enthusiasts of aristocratic descent, although the latter had been prominent in the Labour Party in Keir Hardie's day. A resolution passed by the demonstration demanded that 'a National Parliament be at once re-established in Scotland' and was supported jointly by Cunninghame Graham (SHRA president), Erskine of Marr (president of the Scots National League) and Lewis Spence (president of the Scots National Movement).

In April 1928 two issues provoked a powerful backlash from the labour-movement supporters at the SHRA's annual general meeting. The first, Roland Muirhead's independent candidature in West Renfrewshire, had been brewing for some months. Muirhead had announced that he intended to contest West Renfrewshire as an Independent Scottish Nationalist. Reluctant to break totally with Labour, he at first justified his candidature on the ground that no Labour nominee was in the field. After Labour had nominated Wedgwood Benn for the seat, however, Muirhead persisted in his campaign, despite a lack of support from the SHRA General Council. The second issue was the formation of the National Party of Scotland, which was the outcome of a series of meetings convened by Glasgow University Scottish National Association, to which the SHRA had sent representatives 'with a watching brief'. Delegates attended the annual general meeting in force, and from the start it was clear that the SHRA would have no truck with Muirhead's candidature or the new party he had helped to found. Peter Webster for the STUC immediately moved suspension of standing orders, so that the question of a National Party could be discussed.

Muirhead explained that he had become a member of the Provisional Committee of the National Party of Scotland, along with members of Glasgow University Scottish National Association, the Scots National League and the Scottish National Movement. All were members of this Provisional Committee in their individual capacities, and not as representing their organisations. The Provisional Committee had resolved 'That this meeting of Scots men and women . . . hereby constitutes itself the National Party of Scotland.' The party had no provision for affiliation, and so Muirhead proposed a resolution simply calling on all individual members to join the new party.[68]

Webster then argued forcefully against the formation of the new party. Labour had been fully committed to devolution, but, although it had held office in 1924, it had never held power, and was unable to obtain a majority in the Commons for many desired measures.

> If the Association deliberately decided to pass the Resolution and ask them to recommend people to leave their Parties and join another Party, then as politicians with traditions behind them, fundamental beliefs behind them, then he would say quite frankly he for one would be compelled to advise his organisation, a rather powerful organisation in Scotland, to withdraw from the SHRA. They had had to fight to maintain their identity as a Scottish Trade Union Congress, and they had maintained it by an overwhelming majority. He represented one of the few Trade Unions which had distinctly maintained their Scottish traditions (the Scottish Horse and Motormen), but these things have been maintained simply because of the political ideals and political beliefs, the foundation of which we are not prepared to

throw lightly away, and while he could agree that Scots
Home Rule was an important subject, he could not forget
that there were other important subjects.

The resolution was withdrawn, but the SHRA had received its
death-blow. Labour reacted to the formation of the National Party
by a Scottish Executive resolution declaring it to be in the same
category as 'the Communist or other party which it is not eligible for
us to affiliate or become members of'.[69] Webster's report to the
STUC General Council of the SHRA annual general meeting led
W. Leonard and J. Walker to move that they withdraw from the
organisation, but reaffiliation was moved by Webster and Duncan
and was carried by five votes to four. By June 1928 Barr was refusing
to attend SHRA demonstrations, because he believed the
Association to be endorsing candidates in opposition to Labour.
Within the SHRA the Edinburgh branch protested against the
action of Muirhead and of Cunninghame Graham in standing as
Nationalist candidates. They tried to keep up the old style of non-
party activity, but a demonstration in Edinburgh that September
attracted a 'disappointing' 200 people, including only two politicians, Mathers (not yet in Parliament) and E. Brown, the new
Liberal MP for Leith. A report of the meeting attempts to make a
virtue of the obvious lack of fervour shown: 'There was a total lack of
emotional rhetoric. Scottish Home Rule was advocated as a
business proposition and as a matter of ordinary common sense and
justice.'[70]

By March 1929 a less sympathetic source, the *Aberdeen Press and
Journal*, was commenting:

> For years now the Association under its non-party name has
> been mainly socialistic in ideas and composition. Now all the
> Socialists are flocking from it: some to join the new
> Nationalist Party – an offshoot of the Association – and the
> rest because it has given birth to the Nationalist Party.[71]

In reality it was Muirhead and his fellow nationalists who had
forced the parting of the ways. The Labour element won all the set-
piece battles in the General Council or the annual general meeting,
but found that with the formation of the new party Muirhead's
sponsorship of the SHRA went with him, while his call for
individuals to join the new party decimated the grass roots of the

SHRA. In Perth, the local branch decided to dissolve itself in January 1929, despite the attempt by the Trades and Industrial Council to keep the branch going. At the 1929 annual general meeting, in April, because of the withdrawal of members and financial sponsors and following the resignation of Muirhead, the SHRA voted to dissolve itself.

The first few nationalist candidatures were reported to have led some Labour MPs, worried about the electoral consequences, to revive their flagging support for Home Rule, but, as the complete failure of these candidates demonstrated the lack of political mileage to be made out of Scottish nationalism at this time, Labour interest waned still further. Indeed, the nationalist attack was one factor leading Labour to stress the unionist aspect of its policy, while continuing to pay lip service to Home Rule. The Home Rule wing of the labour movement, men such as Webster of the Scottish Horse and Motormen's Association and Mathers of the Railway Clerks' Association had had their fingers badly burnt and were no longer inclined to push Home Rule with the same degree of enthusiasm.

In 1928 Labour's national conference endorsed the programme of *Labour and the Nation*, which called for 'the creation of separate legislative assemblies in Scotland, Wales and England with autonomous powers in matters of local concern', but this was a formal repetition of the policy of the 1918 programme and attracted little attention in the debates. During the 1929–31 Labour Government, the issue never assumed great importance. Shortly before taking office, Ramsay MacDonald declared that he was still a supporter of Home Rule but qualified this heavily, adding that the United Kingdom was an economic unit and that labour and industrial legislation must be the same throughout it. Other questions were more important and a Labour Government could not give over a whole session to Scottish Home Rule.[72] Later in 1929, as Prime Minister, he said that, when the new Local Government Act had run for a year, the Government would consider devolution, but indicated that it would need five years in power before being able to do anything.[73] Reminded of this exactly a year later by George Mathers, he declared that the time had not yet come.[74]

To maintain the alliance between Home Rulers and Labour would have needed both a greater degree of commitment from Labour and more agreement on the meaning of 'Home Rule' itself. A general consensus on the need for more self-government for Scotland was a long way from agreement on a specific measure, and, as the meaning of Home Rule became clearer, Labour MPs began to back away from it. The economic consequences, in particular, had concerned Labour and trade-union leaders, but, if Home Rule were defined so as to exclude all economic matters, it would be of little importance to the labour movement and of little interest to dedicated Home Rulers.

The Labour Party had opted decisively for a UK strategy and the pursuit of power at Westminster could not easily be combined with vigorous advocacy of a diminution of Westminster's power. Nationalism could be harnessed to a movement striving for recognition and challenging the established political order but was a danger to a party seeking to achieve its aims within that political order. It might be an appropriate ideology for a movement of the periphery, but, as soon as that movement became serious about capturing power at the centre, its nationalist credentials became suspect. A parallel can be drawn with the earlier history of the radical Liberals. In office, Lloyd George had shown himself no more ready than Ramsay MacDonald to devolve power.

However, the Labour Party was not yet ready to repudiate the idea of Home Rule for Scotland, and, for a long time after it had ceased seriously to figure in Labour's programme, it continued to be accepted as desirable as a vague aspiration for the future. This allowed the party in later years to claim that it was still 'sound' on Home Rule and allowed its more nationalistic supporters to claim that they were reflecting long-standing party policy in their demands. Very importantly, it also meant that Scottish nationalism was a force with which it felt able to make compromises, as devolution continued to be politically 'respectable'; but at the same time, in the absence of a significant external nationalist threat to its position, Labour was able effectively to suppress the nationalist dimension in Scottish politics while claiming itself to represent Scotland's best interests.

4 Nationalism on the Fringes

I. LABOUR AND SCOTLAND IN THE 1930s

The break-up of the old Home Rule coalition after the failure of the 1927 Bill heralded a progressively widening split between the forces of Scottish nationalism and the labour movement during the 1930s. The break-up itself resulted from the contradiction between a vigorous nationalism and Labour's aspirations for power at Westminster. As we have seen, the contradiction had been largely settled in favour of the UK strategy by 1924, after the failure of the nationalist impetus of the post-war period to set the movement on a separatist road. During the 1930s, forces were at work pushing the movement yet further away from identification with the cause of Home Rule.

Dominating Labour's thoughts in the 1930s was the economy. Scotland's economic decline relative to England, which, in retrospect, can be seen to have set in immediately after the war, was deeply ingrained in the minds of contemporaries by the 1930s. Scotland's industrial dependence on heavy industries had left it dangerously exposed in the slump which followed the brief post-war boom of 1918–21. The crash of 1929 found it equally vulnerable and, in the depression of the early 1930s, it suffered particularly badly. Scottish unemployment, which has been higher than that in England since 1923, became proportionately worse, reaching a high of 27·7 per cent in 1932.[1] Emigration overseas, which may have helped to hold down the figures in the earlier period, had virtually stopped by 1931, as a result of restrictions imposed by depression-bound host countries; but the southward drift to England continued and the Scottish population, after a fall between 1921 and 1931, remained virtually static through the 1930s.[2] Scottish incomes, and particularly wages, followed the same trend as unemployment. A precipitous fall in Scotland's share of the national income was not halted until the mid 1930s, when, at its lowest, income per head was only 87 per cent of the UK average.[3] Between 1929 and 1932 alone, Scottish income fell by 22 per cent, as compared with 15 per cent for the UK.[4] Scotland was thus left with a diminishing share of a reduced national cake and, with an industrial structure geared to an earlier age, little prospect of reversing the trend without radical measures of reconstruction. There was little sign of industry's responding to this need. On the contrary, a dominant feature of the Scottish industrial scene remained the 'drift to the south'. In 1932, for example, 626 new factories were opened in England and 130 closed, a net gain of 496. In Scotland, twenty were opened and thirty-six closed. In the following year, England's net gain was sixty-nine and Scotland's loss fifteen.[5] Over the period 1932–7, of 3217 factories opened in Great Britain, only 127 were in Scotland and those were more than counterbalanced by 133 closures.[6] As a result, Scotland's share of British industrial production fell from 9·9 per cent in 1924 to 8·2 per cent in 1935.[7] Particularly hard hit were the heavy industries, such as ship-building[8] and coal-mining,[9] and the engineering industries dependent on them. It was in these industries that the Scottish labour movement was most strongly based and from which it drew its strength and confidence. The industrial wing of the movement, still weakened by the after-effects of the General Strike, found it difficult to hold its own in such a climate, let alone advance in strength and numbers. Its weakness was reflected in a fall in affiliations to the STUC.[10]

The position of Labour in the Scottish political structure at this time was not a strong one. The election of 1931 left Labour with only seven seats in Scotland, and while, in terms of seats though not of votes, this represented a stronger Labour presence in Scotland than in England, the overall position was so weak as to render this irrelevant. The Labour Party in Scotland received a further blow in 1932 when four of its seven Scottish MPs defected as a result of the ILP disaffiliation. A further consequence of the ILP breakaway was the virtual disappearance of Labour's constituency organisation, which in Scotland had consisted largely of ILP branches. In the years following, much effort was devoted to rebuilding the machinery and to establishing a strong Labour presence in local government, while Labour's weakness in Scotland led to close association with, and dependence on, the party nationally.

In terms of policy, a concentration on immediate, practical measures to alleviate Scotland's plight replaced the earlier, utopian visions. When general policies to tackle the economic ills of the 1930s were considered, Labour turned to the remedies of planning and public ownership. For the ILP and the Communists, the rhetoric was stronger and the measures proposed were more radical, but they pointed in the same direction, to state action and greater state control. After the launching of the first Soviet five-year plan, in 1928, 'planning' became a key word in the socialist vocabulary.[11] Even outside the labour movement, the vogue for planning took hold. Political and Economic Planning was founded in 1931, and the publication of works such as *The Next Five Years: An Essay in Political Agreement* by an all-party group in 1935 and Harold Macmillan's *Reconstruction: A Plea for a National Policy* in 1933 testified to the appeal of the planning idea. Within the labour movement, a clear statement of the case came in Barbara Wootton's *Plan or No Plan* in 1934.[12] Examples of public ownership in the Commonwealth, and the BBC and Central Electricity Board in Britain provided models of direct state involvement in industry, later developed as the centralised 'Morrisonian' corporations. The difficulties of the depressed areas, too, pointed to the need for state action, and government's response, in the form of the Special Areas Act of 1935 and its amendment in 1937, while having comparatively little effect on the problems themselves, at least showed the way for future developments.

Scottish Labour shared fully in this trend of thought and also in the assumption that the extra responsibilities would be assumed by a *British* state. Advocacy of radical measures of devolution was not easily compatible with the construction of a centralised, planned economy and interventionist state in any circumstances, In the case of Scotland, dependence upon the United Kingdom was dictated by the economic decline and the drift of industry to the south. These could only be halted by a strong government at the centre, willing and able to take positive action to redistribute resources and help ailing regions. Anything which could prejudice this objective was to be avoided. Thus, the need to maintain the economic unity of the United Kingdom forms a constant theme of Labour and STUC conferences in the 1930s – a change in emphasis from the earlier period typified by the changing ideas of Tom Johnston. An enthusiastic Home Ruler until the early 1920s, he had backed Barr's bill of 1928, though he later admitted to having had reservations about it, particularly in respect of the proposal to withdraw Scottish members from Westminster.[13] In the second Labour Government, he served first as Under-Secretary for Scotland, then, briefly, as Lord Privy Seal, in charge of measures for dealing with unemployment. While he always maintained his belief in the desirability of Home Rule, during the 1930s he became increasingly concerned with practical measures to build up the Scottish economy. Only with a sound economic structure would it be possible to embark on Home Rule. He later wrote,

> For many years past, I have become, and increasingly
> become, uneasy lest we should get political power without
> our first having or at least simultaneously having, an
> adequate economy to administer. What purport would
> there be in getting a Scots Parliament in Edinburgh if it has
> to administer an emigration system, a glorified Poor Law and
> a graveyard?[14]

While Home Rule was thus rejected as a solution, the focus was nevertheless on *Scottish* problems. Johnston remained a patriot at heart and a Scotsman first. What had changed was his view of how Scotland was best to be helped. In the late 1930s he was to try and reconcile Home Rule with Labour's belief in planning, and from the 1940s he developed the view that Scotland's problems could be solved on a non-partisan basis by the coming together of Scotsmen of goodwill; but Home Rule itself was not a priority.

Indeed, the very concept of 'Home Rule', the rallying cry of radicals and the advancing left up to the 1920s, was rendered largely obsolete by the demands of the 1930s. Its formulation in the days of the non-interventionist state had been at best vague, but at a time when government was looked to for economic salvation it offered no obvious remedies. If Home Rule extended to economic and industrial matters it could only hamper central policies of planning and intervention. Drained of economic content, it was irrelevant to the problems of the day.

This dilemma comes out clearly at the 1931 congress of the STUC. A motion from the Scottish Horse and Motormen's Association called for a renewal of the commitment to Dominion status, sparking the first debate on the subject since 1923. Challenged on the benefits to Scottish workers of self-government, the mover, who had started by maintaining that one could not separate politics from 'industrial issues', was forced to admit that 'no-one suggested it would make any difference to the workers' lives'. The motion, caught in a cross-current of other issues, was lost by a large majority. The same dilemma faced that year's president, the veteran Home Ruler C. N. Gallie of the Railway Clerks' Association. In his address he pressed the cause of Home Rule but added that 'no person in industry believed that Scotland could survive a separate economic unit'[15] and that 'every trade unionist knew that, in respect of national social services and industrial legislation generally there could be no administrative barrier between this country and England, nor could there be a different fiscal policy'.[16] This problem was to bedevil Home Rulers in the labour movement at least until the concept had been reformulated in the late 1930s.

The old Home Rule concept also proved unable to cope with Britain's changed position in the world. In the aftermath of the First World War, with the Empire still apparently strong, though developing politically, the concept of Dominion status, as well as being conveniently vague, had the merit of enabling its advocates to avoid the dreaded charge of 'separatism'. An imperial federation was much favoured by certain thinkers on the left,[17] as a means of ensuring free trade, co-operation and unified defence and foreign policies, together with equality of democratic rights throughout the Empire. To admit Scotland as a self-governing member of such a federation did not seem to raise insuperable problems. Indeed, Barr's Bill of 1927 and Buchanan's of 1924 were envisaged by their supporters as merely the first stage of such a general reform. By 1931, the meaning of Dominion status as virtual independence had been officially sanctioned by the Statute of Westminster and the idea of imperial federation appeared increasingly unrealistic. The danger of Scotland's political and economic isolation in a competitive and hostile world thus led Scotsmen to seek shelter in the British state. Interestingly, this directly contradicts that school of thought which holds that the emergence of Scottish nationalism can be attributed to the decline of the Empire, revealing the absence of a specifically British national identity. Some[18] locate this development in the period after the Second World War or after the Suez operation, while others plump for the 1930s.[19] The significance of other nationalist developments in the 1930s is considered below, but for the labour movement the logic of the position was clear. Britain's position in the 1930s presented it with a choice of endorsing a separatist policy or of accepting a very limited and possibly meaningless form of devolution. The middle road of Dominion status was no longer an option, if it ever had been. Even in 1928, the separatist implications of Barr's bill had worried some of its own supporters. After the political and economic events of 1929–31, such a bill would have worried them a great deal more.

The Red Clydesiders of the ILP had moved a long way from the heady nationalism of the post-war years, while nationalism itself was tainted in the 1930s by its association with right-wing regimes in Europe and was no longer generally regarded as the ally of progress and socialism. The old dispute on the left between the advocates of national liberation and of international socialism revived and were usually settled in favour of the latter. In Scotland, the rise of 'bourgeois' nationalist parties distracting attention from the class struggle and attempting to divide the workers provided the incentive for an attack on nationalism. Jimmie Maxton, the nationalist demagogue of former days, never abandoned his belief in a Scottish Parliament, but by the 1930s he had come to believe that national self-determination should follow, not precede, the establishment of socialism. In 1932 he declared that 'a struggle these days for mere political liberty is out of date, whether it takes place in India, Ireland or Scotland'.[20] By 1942 he was saying, 'We as a party [i.e. the ILP] are not impressed with the resurgence of nationalism, which synchronises with the rise of national socialism in Germany'.[21]

While the ILP and the Communist Party, as befitted their more ideological stance, developed an anti-nationalist line, though still believing that self-determination would be an aspect of the socialist state, the Labour Party merely allowed the Home Rule commitment to lapse as other issues gained in importance. The issue was not raised at Scottish Labour conferences between 1930 and 1937. What was notable in the solid centre of Scottish Labour and trade union opinion was, on the one hand, a continuing lip service to the old idea of Home Rule, and, on the other hand, a growing support for administrative devolution, a development which expressed a continuing concern with the promotion of Scottish goals and benefits while avoiding the dangers of constitutional change.

This was particularly noticeable in the STUC which, after the failure of the 1931 motion on Dominion status, turned its attention to practical administrative measures for improving Scottish government and promoting development within the context of the unified economy, to which it was now firmly committed. In 1932 the General Council reported that it had 'examined the effect a change in the government of Scotland might have upon industrial legislation'. It had not investigated 'the wider question of Scottish Home Rule', but recommented that 'in any system for the government of Scotland, provision should be made for the same industrial legislation being applied throughout Great Britain'. In 1935 Congress called for an 'authoritative body' to co-ordinate Scottish economic development, and in 1936 for a 'national administrative and rating body for Scotland' to take over local authority functions. The latter was clearly a centralising measure, and its proposer, C. N. Gallie of the General Council, formerly a strong Home Ruler, was careful to distinguish it from 'economic nationalism or even Scottish Home Rule'. A miners' delegate commended the motion, remarking that, 'as a socialist, he was in favour of centralisation'.

The advocacy of administrative devolution was not confined to the labour movement. Scottish administration in the inter-war period was very fragmented, with responsibilities shared between the Secretary for Scotland, who in 1926 became a Secretary of State; administrative boards; UK departments; and a large number of local authorities, many of them extremely small. In 1928 the Conservatives reorganised the Scottish Office, converting all but two of the boards into regular departments.[22]

In 1929 local government was reorganised, the parish councils being abolished and the small burghs divested of many of their functions.[23] Nevertheless, compared with England, local government in Scotland was still fragmented and many authorities lacked the resources to undertake ambitious development projects or even efficiently to discharge their functions. This underlay much of the Labour and trade union concern about local government. At the Scottish level, the process of administrative reform culminated in the implementation by the Conservatives of the Gilmour Report of 1937. The remaining Scottish boards were reorganised as departments of the Scottish Office under the Secretary of State, and the great bulk of the Scottish administration was transferred from London to St Andrew's House in Edinburgh.

The attitude of the Scottish Council of the Labour Party, the Scottish Labour MPs and the STUC was to welcome these developments and to press for the administrative devolution of more economic and industrial powers. This set a pattern which was to persist for many years, based on the view that Scottish interests were best promoted by a strong UK government, with a strong Scottish Labour presence at Westminster and a large measure of administrative devolution to ensure that Scotland's voice was heard, that Scotland received a fair share of the UK cake and that special Scottish conditions were recognised in the administration of policy. Such a view accorded well with the general practical bent of Labour Party thought in the 1930s, which was to culminate in the notable Secretaryship of State of Tom Johnston during the Second World War.

So, for most of the Scottish labour movement during the depression years of the 1930s, Home Rule and nationalism were side issues. For the left, it was at worst a positive evil, the ally of fascism and the enemy of socialism and, at best, an issue to be considered after the attainment of the socialist millennium. For the right and centre, it was at worst a threat to sound government and economic recovery and at best an issue to be postponed until more immediate problems had been settled. Only among old-fashioned radicals such as James Barr was it seen as an important aim in itself and a means to the attainment of other aims, and Barr himself was increasingly absorbed in ecclesiastical politics and Westminster business. Another exception to the general rule was Davie Kirkwood, one of the Clydesiders, described in 1935 as 'dividing his affections among porridge and politics, the Bible and Burns, Scottish Home Rule and Socialism, his family and "ma people in Clydebank" '.[24] The Home Rule issue was kept alive in the labour movement of the 1930s by such people and by a lingering but widespread sentimental attachment to the old cause. So, although by this time the emotional nationalistic impetus had largely gone out of the Scottish labour movement and it became fashionable to decry the 'sentimental, flag-wagging' type of nationalism which had characterised the early period, a vague feeling that Home Rule was a 'good thing', other things being equal, persisted. Labour has always found it difficult to jettison ideas once regarded as sacrosanct, and, for a long time after it had ceased to be taken seriously, Home Rule continued to form part of the ideological baggage of many Scottish radicals. Thus, in 1931 a poll conducted by the *Daily Record* showed all the Scottish Labour MPs to favour Home Rule in principle,[25] and, as Minister of Mines in the same year, Emmanuel Shinwell declared that, while he was opposed to economic separation, 'I am a strong upholder of Scottish interest and would gladly see Scottish affairs dealt with in a Scottish Parliament.'[26]

Emotional cultural–political nationalism was now largely the property of the adherents of the separatist parties. It is the founding and vociferous campaigning of these parties, together with the literary renaissance, which has led some writers to characterise the 1930s as a period of rising Scottish nationalism. Thus, Nairn sees the birth of politico-cultural nationalism in the late 1920s with the foundation of the SNP and the publication of Hugh MacDiarmid's *A Drunk Man Looks at the Thistle*.[27] Ferguson maintains that the rising national consciousness associated with the literary renaissance was reflected in Barr's Bill of 1927.[28] In later years, Labour leaders too liked to describe the 1930s as a period of nationalism, because this allowed them to dismiss nationalism as a reaction to the policies of the Tory–National governments and as such certain to disappear as soon as Labour started to implement progressive policies.

The 1930s did indeed see a new phase in the development of Scottish nationalism. The break up of the all-party Scottish Home Rule Association led to the foundation of the National Party of Scotland (NPS). In 1932, a breakaway group of the Cathcart Conservative Association formed the Scottish Party under the patronage of the Duke of Montrose and Professor Alexander Dewar Gibb, committed to a moderate Home Rule policy. In 1934 the two amalgamated to form the Scottish National Party (SNP). These developments, however, represented not an advance for Scottish nationalism, but a retreat. The foundation of the NPS was a result of the decline of nationalism in left-wing and radical circles and the despair felt by Roland Muirhead and other nationalists of getting any action on the subject from the Labour Party. In later years, Muirhead regretted the break-up of the Home Rule alliance of the 1920s and his own decision to work outside the Labour Party,[29] but he was certainly right in his belief at the time that Home Rule was not to be attained through Labour. This 'outsider' strategy in turn failed because of the absence of a popular and politically salient nationalism. A realistic interpretation of Barr's Bill of 1927 is that it represented the last fling of the old Home Rule coalition, not the first effort of a new nationalism. Its failure demonstrated the weakness of that coalition and the outdated nature of its common aim.

The literary movement was marked by a revival of interest in Scottish culture and by the invention of a Scots literary language, 'Lallans' – this being particularly associated with Hugh Mac-Diarmid, who, as a cultural and political nationalist, believed a language to be essential to a nation struggling for independence.

Apart from MacDiarmid, however, the connection between literature and political nationalism is often tenuous. Scottish political
nationalism has long been distinguished by the absence of a literary
dimension, and a vernacular writer such as Lewis Grassic Gibbon,
in his *Scots Quair*, which deals in political and socialist as well as
Scots themes, could make clear his view of Scottish nationalism as a
mere refuge for disillusioned Tories.

One can thus take issue with Nairn's contentions that politico-
cultural nationalism 'did not even dawn until the 1920s, after all-
British imperialism had received its first shocks and begun to enter
on its long decline',[30] and that, while the old Home Rule
movements were remarkable in a wider perspective for their
feebleness and political ambiguity, the formation of the NPS in 1928
and, 'just as important', the appearance of MacDiarmid's *A Drunk
Man* in 1926, are of great significance.[31] Certainly, the old Home
Rule movements contained crucial ambiguities, but it is difficult,
even with hindsight, to attribute this degree of significance to
MacDiarmid's poem or to rate the fledgling NPS of 1928, or even
the SNP of 1935, as more important than the earlier radical Home
Rule movements. The SNP of the 1930s was itself feeble and
ambiguous in its aims, divided between moderate Home Rulers and
extreme separatists, with several shades in between. Nor was the
international climate of the 1930s favourable to a major revival of
Scottish nationalism. Britain's imperial decline occurred in a world
marked by international tension in the military and economic
spheres, an unlikely setting for the growth of post-imperial Scottish
nationalism, either in the 1930s or in the Cold War of the 1950s.

The economic depression too has been credited with stimulating
a revival of Scottish nationalism.[32] In fact it seems to have weakened
it, and, indeed, taking a longer historical perspective, nationalism
has usually been associated with relative prosperity or rising
expectations in Scotland, not with depression and dependence on
the English connection. In so far as discontent with the economic
condition of Scotland received political expression, it was chan-
nelled through the parties of the left, which were themselves
increasingly committed to the unity of the UK.

Election results provide the strongest evidence of the weakness of
political nationalism in the 1930s. Nationalists contested two seats
in the General Election of 1929, polling 4·9 per cent in Glasgow
Camlachie and 5·4 per cent in West Renfrewshire. In 1931 five
Nationalist candidates polled 12·4 per cent of the total poll in the

seats contested. In 1935, at the height of inter-war nationalist activity, the newly founded SNP fielded eight candidates, only to see the Nationalist share of the vote in seats contested fall to 9·9 per cent.[33] Three deposits were saved in 1931, two in 1935. The best Nationalist performance was in the idiosyncratic constituency of the Western Isles, where in 1935 Sir Alexander McEwan, the former Liberal provost of Inverness and, from 1931, a county councillor for one of the isles, polled 28·1 per cent of a low poll.[34] Nor was the Nationalist performance in by-elections before the war particularly notable. Only when special circumstances were present did their candidates show at all strongly. In 1931, at the end of the second Labour Government, which was suffering a string of by-election reverses, Miss E. Campbell polled 15·1 per cent at Glasgow St Rollox, an area hit by the recent closure of the railway engineering works. In 1933 MacEwan, as joint candidate of the NPS and Scottish Party, managed 16·9 per cent at Kilmarnock in an election contested by National Labour, Labour and the ILP but not by the Conservatives. Even so, he came bottom of the poll.

The first few Nationalist candidatures were reported to have led Labour MPs to revive their flagging interest in Home Rule, but the failure of these candidatures caused interest to wane still further. As the belief strengthened that nothing was to be gained from Labour, nationalists began to form alliances with groups hostile to the party and the gap between the two movements widened. Increasingly common were attacks such as that of the STUC president of 1931. While supporting Home Rule he declared that

> such obstacles as existed had not been removed, rather they had been accentuated by a few doctrinaire people who still lived in the dead pages of Scottish history, giving voice to proposals which were ludicrous and unworkable. So much sentimentalism had been wound around the subject that its real use or value had been obscured.[35]

One of the more bizarre alliances which the Nationalists formed was with Lord Beaverbrook, proprietor of the *Daily Express*. This was the work of John MacCormick, a Glasgow lawyer and former student ILP-er and an increasingly prominent figure in nationalist circles. The *Express* was in the midst of a circulation war with the *Daily Record*, each paper vying to prove its Scottishness. By 1932 the *Express* had adopted the prefix *Scottish* and come out openly for

Scottish nationalism. For a time MacCormick was a regular visitor to the Beaverbrook offices, though it is not clear if the promised finance for the Nationalists ever materialised.[36] In 1933 Beaverbrook dropped Scottish nationalism as quickly as he had adopted it, but MacCormick's search for allies continued. In view of the increasing left-wing hostility to nationalism, it is perhaps surprising that he should next have co-operated with the Communist Party.

The adoption in 1929 of the 'New Line' had inaugurated the Stalinist 'Third Period' in Britain, during which the Communist Party was to attack the Labour Party as 'social–fascist' and denounce ILP-ers such as Maxton as props of the social–fascists. Building the Communist Party at the expense of Labour now became a crucial goal, and the methods extended to the formation of breakaway revolutionary trade unions in certain circumstances and the standing of candidates against Labour candidates in Parliamentary and local elections.

In Scotland the Communist Party and the National Minority Movement, which it dominated, had built up considerable support in the mining districts, and by 1928 were locked in a bitter struggle with the right wing, culminating in the decision to form a breakaway 'United Mineworkers of Scotland'. At first sight, such a development may seem to have offered scope for a tactical espousal of Home Rule. But this would be to misunderstand the basis of the Communist Party's strength in the mines, which rested on the militancy of the miners in the less profitable coalfields and, in particular, their advocacy of the transformation of the Miners' Federation of Great Britain into a united national union which could reverse the setback in wages and hours sustained after the General Strike. The Communist Party's view was thus epitomised by a Central Committee resolution in March 1930 which stated that

> the rise of this organisation [the United Mineworkers of
> Scotland] is not a mere incident in the history of the Scottish
> miners, but the beginning of a profound revolutionary
> development throughout the coalfields destined to supersede
> the MFGB, and unite the mineworkers of Britain in a single
> miners' union for the whole of Britain.[37]

Thus, the replacement of the slogan 'All power to the General Council of the TUC' with the policy of independent revolutionary

leadership did not alter the internationalist flavour of Communist Party agitation.
Outside the mines, the Communist Party had little industrial base in Scotland and in 1931 Peter Kerrigan pointed out that the party had been successful in getting the unemployed out on the streets in mass demonstrations, but had failed to lead strikes:

> In most areas in Scotland there is a steady stream of recruits coming in. . . . Wherever it has been possible to get information regarding the social composition of recruits made (Glasgow, Uddingston) this information bears out our basic weakness, namely, failure to get established in the factories because over 90 per cent of those coming in are unemployed.[38]

While there was no hint of nationalism in the Communist Party's industrial efforts, its political intervention against Labour, coming at the same time that the nationalist movement was beginning to stand independently, confronted the party with the need for a policy on Scottish Home Rule. This was recognised by Willie Gallacher, commenting on the Dumbartonshire by-election of 1932, where the Scottish nationalists gained 13·4 per cent of the poll, as against the Communists' 7·5 per cent:

> We did not do anything like sufficient to expose the Scottish Nationalists. This movement is becoming an increasing menace.
> The Scottish Nationalists have their roots in the universities. Many of the students in these institutions are faced with the fact that when their studies are over there is little for them but the scrapheap. The professions are overcrowded. . . .
> Amongst the students the idea of a Scottish Parliament has made great headway as a means of solving the crisis for them. But then in Scotland, there are problems that confront agricultural workers and fishermen, then there is the heavy collapse of the basic industries and the feeling that somehow England is given preference.
> It is necessary that we should make a thorough study of all the problems that confront the Scottish workers so that we

can effectively deal with the Fascist demagogy of the Scottish Nationalists.[39]

Gallacher's call was taken up by writers in the *Communist Review* in the following year. Helen Crawfurd analysed the petty-bourgeois support for the movement as a response to economy cuts and to the relatively poor position of Scotland – for example, what she sees as its poor share of national expenditure and of grants to the social services and to industry.

> Lord Beaverbrook and certain sections of the capitalist class who are supporting this movement are fully aware of its potentialities as the basis of a fascist movement, and see the possibilities of attracting the youth of Scotland away from the class struggle to follow this Will-o'-the-wisp.

Nevertheless, the party should, she felt, analyse the economic content and cause of the movement, and as soon as possible make its position on the question clear (which confirms the lack of definite Communist policy on Scottish Home Rule at this time).[40]

Oliver Bell, whose analysis stressed the support nationalism received from the crofters of the Western Highlands and the Western Isles, the farmers suffering from the economic crisis, and the middle class, also called for the party to 'make our position clear in the very near future'.[41]

However, there was no major initiative in response to this evidence of disquiet at the lack of policy on Home Rule and nationalism. It may be surmised that, in the period of militant 'class against class' politics, the Nationalist parties had to be denounced as fascist or semi-fascist, while any attempt to woo their base of support in the disgruntled middle classes by advocating Home Rule would have been seen as trying to beat them at their own game. On the other hand, outright opposition to Home Rule might have offended the sentiments of many potential recruits, since in practice there was some overlapping in the social groups from which both Communist and Nationalist parties were able to recruit during these worse years of the Depression.

By 1935 the Seventh Congress of the Comintern confirmed an abrupt turn in Stalin's strategy for the Third International. This was to open up the possibility of a new initiative by the Communist Party of Great Britain on the Scottish question. The sectarianism of the Third Period was replaced by a policy of a popular front against fascism. Unity of the working-class parties was supplemented by efforts to embrace 'progressive' elements of the bourgeoisie in the anti-fascist fold.

By 1937 the CPGB had begun to grasp the opportunities presented by the new strategy. Ted Bramley referred to the need to 'pay more attention to studying outlook, prejudices, etc., of all sections of the people to find the most suitable form of approach, and to avoid a stereotyped appeal'.[42] He felt that, while Communists could not carry the Union Jack, the party could certainly develop a more positive attitude to England.

A writer on the problems of propaganda in Wales referred to the need to 'pay attention to the national characteristics, prejudices and traditions of Wales': 'Not half enough attention is paid to those things that have agitated the Welshman for centuries, such as the right, free from restrictions, to develop the Welsh language and culture, and the right of Wales, at least to a greater degree of administrative autonomy'.[43]

Thus, when J. R. Campbell referred at the Fourteenth congress, in 1937, to the need for 'a big change in our propaganda methods' in Scotland, he did so in the context of an overall policy initiative. He pointed out that a high proportion of party members still came from the ranks of the unemployed, 'signifying that our work has not yet swung round strongly enough to the employed workers in the factories, winning workers in the Labour Party, getting contact and influence amongst the middle classes'. The party was thus now directly in competition with the Nationalists for middle-class support: a dramatic turn around from the 'class against class' position of five years previously. Campbell noted that Scottish comrades were 'now preparing publication of a whole series of pamphlets dealing with problems confronting the Scottish people'.[44]

It was this change of line by the Communist Party which made possible a move towards the SNP. Around 1936 Aitken Ferguson started negotiations with John McCormick and Roland Muirhead, the outcome of which was a statement supporting a Scottish Parliament. Although rejected by the Scottish Committee of the party, this was supported by the National Committee in London, which then proceeded to call an extended Scottish Committee to ratify the decision.[45] The Communist Party now threw itself into the Home Rule fight with great vigour.

The main propaganda contribution was a pamphlet by Aitken Ferguson entitled *Scotland* and embodying a 'Programme for Scotland'. In 1927 he had criticised Duncan and Gallie of the STUC for 'donning the tartan'; now it was his own turn, a decade later, to do so! The pamphlet began with tributes from two nationalists, one of whom, John MacCormick, praised it as 'a decided contribution to the fight for Scottish Freedom'. After dealing with the depression and its economic causes, and discussing the plight of the Highlands and the miserable social conditions prevailing in Scotland, an enormous catalogue of proposed measures was set out ('The Communist Plan to Save Scotland'). Ranging from improved housing schemes, higher wages, and road- and bridge-building and tourism projects to overcome unemployment, to grants and credits to aid smallholders and fishermen, the plan fulfilled the propaganda needs identified as long ago as 1932 by Willie Gallacher. The 'bureaucratic way in which Scottish affairs are mismanaged' was criticised, and the realisation of the proposed social and economic programme linked to the need for 'a new legislative body in Scotland, with a Socialist and democratic majority elected on a basis of full joint suffrage and with wide powers to go ahead'. Powers demanded included the 'power to tax and levy, power to budget' and 'power to compel reactionary elements to toe the line'.

Would not such a body doing such a job inevitably mean a parliament in Scotland, and thus the splitting of the British working-class movement? On the first point, Ferguson was clear: 'Such a body, such a national organisation is necessary and imperative, and such powers are needed and can be forced from the House of Commons.' The second point was answered, in a manner to become characteristic of Communist rhetoric on Home Rule, not by a discussion of the actual effect of a separate parliament, but by the assertion of the need for working-class unity: 'Just as we stand for "Scotland's Nation", so at the same time we stand for strong, centralised organisations of the *British* working class on a democratic basis, both for the industrial and political fight'.

Despite the earlier call for a 'legislative' body, and reference to a 'Parliament in Scotland', the chapter headed 'Self Government for Scotland' stated that 'the Communist Party advocates the establishment of a central administrative body for Scotland' which 'should have the administration of all Scottish affairs delegated to it by Parliament'. Vaguely defined control over 'the disbursement of the

Scottish Estimates' and rating, finance and budgetary powers would be necessary to make this administrative body effective. Pending a promised more detailed statement of the Communist Party's position on the national question, support was offered initially, 'as a step on the road to Scottish Self Government', to the proposals made by Tom Johnston MP and Willie Gallacher, Communist MP, for 'the meeting in Edinburgh of all Scottish MPs in the Scottish Grand Committee to discuss the Scottish Estimates'.

Thus, the Communist Party's policy swung from confused rhetoric designed to appeal to those with nationalist sympathies, to support for the renewed interest in Home Rule within the Scottish Labour Party. It was a 'lefter than thou' *and* 'more nationalist than thou' version of the *Plan for Scotland* issued by Tom Johnston's London Scots Self-Government Committee in 1937. Confirmation of the new importance attached to the issue came with the full-time attachment of Aitken Ferguson to McCormick's projected 1939 convention,[46] which we examine below.

II. HOME RULE AGITATION REVIVED

Scotland shared in the general recovery from the Depression from about 1934 onwards. Wage levels, which had fallen further than those in England during the slump, recovered and, from 1934, rose more rapidly than the UK average, so that Scotland enjoyed an increasing share of the national wages bill up until the end of the war, when the share began to decline again.[47] Even at its new height, in 1945, however, Scotland's share of UK wages was lower than it had been in 1924.

In terms of employment, Scotland's industrial structure and the failure to attract new industry prevented as rapid a recovery as in England, but, apart from a slight hiccup in 1938, Scottish unemployment fell steadily in the late 1930s.[48] In the coal and shipbuilding industries, some recovery was under way by 1935,[49] and when, in 1937, the recovery looked like faltering, the rearmament programme, begun in earnest in 1936,[50] soon picked up the slack. Rearmament, as some contemporaries warned,[51] was a mixed blessing to the Scottish economy, carrying as it did danger of a return to dependence on heavy industry, but in the short run it certainly gave the Clyde industries a new lease of life. While the Scottish economy in the late 1930s was hardly booming, then, there

had been a substantial recovery from the depths of the Depression
and Scotland's standing in the United Kingdom was no longer so
obviously that of a 'poor relation'.

This period also saw some revival in Labour circles of support for
Home Rule. Several features distinguish this renewed agitation in
kind from the earlier phase. It was not general, but confined to
certain sections of the movement; in particular, the trades unions
were hardly involved. It had little effect on the leadership, which,
especially after the election of the Labour Government of 1945,
strived to keep it under control. It generally lacked the emotional,
nationalistic fervour of the earlier days. Finally, there was now a
nationalist party outside the labour movement, challenging Labour
and putting it, as a UK and, in due course, a governing party, at the
receiving end of nationalist pressure. Labour's policy must therefore
be understood partly in terms of its own thought and partly in terms
of its being infected by, or needing to react to, an external
nationalism of varying strength.

The renewed interest in Home Rule was led by a few middle-class
professionals, writers and MPs. In 1936 Tom Johnston founded the
London Scots Self-Government Committee, a group of Labour
Party members, with the aim of converting the party to the need for
Scottish Home Rule and producing a scheme which would
reconcile this with the planned economy. Johnston himself, who
became president of the committee, was disillusioned with
Westminster politics, and, having decided by 1937 to retire at the
next election to concentrate on his writing, was concerning himself
increasingly with Scottish questions. The chairman of the committee was the old Home Ruler James Barr, and vice-presidents
included nine MPs and the author Naomi Mitchison. The secretary
and treasurer respectively were Norrie Fraser and Thomas Burns,
and among the active members was Douglas Young, later to
achieve prominence in the SNP. The group held regular meetings
and dinners in London, at which prominent Labour leaders such as
Herbert Morrison were the guests, and in 1937 issued a pamphlet,
Plan for Scotland, written by Thomas Burns, with a foreword by
Clement Attlee himself. This firmly declared that only through
Labour and progressive politics could self-government be brought
about, and put forward a series of proposals for discussion, 'not in a
spirit of dogmatism'. A federal system was envisaged, with a Scottish
Parliament responsible for everything except the Crown, Army,
Navy, peace, war, foreign affairs, imperial affairs, currency and the

Post Office. The 'ticklish "tariffs at Gretna" question' would be eliminated by conducting all foreign trade through an imports and exports department. The Scottish Treasurer would pay an imperial contribution and Scottish MPs would remain at Westminster, in reduced numbers and with no voting powers on English affairs. The causes of socialism and of self-government in Scotland were declared to be one and indivisible and the emphasis throughout the document is on the need for planning in Scotland, with close co-ordination between Scottish and English plans. UK-wide trades unions and their direct involvement in planning would prevent any weakening of the united working-class movement. The plan, in its lack of any nationalistic or anti-English tone, is typical of the committee's approach, declaring, for instance, that 'Scotland has indeed been ruthlessly exploited and bled white, not by England, but by her own industrialists'. In his preface Attlee extolled the virtues of national sentiment, but warned that much spadework still needed to be done and commended 'the careful consideration of the economic questions which so many nationalists ignore'. The plan's significance lies not so much in its detailed content as in its being the first reformulation of the Home Rule concept since the general abandonment of the aim of Dominion status. In its cautious tone it recognised the many difficulties in the way of Home Rule, but it did provide a starting point for the serious reconsideration of the issue.

As a result of the committee's work, some interest in the matter was rekindled. In 1937, on the eve of the Scottish Labour conference, Scottish Labour MPs, reportedly angry that Home Rule had been left out of the 1937 programme, were told that, in the view of the National Executive Committee, this was not as important as some of the other items in the programme.[52] The MPs may have had an eye on the conference, at which an Executive resolution calling for 'an adequate measure of self-government' was passed overwhelmingly, against an amendment from Stirling, Falkirk and Grangemouth Divisional Labour Party condemning 'self-government under capitalism' – a reminder that in the Labour Party and the ILP the left tended to oppose Home Rule, though, further to the left, in the Communist Party, nationalism was, as we have seen, becoming respectable again.

In 1938, in Scotland, a group similar to the London Scots was founded, the Labour Council for Scottish Self-Government. In 1939 it issued a pamphlet,[53] penned by W. Oliver Brown. This gave a list of examples of Parliamentary and administrative neglect of Scottish affairs, repeated the old argument that, as Scotland is more progressive than England, it can attain socialism sooner, and claimed that, as Labour's nationalisation programme would place great burdens on the administrative machinery, decentralisation was essential. In 1939 the council offered to help the Scottish Council of the Labour Party with its economic survey of industry, but this appears to have been overtaken by the war.

The activities of these bodies formed part of a general concern felt by professional people, academics and writers of the late 1930s about the condition of Scotland and particularly about its economic and industrial problems.[54] A stream of books appeared dealing with these themes, and, while most of them did not take an overtly nationalist stance,[55] a need was usually felt to relate the diagnosis and remedies to the fact of Scottish nationhood and, at least, to consider their constitutional and political aspects. By and large, however, a sound economy was seen as a prerequisite of constitutional change. The concern over the condition of Scotland also found expression in the foundation of bodies such as the Scottish Development Council, the National Trust for Scotland, the Scottish Economic Committee, the Saltire Society and the Scottish Council for Social Service, which sought remedies in social and environmental planning and control. Regional policy and planning provided the basis for a Scottish lobby, encompassing both labour and capital. Left-wing indignation at such class collaboration and demands for direction of industry to replace the policy of incentives to invest in depressed areas were of little avail and had largely died down by the outbreak of war.

By the late 1930s John MacCormick had realised the potential of this developing Scottish lobby as an ally in the Home Rule cause. Although he had been a founder of the NPS and SNP, he was never comfortable in the company of thoroughgoing separatists, and, following the SNP's electoral failure, he proposed a return to the all-party approach of the Scottish Home Rule Association. A Scottish convention was arranged for 1939, and, although it had to be postponed on the outbreak of war, it attracted widespread support, including that of the Communist Party, James Barr, William Gallacher of the Scottish Co-operative Wholesale Society, J. McKendrick, secretary of the Lanarkshire Miners' Union, and J. McBain, Scottish organiser of the foundry workers. Officially, the Labour Party, while not joining the convention, observed a benevolent neutrality.

The war saw several notable developments in the Scottish political and administrative scene. In 1940 Churchill persuaded a reluctant Tom Johnston to take the post of Secretary of State for Scotland. Johnston, though much mellowed politically since his radical days as editor of *Forward*, was an energetic and decisive administrator. Convinced, in line with the 'middle opinion' characteristic of much 1930s thinking, that what Scotland most needed was a consensus approach to vital economic and industrial issues and sound, practical measures rather than high-flown theories, he set about putting his ideas into practice, with unprecedented vigour. The consensus approach produced the 'Council of State', a group of all the living ex-Secretaries of State, which, when in agreement, carried great weight, in government and with Churchill. With the backing of the council, Johnston was able to set up the North of Scotland Hydro Electricity Board, to promote electrification and industrial development in the Highlands. In 1942 he set up the Scottish Council on Industry, a semi-official group bringing together government and industry to promote development. Later it amalgamated with a similar private group to form the Scottish Council (Development and Industry). Johnston insisted on the Secretary of State's being the planning minister for Scotland for the purposes of wartime and reconstruction planning and improved the co-ordination of plans by setting up regional bodies of local authorities for east and west Scotland.[56] By fighting hard in Cabinet, he secured favourable treatment for Scotland on a whole range of issues, from the length of the tomato-growing season to industrial development. Although now distant from Scottish nationalism, he was not averse to turning it to his own advantage. In his Cabinet battles, a favourite ploy was to remind his colleagues of the threat of nationalism to Labour's position – a technique which was to be emulated by later Secretaries of State with similar effect. The result of these efforts was a Scottish administration which was both responsive to Scottish demands and effective. Agriculture and industry revived and the drift to the south was stemmed. It was a great vindication of the policy of administrative devolution, and, shorn of its non-partisan trappings, formed the model for Scottish Labour's approach to Scottish affairs for the next thirty years. Though in the post-war period the Scottish Office fell from the heights of influence and prestige which it enjoyed under Johnston, he had shown how Scottish aspirations could be combined with national unity and special consideration given to Scottish problems without courting the dangers of separatism. So, although Johnston himself saw the building of a sound Scottish economic and administrative base as a prerequisite for Home Rule, the result of his success was to weaken further the argument for a Scottish Parliament and its priority for Labour.

The war itself had produced convulsions within the SNP and, for a short time, a considerable upturn in its fortunes, despite the continuing tension between the Home Rulers and the separatists. The electoral truce observed by the major parties during the war gave it a unique opportunity, which was seized in the Argyll by-election of April 1940. In a straight fight with the Conservative, the SNP candidate polled 37·5 per cent of the vote. The reasons for this result have been the subject of varying interpretations,[57] but one effect was certainly to put nationalism back on the political agenda. However, the scene was again transformed shortly after, by a split which developed over the party's attitude to the war. Douglas Young, a lecturer in Greek at Aberdeen University and former Labour Party member who continued to identify with the labour movement, refused to be conscripted for military service other than by a Scottish government. In 1942 he was sentenced to a year in jail, having gained a great deal of publicity through the protracted proceedings in the conscription tribunals. The publicity, however, did the party no good at the polls, as in April 1942 an SNP candidate at the Cathcart by-election received a mere 5·5 per cent of the poll. The split in the party came to a head at the annual conference in June of that year. MacCormick and most of the leadership determined to repudiate Young and also the policy of contesting elections and instead to return to the all-party Home Rule approach.[58] Their opponents nominated Young as chairman, and, after Young had won by four votes, MacCormick and his followers seceded to form the Scottish Union, later named the Scottish Convention. The Convention was to make its major impact after the war, but meanwhile the SNP experienced another remarkable upturn in its fortunes. Party membership rose[59] and in 1944, at a by-election in Kirkcaldy, Douglas Young polled 41·3 per cent. The following year, Robert McIntyre became the party's first MP, after securing 51·4 per cent of the vote in the Labour stronghold of Motherwell.

By 1944, then, the nationalist movement outside the Labour Party had revealed itself as a potent threat, a force to be taken seriously. After the war, the electoral pressure of the SNP was to be replaced by the popular pressure of the Convention, so that it becomes impossible to understand Labour's attitudes apart from developments in the rival nationalist movements. Labour could be affected by a revival of popular nationalism in two ways: it could be infected itself with the nationalist mood, or it could be forced to accommodate itself to it. There are several reasons why Labour politicians and activists could be expected to possess a degree of immunity from the popular infection. Their ideology might incorporate universalist elements antagonistic to nationalism. Such elements were an influence on the left and in the ILP in the 1930s and 1940s, but for many Labour activists Home Rule was a traditional and respectable part of the programme and its accommodation posed few ideological, as opposed to practical, problems. Labour's leaders, on the other hand, might be less sympathetic to Home Rule now that they had become part of the UK political structure and gained status and influence with it. So, far from seeing any appeal in Scottish nationalism, they might resent it personally as a threat to their own position. In turn, their integration into the UK political structure could take two forms. On the one hand, they might by now have become part of a nationalised, homogeneous UK political system concerned with the promotion of UK policy goals; some Scottish Labour politicians had become national and were no longer primarily concerned with Scottish affairs, but in the Labour Party, as opposed to the ILP or the Communist Party, these were few. On the other hand, Scottish Labour leaders may have carved out a role as brokers for Scottish interests at the UK level, while also influencing UK policy; this was true of most Scottish MPs. It was not, therefore, that they saw a conflict between Scottish and UK goals and chose the latter but that the two sets of goals had merged so that Scotland's interests were almost regarded as synonymous with the election of a Labour government.

Thus, the Labour leadership, including the MPs, the leaders of the Scottish Council and the national leadership in London, was faced with expressions of nationalism within and outside the party and was forced to react to it. Until 1945 the token disposition towards Home Rule is still in evidence, with the Scottish leadership prepared to consider ways in which this traditional item of Labour's package can be incorporated into the programme. With the election of 1945, the emphasis changes to strong opposition to all varieties of Home Rule, with continuing pressure from the nationalist elements among the rank and file being met by only limited

concessions in administrative devolution and Parliamentary reform.

The question of Home Rule came back onto the Labour Party
agenda in connection with post-war reconstruction. In 1940 the
Executive of the Scottish Council of the Labour Party appointed a
committee to review and report on the findings of the Royal
Commission on the Location of Industry. The following year, its
terms of reference were extended to cover the whole question of
post-war reconstruction in Scotland. In August 1941 it reported,
producing the document *Plan for Post-War Scotland*. On the question
of Scottish government, it came down firmly on the side of
devolution, recommending 'an executive authority in Scotland
with legislative and administrative power to deal with all matters
that have solely Scottish import and with the Scottish aspects of
social and industrial legislation'. On the composition of this body,
the committee was less firm, advocating that, initially at least, it
should comprise the Scottish Members of Parliament. There
followed a complex series of negotiations with the National
Executive Committee and its Central Reconstruction Committee,
determined now to keep the Scottish Council on a tight rein and to
prevent party commitments from being made in Scotland which
could later prove embarrassing or damaging to Labour's national
programme – an interesting contrast to the First World War, when
the party, remote from power, happily took on sweeping commitments to Home Rule all round. Now the emphasis was on detailed
planning and realistic measures. The National Executive, worried
lest the *Plan for Post-War Scotland* be seen as official party policy,
agreed that the document should be *presented* to the annual Scottish
Labour Conference of 1941, but insisted that detailed discussion be
postponed to a special conference to be attended by its own
representatives. This would enable 'the Scottish movement [to]
assist them in drafting the Scottish section of their report'.[60]

This cautious approach was continued at the special conference
of December 1941. Emmanuel Shinwell and Morgan Philips from
the Central Reconstruction Committee attended and made it clear
that the suggestions of the document were no more than *suggestions*
by the Scottish Executive and should not be taken as the final word
on policy. General approval was given to the plan, on the
understanding that the Scottish Executive would re-examine each
section and continue to give careful and detailed consideration to
the whole question of post-war policy. Shinwell and Philips,

requesting close collaboration with the Central Committee, promised full consultation between the committee and the Scottish Executive. Following this special conference, the Reconstruction sub-committee was reappointed and met the Machinery of Government sub-committee of the Central Committee, but little progress was made and by the end of the war no definite plan had emerged.

Towards the end of the war, some sections of the Labour Party turned again to Home Rule. At the 1944 Scottish Labour conference two resolutions, from the Railway Clerks' Association and Dumbartonshire Divisional Labour Party, called for an inquiry into devolution. The Scottish Executive responded to the nationalist mood by tabling a resolution declaring the need for a Scottish parliament but carefully qualifying its enthusiasm by proposing a committee of inquiry, to report to the next conference. The report and the views of the conference would then be placed before the *following* conference. Although the resolution was carried, the committee seems to have disappeared into the same obscurity as had enveloped its predecessor. In 1945 the issue again appeared on the agenda, with four motions favouring Home Rule, one of which reminded Conference of National Conference decisions in 1918 and 1928 and of the special Scottish Conference decision of 1941. The composite resolution, which was passed by 97 votes to 67, expressed the opinion that the existing machinery for dealing with Scottish affairs was unsatisfactory and that the time had come to consider whether a Scottish legislative assembly was desirable. The Government was urged to establish a representative committee to consider the matter, the report of this committee to be considered at a specially convened Scottish Conference. T. Scollan, the candidate for West Renfrewshire, said that he had committed himself to a Scottish parliament and could not betray that pledge. Pressure was also kept up from the sidelines. In 1944 a group under the chairmanship of the Labour MP William Leonard, including several well known Labour and Liberal figures, as well as members of the Scottish Convention, issued a 'Declaration on Scottish Affairs', calling for a federal system.[61] In 1943 the London Scots Self-Government Committee and the Labour Council for Scottish Self-Government merged to form the Scottish Reconstruction Committee, under the leadership of Tom Burns and Norrie Fraser. This kept up a vigorous campaign for socialism and Home Rule until the late 1940s. In 1945 it launched a journal, the *New Scot*, and an impressive series of papers on aspects of a Scottish political, social and economic life.

The party thus approached the 1945 General Election with a vague pledge to do something about devolution in the course of reconstruction, with some Home Rule pressure from the rank and file but a leadership which was very cautious and in its turn kept firmly in line by the national leadership. The environment of post-war Scottish politics was as yet unclear. The SNP appeared set to pose a considerable threat to Labour, and the Convention movement was beginning to mobilise, but for the Labour Party the first priority was the election of a Labour government and the enactment of its programme of nationalisation and welfare provision.

This situation was very different from that following the First World War. Labour was now poised to take power and rash commitments to schemes which could frustrate the exercise of that power were to be avoided. The nationalist fervour of the earlier period was absent from the party and, as far as the UK party was concerned, Scottish devolution came well down the list of priorities. In these circumstances, it is perhaps not surprising that the Labour Party equivocated. Home Rule was not mentioned in the 1945 Labour Manifesto but the Scottish Council of the party issued speakers' notes which listed, as the second priority after the defeat of Japan, 'a Scottish Parliament for Scottish Affairs'. In a reply to a questionnaire from the Scottish Convention, twenty-three out of thirty-seven successful Labour candidates pledged support for a measure of Home Rule, while a further four gave qualified support.[62] In a letter to a Scottish Home Ruler, Attlee gave general support to devolution but warned that the subject needed careful consideration and carefully avoided any commitment. Such vague commitments could not long survive the election of the Labour Government in 1945 and the bandwagon success of the Scottish Convention. At the 1945 General Election, the Labour Party in fact did less well in Scotland than south of the border but the sweeping overall Labour victory directed attention firmly in the direction of Westminster and Whitehall. The poor showing of the SNP, which only managed to save two deposits, relieved the pressure on many MPs to emphasise their Home Rule credentials. On the other hand, MacCormick's Scottish Convention appeared a runaway success and its activities and relations with the Labour Government and

Party provide the background to Labour's manoeuvrings over devolution in the late 1940s.

The Convention, which had started life in 1942 with 342 members,[63] began to build up momentum after the war. Most of the members were defectors from the SNP, but by 1943 it had been established that the Labour Party had no objection to its members' joining and Neil Maclean MP and William Gallacher the Co-operator, as well as Willie Gallacher the Communist MP, became active in it. A rather distant and uneasy relationship was maintained with the Scottish Reconstruction Committee, which the Convention leaders seemed to suspect of usurping their proper role, and the movement was tolerated rather than supported by the Labour Party and the STUC. In 1946 the Convention decided, like the Scottish Home Rule Association before it, to summon a representative national assembly. This met in March 1947, attended by representatives of MPs of all the parties, over fifty town councils, county councils, churches, trades unions, commercial and industrial associations, Co-operative societies and social and cultural bodies.[64] A resolution calling for a large measure of self-government was passed and a committee appointed to draw up a scheme. The following year, the committee's report *Blue Print for Scotland* was accepted by a second assembly. By this time, however, the limitations of MacCormick's all-party approach were already apparent. Attacks in the Convention on 'London Government' could all too easily be interpreted as attacks on the Labour Government struggling amid a deepening economic crisis. In 1948, relations with Labour received another blow. MacCormick, who had stood as a Liberal in the 1945 election, had been adopted as a Liberal candidate for Paisley, where a by-election now occurred. During the previous year, ever in search of a broader alliance, he had been negotiating with certain Unionist, National Liberal and Liberal leaders to secure a fusion of the three parties, the price of which, from the Unionist point of view, would have been acceptance of a measure of Home Rule. A few Unionists had been active in the Convention and others had been exploiting the Convention's attacks on centralisation to attack nationalisation and planning – a tactic endorsed by Churchill early in 1950, when he declared,

The principle of centralization of government in Whitehall and Westminster is emphasized in a manner not hitherto

experienced or contemplated in the Act of Union. . . . If
England became an absolute Socialist State, owning all the
means of production, distribution, and exchange, ruled only
by politicians and their officials in the London offices, I
personally cannot feel Scotland would be bound to accept
such a dispensation.[65]

MacCormick accordingly decided to use the Paisley by-election to
advance this potential new alliance.

Paisley Unionists active in the Convention persuaded their party
not to put up a candidate, and the party, anxious to embarrass
Labour and knowing that it stood no chance of winning the election
itself, agreed. The Paisley electorate were thus treated to the strange
spectacle of the nationalist MacCormick sharing his election
platform with such stalwart Tories as Walter Elliott, Manningham-
Buller and Peter Thorneycroft. Naturally, the Labour Party was
furious, and it became impossible to convince Arthur Woodburn,
the Secretary of State, that Convention was anything more than a
Tory plot. It is difficult to absolve MacCormick from the charge of
political naïveté over this incident. He had already, in the 1930s, by
his relationships with Lord Beaverbrook and the Communists,
shown himself ready to accept any allies without questioning their
motivation. His action in Paisley in 1948 now broke the all-party
front, without extracting from his new allies any firm pledge of
action. On the other hand, without any electoral muscle the
movement was powerless. In 1949 James Stuart, chairman of the
Scottish Unionist MPs, told MacCormick as much, pointing out
that in Britain the public's wishes were made known through the
mechanism of Parliamentary elections.

After the 1948 assembly, delegates were sent to see Attlee. He
refused to see them and referred them to Arthur Woodburn, who,
still smarting from Paisley, where MacCormick had given Labour a
severe fright, said that, although the proposals sounded reasonable,
there was no evidence of widespread support for them. Convention
therefore launched its last major initiative and revived an idea
which had been floated during the war. At the third assembly, in
1949, a national covenant was launched. Although this eventually
collected more than 2 million signatures (some of them later found
to be duplicated) and provided an impressive demonstration of the
breadth of support for some measure of Home Rule, its launching
reflected the movement's essential weakness, its inability to con-

vince either of the major parties or to mount an electoral challenge itself. Home Rule may have been supported by a majority of Scots, but it was not a matter about which they felt sufficiently strongly to upset their normal pattern of political behaviour. With no tangible results, it was impossible to keep up the momentum of the Convention, and after 1950 it rapidly declined.

The election of the Labour Government had completely changed the nature of the debate as far as the Labour Party was concerned. The Convention had attracted considerable support from rank-and-file members in the constituencies, but, with a Labour Government in office, it was no longer possible to identify Home Rule with the advancement of socialism or to join in attacks on 'London government'. The Convention also came under suspicion because of the presence of anti-Labour elements within the ranks. Faced with the choice of pushing for Home Rule or giving solid support to Labour in government, there was little doubt as to which way the Labour leadership would go and the post-war years saw a prolonged attempt by it to extricate itself from its Home Rule commitment, in the face of continuing agitation by Convention supporters and the traditional party support for the policy. Unlike the Home Rule agitators in the period following the First World War, the Convention supporters were predominantly constituency activists, with little support coming from trades unions and the STUC. They suffered from the weaknesses of the Convention itself. If Home Rule was a purely 'political' concept, then it was at best irrelevant to Scotland's needs and almost impossible to define except as a vague aspiration. If it were to involve Scottish autonomy in economic matters, then it could be a positive menace to Scottish interests. Complaints about the centralising tendency of many of the Labour Government's measures might gain some sympathy from the public at large, including many Labour supporters, but they cut little ice with those who saw these measures as an essential part of the new order and as the only way to mobilise resources to meet Scottish needs.

Following the 1945 resolution, the Scottish Executive established a special sub-committee under the chairmanship of A. Anderson MP. By the 1949 conference, this group was reported to have made some progress and to be 'still proceeding'. The Executive, now determined to restrain the calls for devolution, or even an inquiry, opposed a motion in similar terms to the 1945 resolution, calling for a Government inquiry. The resolution was nevertheless carried by

97 votes to 67, with 68 abstentions.[66] At the same conference, a motion from the Amalgamated Engineering Union was passed calling, in line with the trade unions' preference for administrative devolution of economic matters, for Scottish departments of the Board of Trade and the Ministry of Labour and for a Scottish Planning Commission. This was referred to the sub-committee considering the 1945 resolution, which, despite claiming difficulties in reconciling the two resolutions, pursued them both with the Government and the party. No progress was made. They met with a committee of the National Executive Committee (NEC), with Herbert Morrison and Joe Westwood, the Secretary of State for Scotland, present, for a general discussion. Then they met with Westwood and representatives of the Parliamentary Labour Party, who tried to dismiss them by suggesting that they take the 1945 resolutions back, to consider the terms of reference of the proposed commission. This they refused to do, as they were bound by the conference decision, so they sent the resolution to the NEC and to Herbert Morrison. The Scottish group of Labour MPs had a similar experience. After affirming its support for the resolution, the group met a number of times with Morrison and Westwood and requested a decision by October 1947. The NEC at first decided to launch its own investigation, then, on Morrison's suggestion, agreed to arrange a meeting between its policy sub-committee and the Scottish Executive and MPs. This was immediately overtaken by the economic crisis, pushing Scottish devolution even further down the list of Government and NEC priorities. Westwood was sent to see representatives of the MPs and the secretary of the Scottish Council to convey the Government's view. This was that the Government was not in principle opposed to an inquiry, but that questions of the general policy of the Government and the Labour Party and the administrative structure of the nationalised industries and services should be excluded from its terms of reference. Westwood asked the Scottish Executive to appoint two or three representatives to consult with him on possible terms of reference. John Taylor, secretary to the Scottish Council, was now a determined opponent of devolution and attacks on him by nationalists only strengthened his resolve to make no compromise with them. He recommended that the Scottish Executive accept the Government's reasoning and that the Conference should be urged to reject all resolutions on devolution on the grounds that the Government's hands were full with their basic programme and the

economic crisis and that the matter should be left to the Executive's continuing negotiations with the Government. This was accepted by the Executive, the only dissentient being Sinclair Shaw, a long-standing supporter of Home Rule.

At the 1947 conference there was an open split on the issue. A motion expressing concern at the Government's delay in implementing the 1945 resolution for a committee of inquiry was opposed by the Executive. John Taylor, who during the war had argued for devolution,[67] deployed the now standard arguments of the leadership. Support for devolution in the past had merely been a reaction to Tory misgovernment, but under Labour was a low priority. In any case, it was impossible to be both a nationalist and a socialist. On this occasion, it failed to convince; the motion was carried by 111 votes to 82.

In January 1948, the Government unveiled its own proposals for change, drawn up by the new Secretary of State, Arthur Woodburn, in response to Labour and Covenant pressure, and pushed through a reluctant Cabinet. The White Paper rejected the idea of a commission of inquiry on the grounds that its scope would include matters affecting England and Wales; that an inquiry into Parliamentary devolution, administrative devolution and financial relationships could properly be conducted only by MPs; that it would need the services of financial experts, who could not be spared; and that it would take at least two years to complete. Instead, various Parliamentary reforms and a representative Scottish Economic Conference were proposed. By a majority vote, the Executive accepted the White Paper and agreed to recommend it to Conference.

At the 1948 conference, a resolution was moved by Galloway Divisional Labour Party, again urging a royal commission. It recalled the 1945 Scottish Labour election pledge and the fact that the 1948 national conference had not rescinded the party's federal devolution policy.[68] Before the conference, the mover of this resolution, James Urquhart of Galloway, had attacked Labour leaders for abandoning their previous devolution policy. At the conference itself, however, a semblance of unity was preserved. The Executive report, endorsing the Government's White Paper, was accepted, in return for an undertaking by John Taylor 'to approach the National Executive to ensure that Scottish affairs, in keeping with previous Conference decisions, demanding a royal commission of enquiry into devolution, are given adequate representation in the party's programme for the next General Election'.[69]

The Executive was clearly winning its battle now. Its victory was completed at the 1949 conference. A policy document, *Forward Scotland*, presented to Conference, dealt with Scottish government in a mere fifteen lines, praising the Woodburn reforms. It was challenged by Midlothian and Peebles and Galloway Divisional Labour Parties, which reminded Conference of the 1948 agreement and regretted that the national policy document *Labour Believes in Britain* contained no reference to an inquiry on devolution. However, a composite resolution, moved by Dumfries Divisional Labour Party, urging the NEC to establish an inquiry, was defeated overwhelmingly. The leadership had at last brought its followers into line – helped, it seems, by the precariousness of the Government's position and the need for unity in the approaching election, and by the attacks of the nationalists, particularly after Paisley. As for the Scottish Labour MPs, any enthusiasm they might have had for devolution had cooled and they appeared generally well satisfied with the new Parliamentary arrangements, which enhanced their positions as the sole political representatives of Scotland.

Labour thus went into the 1950 General Election for the first time without a commitment to Scottish devolution. The result of the election left the parties evenly balanced in terms of English seats but with Labour retaining the advantage in Scotland. Just as Scotland had swung less strongly to Labour in 1945, so in 1950 it swung less strongly to the Conservatives. This, however, had little bearing on the party's attitude to devolution. The party's precarious position in government and the likelihood of another election at an early date, though, did put a premium on unity and meant that the party could not afford to dismiss the apparent mass support of the Covenant, which, by 1950, had reached the peak of its influence. Arthur Woodburn was dismissed as Secretary of State and replaced by Hector McNeill, who in 1950, following further pressure from Scottish MPs, appointed the fact-finding Committee on Scottish Financial and Trade Statistics under Lord Catto. Its terms of reference were to report on the statistics and not to make constitutional recommendations, but even this was a considerable advance on the Government's previous position. In 1951 the Scottish conference met on the eve of the election, and once again unity was the keynote. A mammoth, 600-word composite resolution contained something for all points of view. The nationalists were attacked, the Government was congratulated at length for its efforts on behalf of Scotland, and the establishment of the Catto Committee was praised, and, finally, a royal commission to examine the question of a Scottish Parliament was requested. Sinclair Shaw supported the resolution, pointing out that it did not commit the party to a Scottish Parliament, and, from the anti-devolution side, John Taylor, now prospective candidate for West Lothian, claimed that it indicated the extent of common ground within the party on the devolution question.

By 1952, with the Conservatives in power, Labour no longer felt so constrained and the demand for an inquiry into devolution could be more strongly urged. However, the steam had gone out of the issue and Labour's return to opposition failed to rekindle interest in the subject. The fight had generally gone out of the Home Rulers. Even the Scottish Reconstruction Committee had lost its earlier drive, and the *New Scot* devoted less and less time to political and economic matters and more and more to short stories of the 'kailyard' variety. In 1949 the Golden Eagle Press, which Burns and Mrs Fraser had established to publish the journal, went bankrupt and the committee ceased to exist. In 1952, following the report of the Catto Committee, the Conservatives announced the appointment of a Royal Commission on Scottish Affairs, and the Scottish Executive was able to tell the 1953 conference, which had before it a resolution demanding a Labour inquiry, that it was delaying consideration of the matter pending the report of the Royal Commission.

The Communist Party reacted to the revival of nationalism with more enthusiasm. In 1943 its Scottish congress restated its demand for a 'Parliament for Scotland', which was to 'have the administration of all Scottish affairs and deal with Scottish aspects of social and industrial legislation'. In October 1945, shortly after the General Election, the Scottish Committee of the party issued a pamphlet entitled *Whither Scotland?*, which placed the demand for a Scottish Parliament in the context of economic policies required for the whole of Britain. A Scottish Planning Commission would draw up a plan for Scotland, but this would 'dovetail in with the bigger national plan' to be prepared by a National Planning Commission. Coming down to more immediate measures, *Whither Scotland?* called for Scottish MPs to meet separately in the Scottish Grand Committee, with co-opted members from the local authorities, to discuss the Scottish estimates; for an extension of the administrative

machinery of St Andrew's House to direct post-war reconstruction
from new Scottish departments; and for an all-Scottish convention
to which all comers would be invited, to 'discuss and draw up a
common programme of action for the future development of
Scotland'. Significantly, at national level the Communist Party was
less enthusiastic in advocating a Scottish Parliament. At the 1945
congress a motion giving wholehearted support to the plans for a
Scottish Parliament as outlined in *Whither Scotland?* was not carried,
and the resolution on Scotland stressed the need for planning for
Scotland, for the direction of industry to the region, and for new
Scottish departments, but omitted to call for a Scottish Parliament.
Vague reference to a 'Scottish Parliament for Scottish Affairs' was
made in the resolution on Wales, but the powers of such a body were
not specified.

In 1948 the Communist Party line was spelt out in more detail in
John Gollan's *Scottish Prospect*,[70] an immensely detailed account of
Scotland's economic and industrial development and future prospects. Striking a distinctly technocratic tone, this steered clear of
the wilder enthusiasms of nationalism and maintained that, while a
Scottish Parliament was vital to Scottish industrial development, it
would not in itself guarantee development. Working-class forces
must first establish their strength so that the 'change in the political
balance of power . . . will make way for self-government. In this
sense, the issue of self-government is subordinate to, and is decided
by, the wider issues of the political struggle.'

So the fundamental dilemma between supporting centralising
measures and going for Home Rule was neatly glossed over. The
definite commitment to self-government allowed the Communist
Party to support the Convention movement, and the party's only
MP, Willie Gallacher, played a prominent part in its proceedings.
By the 1950s, however, as the Home Rule issues declined in
importance, the Communist Party began to stress the centralist
aspects of its policy. So, in evidence to the Royal Commission on
Scottish Affairs in 1953, while supporting the creation of a Scottish
Parliament, it insisted on such safeguards for UK-wide interests as
to circumscribe severely the powers of such a body;

The provision should be written into the Constitution of any
future Parliament in Scotland, that industrial standards
legislated by a Scottish Parliament and levels of social
security and unemployment insurance, food subsidies, etc.

should not be less than those prevailing in the UK as a whole.[71]

The trade union movement was little affected by the Home Rule agitation of the post-war years, preferring to concentrate on practical measures of economic development and, where appropriate, administrative devolution. Its strategy bore fruit. During the war years the STUC grew greatly in status and influence, a trend reinforced after the election of the Labour Government in 1945. For its leadership, the main tasks were seen as being to reduce Communist influence, to support the Government and protect it from its enemies, and to ensure that Scottish interests were catered for in the Government's programme. What Home Rule agitation there was came from three sources: the traditional Home Rulers; the Communists; and a few trade unionist supporters of the Convention. The General Council, like the Labour Party leadership, tried to restrain the nationalist elements within the movement while itself pressing for more administrative devolution, particularly in economic and industrial affairs. Its attitude to nationalism was one of increasing hostility. At the same time, the Home Rule issue became entangled in the wider division between Communists and non-Communists which nearly split Congress in the late 1940s and early 1950s and led to the disaffiliation of Glasgow Trades Council in 1950 and the exclusion for some years of the leaders of the Communist-led Scottish miners from the General Council.

In 1947 Congress was able to agree unanimously on a resolution from two traditional Home Rule unions, the Scottish Horse and Motormen's Association and the Railway Clerks' Association. This praised the Labour Government but expressed the view that 'a wider measure of autonomy' over Scottish affairs would be desirable and called on the Government 'to enquire into the advisability of the setting up of a Scottish body with special powers in order that problems peculiar to Scotland, which arise from time to time, can be expedited'.

While unanimous agreement on such a general formulation was not difficult to achieve, it was not so easy to agree on the correct response to the immediate questions raised by the Convention movement and its success in mobilising widespread support in Scotland, among all sections of the population, including Scottish trades unionists. In 1948 Congress was presented with the White Paper on Scottish Affairs and a motion from the National Union of

Railwaymen deploring the spread of nationalism in the trade union movement. The motion declared that nationalism was leading the movement to back uneconomic projects and that only 'economically sound' projects should be supported. This was clearly an attack on some specific set of projects dear to another section of the movement, probably the proposals for road bridges over the main estuaries, and as such could only be divisive. It was referred to the new General Council, which simply let the matter drop. The response to the White Paper took the form of a composite resolution criticising the proposals as falling 'far short of the needs and expectations of the Scottish people'. The Economic Conference and new Parliamentary arrangements were criticised in terms which could be interpreted by those so inclined as pointing to the need for a Scottish Parliament, while, in practical terms, the resolution limited itself to three proposals. These were for the establishment of a National Planning Commission, the creation of Scottish Departments of Trade and Labour and the formation of a Scottish 'Cabinet' of representatives of Scottish and UK departments. The resolution was carried by a large majority. Earlier, Arthur Woodburn, the Secretary of State, had addressed Congress and poured cold water on the idea of devolution, asking pointedly if Scottish trades unionists wanted separate wage negotiations which would give them lower wages than their English fellow workers.

In 1949 there was a brief skirmish on the issue when Abe Moffat, Communist president of the Scottish miners, moved the reference back of the section of the Executive report containing Woodburn's reply to the previous year's resolution. Apart from Glasgow Trades Council, however, he got little support, and the general secretary pointed out that, while they must give consideration to Scottish affairs, this was not the same as associating themselves with Scottish nationalism.

It was in the following year, 1950, that the issue came to a head. A General Council resolution, without naming names, vigorously attacked the Convention and Covenant and their claim to speak for Scotland. It declared that the STUC, together with the Labour Party, spoke for the great majority of the Scottish people. Two amendments were moved by Covenant supporters. The first, from Glasgow Trades Council, seconded by John Boyd, of Clydebank Trades Council, recognised the primacy of economic affairs and the economic unity of the UK but called for 'a greater measure of self-government'. The second, from the Scottish miners, called for a

Scottish Parliament. The General Council's view was now unequivocal. Administrative devolution could be encouraged but there should be no legislative devolution and no Scottish Parliament. This time Congress too was ready to take a clear decision. After the Glasgow amendment had gone down by a large majority, the General Council resolution prevailed over the miners' amendment by 243 to 78. This represented a signal defeat for those who had tried to push the STUC back on to its old Home Rule track. In 1951 another attempt was made, when a National Association of Scottish Trades Unionists was formed, under the leadership of the Convenant supporter Michael Byrne, secretary of the Scottish TGWU and leader of the Clyde dockers, but it failed to get off the ground. Covenant support in the unions was always confined to a small minority and for most union leaders the movement was at best an irrelevance and at worst a divisive influence which could prejudice the implementation of Labour's programme and the effective organisation of workers.

Nevertheless, an undertow of support for Home Rule did exist, occasionally surfacing when the issue was raised. What was lacking was a clear idea of how the ambiguities of the concept could be resolved and another major issue to which it could be tied. As long as the main issues concerning trade unionists continued to be wages and industrial development, and as long as union interest in these issues dictated support for a united UK economy, Home Rule could never become the leading issue which it had been around the time of the First World War. On the other hand, whenever the question was raised, there was a number of Scottish trades unionists who would declare themselves in principle in favour of Scottish self-government, subject to various conditions about economic and industrial unity. Any raising of the Home Rule issue thus was likely to cause a divison among trades unionists, but with neither side recognising it as an issue of central importance for the union movement.

The STUC's evidence to the Royal Commission on Scottish Affairs in 1951 called for administrative but not legislative devolution, an attitude reaffirmed in 1954 and in 1955, after the Commission had reported. In the latter year, an amendment from Greenock Trades Council calling for a Scottish Parliament was defeated by 209 votes to 118, evidence of a surprising degree of residual support for Home Rule. In 1957, a composite calling for administrative devolution was passed, after the general secretary had drawn attention to the crucial word 'administrative' qualifying 'devolution'.

Meanwhile, the Scottish Council of the Labour Party, which had avoided the issue pending the report of the Royal Commission, was able, in 1955, to unite in condemnation of the Commission's report, on the grounds that its terms of reference had excluded the consideration of a wide measure of devolution. On the positive side, however, Labour was less united, as was shown the following year, when the issue again came up at Conference. Despite an address by Hugh Gaitskell, the party leader, who said that Labour had changed its view on Home Rule because of the growth of economic planning and national wage settlements, a resolution was passed instructing the Executive to study the economic and constitutional issues involved in the proposal for a Scottish Parliament. The report, presented to the 1957 conference by John Pollock, dismissed the idea of a Scottish Parliament 'on compelling economic grounds'. Only one Executive member dissociated himself from the report, but it came under fire at the conference, as much for the offhand manner in which the question had been treated by the Executive as for the substance of the recommendation. Among those attacking it were Alex Moffat of the Miners and two Parliamentary candidates, Judith Hart and John Mackintosh. By 108 votes to 71, the report was referred back,[72] and the Executive undertook to prepare a new report for the next conference. It was soon quite clear that this would be little different in content from the previous one. When, in November 1957, Tom Oswald MP called for a return to the old Home Rule policy, a Scottish Council spokesman was quoted as saying, dismissively, 'Although we as a party do not believe in a Scottish Parliament, we should not stop an MP from saying so. The question is to be raised at our next Conference. But it is a hardy annual and it will no doubt be treated as such.'[73]

Certainly there was no evidence of a widespread demand for Home Rule, but interest in the issue was now briefly revived. The 1958 conference had before it nine resolutions on devolution, eight from constituency parties and one from the Muir Society. As the Executive's report was not yet ready, consideration of devolution was postponed to a special conference later in the year. This was presented with two documents, a general policy statement, *Let Scotland Prosper*, and an Executive special report on devolution. Motions to remit back those sections of the latter which rejected a Scottish Parliament were all defeated overwhelmingly on a show of hands. Thus the leadership triumphed and the Labour Party in Scotland for the first time definitely repudiated the policy of a Scottish Parliament.

It had, of course, been a long time since the party leadership had taken its commitment to Home Rule seriously, and the most striking aspect of the agitation within the labour movement from 1937 to 1958 is its weakness, even at its peak in the late 1940s. Several significant areas of the movement proved quite indifferent to the cause. As we have seen, the trade union leadership was largely unimpressed. Even an old radical such as Joseph Duncan, the founder of the Scottish Farm Workers' Union, could declare in 1948 that he did not favour a Scottish Parliament.[74] The left-wingers in the Labour Party and the ILP now tended to look on Scottish nationalism with contempt. Support came from constituency activists in the right and centre of the party, with the support of a sprinkling of trade unionists, left-wingers and ILP-ers. A separate strand of support for Home Rule came from the Communits, but, as in other matters, their support often tainted the issue in the eyes of Labour Party members. Of course, loyalty to the Labour Government was a restraining influence within the Labour Party and the STUC in the late 1940s, when Convention activity was at its height. With a majority Labour administration in office for the first time and a full programme of reform, there was little inclination to divert attention away from the main tasks, and, the more Home Rulers attacked 'London government' or 'centralisation', the more they alienated Labour's supporters.

Yet, even after the return of the Conservatives in 1951, there was little inclination to pick up the Home Rule question again. On tactical grounds alone, this might have been expected, as in every election since 1950 Labour has secured a larger proportion of Scottish than of English seats. After 1959, Labour also secured a larger proportion of the Scottish than of the English vote, yet it was around that time that Labour finally repudiated Scottish Home Rule. Part of the explanation of this is to be found in the late 1920s and 1930s when, as we have seen, Labour committed itself to a strategy of UK-wide advance. Part of it is to be found in the experience of Tom Johnston's wartime Secretaryship of State and the 1945–51 Government, which showed how access to Whitehall and the centre of economic decision-making could be used to Scotland's advantage. The Labour Party nationally had proved itself able to accommodate Scottish demands and there were no specifically Scottish issues of sufficient salience to fuel a Home Rule campaign.

Indeed, the Home Rule concept continued to suffer from ambiguity and lack of definition, a crucial weakness in the Convention and Covenant campaigns. To express a vague preference for Scottish control of Scottish affairs was one thing. To divide specific functions on this basis was another matter, particularly where economic issues were involved. Once Labour Home Rulers had admitted this problem and agreed that economic matters should continue to be dealt with centrally, Home Rule began to lose its relevance to Labour and trade union interests. Thus arose a difficulty which to this day the Labour Party has failed to resolve.

The 1950s also saw a new downturn in Scotland's economic fortunes, which coincided with a decline in nationalist agitation within and outside the labour movement. The heavy industries, after their gradual recovery in the late 1930s and a boom in the 1940s, which was sustained until the end of the Korean War, began to decline again, and from 1954 Scotland's economic performance began to diverge from that of the UK as a whole. It is estimated that, between 1951 and 1960, Scottish gross domestic product per head fell from 92 per cent of the UK average to 88 per cent.[75] Such a fall may appear marginal and unlikely to influence political behaviour, but the pattern of Scottish economic activity was again beginning to cause concern to politicians. While the composition of manufacturing industry in Scotland closely followed the overall UK pattern, within each industrial group Scotland could be seen to be saddled with low-growth industries.[76] Thus, within the 'vehicles' group there was, in the 1950s, no motor-car manufacture but a very large share of the declining locomotive industry. Net new investment in Scottish industry was low, and suffered particularly severely during periods of recession. Few new firms were coming to Scotland, which thus had to rely on the slow rate of growth of indigenous firms. Consequently, between 1954 and 1960, Scottish manufacturing output increased by only 9 per cent, as compared with 23 per cent for the UK as a whole.[77] Labour and trade union leaders, concerned about these trends, began to demand that the Government take more action to control development in the prosperous areas of England and adopt a vigorous regional policy to save the Scottish economy. From 1960 the Conservatives began to respond, with the first tentative moves back to regional policy, pointing the way to the regional politics of the new decade.

Labour thus entered the contemporary period with its unionist attitudes strengthened and with an official policy of opposition to devolution. Within its ranks were a number of people with an emotional attachment to the idea of Scottish self-government but with little clear idea of what this would mean in practice. Electorally, the party was expanding its base in Scotland, driving the Conservatives from the cities, and there was no effective nationalist party to provide an alternative view of the Scottish interest. Indeed, after the collapse of the Convention, there was no effective voice of Scottish nationalism at all. This allowed Labour to command the centre of the Scottish political stage as never before and to turn the Scottish question to its own advantage in the 1960s.

5 Labour under Assault

I. THE LABOUR ASCENDANCY, 1959–66

The 1950s saw a steady electoral advance for Labour in Scotland. Its share of the vote held up much better there than in England, and, though in 1955 the Conservatives secured a bare overall majority of Scottish votes and seats, there was a swing back to Labour in 1959, giving it a majority of Scottish seats, which it has retained ever since. Particularly marked was the Conservative collapse in Glasgow and the west of Scotland, which thus became a Labour stronghold. The Tories were driven back to their rural fastnesses, which in turn accentuated their upper-class, anglicised image, as these constituencies were inclined to select aristocratic or military public-school products as candidates.[1] This, and the fact that an increasingly Labour Scotland was being ruled by a Conservative England, provided a great temptation for Labour to play the 'Scottish' card for electoral gain. This it did, but not by a simple return to the old Home Rule policy. That was ruled out by a number of factors.

The most important of these was, as we have mentioned, the economic factor. Labour believed that it was the electoral beneficiary of Scotland's economic troubles (though in reality its increased support may have owed more to other factors, such as the decline of religious voting), but it continued to see the solution to these problems as lying at Westminster, where a Labour government, taking the necessary central measures, would in due course gain its electoral reward in Scotland.

Another important factor was a deep hostility to Scottish nationalism. On the left there was still a strong ideological aversion to nationalism, which was seen as a force dividing the workers and diverting attention from the real enemy. In many sections of the movement, the attacks of the Convention movement and the fight at Paisley had left a bitter aftertaste. More important, however, was a strong reluctance to raise the issues which talk of a Scottish

assembly would bring. Of course, the most vital of these was the
threat to the centralised economy if economic powers were to be
devolved; but even an assembly without economic powers would
raise the 'national' question, which Labour wished to suppress; give
credibility to Scottish nationalism – a rival expression of Scottish
aspirations and a potential electoral threat; and, by projecting a
high Scottish 'profile', could raise questions in other parts of the
United Kingdom about Scotland's favoured status.

Labour's attitude to the Scottish question was based upon the
assumptions that the basis of any discontent was economic and that
the electorate were more concerned about the economic goods
which they received than with the constitutional mechanism by
which these were delivered. Labour therefore sought to exploit
Scottish grievances and advance the aims of its Scottish supporters
without raising the constitutional question. This it did by pushing
for greater administrative devolution and special treatment for
Scotland in economic matters, a policy in line with Labour's overall
appeal to the depressed regions of the UK, an appeal based on a
'regionalism', exemplified by economic planning councils and
regional industrial aid, which promised help and greater political
influence to the regions while maintaining an essentially centralised
economic and political system. During the 1950s, the STUC too
pressed for administrative devolution and, in particular, for the
creation of Scottish Departments of Trade and Labour, an idea
adapted from Northern Ireland, though Congress did not favour
devolution on the Stormont model. From 1962, after the Conservatives had been converted to 'indicative planning', the Scottish
Office began to acquire enhanced economic development functions,[2] a trend welcomed by Labour and continued by it after 1964,
pushing 'regionalism' further than in any other part of Britain. As
the Scottish Office put it in a memorandum to the Select Committee
on Scottish Affairs:

The Secretary of State for Scotland's increasing involvement
in problems of economic development flowing from the
increasing expectation that he should interest himself in any
matter affecting Scotland, whether or not it comes within the
scope of this statutory functions, led in 1964 to his being
assigned more explicit responsibilities in the comprehensive
machinery for economic planning which was introduced on
the advent of a new administration.[3]

The Scottish Office, as well as being responsible for administering a large part of Government business in Scotland and, increasingly, making policy for Scotland, has long had a role in lobbying for Scotland and has secured a disproportionately large share of public expenditure in most fields.[4] This was the line which Labour now chose to pursue in its Scottish campaigns, basing its electoral appeals on its ability to gain material benefits for Scotland. This would be achieved partly through the beneficial effects which Labour's overall UK strategy would bring, but partly through the ability of Labour's Scottish representatives to gain special concessions. So, in opposition from 1959 to 1964, Labour's spokesmen, and particularly Willie Ross, made great play of the Conservatives' alleged neglect of Scottish problems. They were thus able to 'sublimate' the Scottish issue and to turn Scottish grievances to their advantage, without making any concession on the constitutional question. The same strategy was carried over into government from 1964, to gain further concessions for Scotland. As long as over forty Scottish seats were delivered at Westminster, this support was maintained and Ross and his team allowed a wide degree of latitude over matters of Scottish policy. In the long run, as we shall see, it was a risky strategy, but in the early 1960s, with no effective challenge from a nationalist party offering a different interpretation of the Scottish interest and with the Conservatives in retreat, Labour was able to play the Scottish card to its own electoral advantage.

The role of Labour's Scottish MPs was consistent with this strategy. Most of them were more concerned with parochial and Scottish issues than with wider UK and international affairs.[5] They tended to concentrate (a) on those matters administered on a Scottish basis by the Scottish Office – there they pushed for more administrative devolution, and separate Scottish legislation; (b) on economic matters administered at the UK level – here they concentrated on securing benefits for Scotland from the centralised economic machinery. They also pushed for administrative devolution of economic matters where this would not prejudice central economic planning. Thus they secured the best of both worlds. They enjoyed limited devolution within the administration and in Parliament, which allowed them, while not being cut off from the source of economic largesse, to articulate distinctive Scottish demands. Most of them opposed the creation of a Scottish assembly, because it would upset their balance. Demands for an assembly would appear to be a criticism of their own role and would raise questions not only about the economic position of Scotland in relation to the United Kingdom but also about the role of Scottish MPs as representatives of Scottish interests. It is therefore not surprising that those MPs who were most deeply involved in Scottish affairs tended to be the most opposed to an assembly.[6] Of course, the more administrative and intra-Parliamentary devolution the Scottish MPs secured, the more they were drawn into a separate Scottish political structure and, as Richard Crossman observed, the more weight was given to the case for devolution.[7]

Labour thus had little incentive to interest itself in the question of a Scottish assembly. On the contrary, it had every incentive to try and suppress nationalist sentiment. Particularly after 1964, as the Scottish political 'establishment', it was itself liable to be the recipient of any nationalist pressure which might develop. Its position was exposed as the weakness of Scottish Conservatism made it possible that discontent with government could be exploited not by a unionist party, as had happened in 1959–64, but by another party, which could play the Scottish issue in a very different way. This is precisely what was to happen.

Labour was also strongly established in Scottish local government, and its representatives there were almost uniformly hostile to the idea of a Scottish assembly, which would rival local government and probably tend to intervene a great deal more than the Scottish Office. In Glasgow, in particular, there was resentment at the thought of being run from Edinburgh, while in Edinburgh and other parts of Scotland there was a fear of domination by Glasgow and the west. Scottish local government in the 1950s and 1960s, outside the big cities, was still highly fragmented, and, while in some parts of the movement there was a certain sentimental attachment to the highly localist Scottish tradition exemplified by the small burghs, Labour was moving towards acceptance of the need for reform. The Royal Commission on Local Government in Scotland, under Lord Wheatley, provided the blueprint. Its 1969 report recommended a radical reform: the creation of seven 'regions' having the authority and resources to establish their independence. These would include a giant western region based on Glasgow and covering half the population of Scotland, which, barring exceptional circumstances, Labour could confidently expect to control. The Wheatley proposals were endorsed by the Labour Party in Scotland, which saw them as an opportunity for strengthening its power base. A Scottish assembly, however, would inevitably pose a threat to the Wheatley plans, as it was difficult to imagine as assembly covering the whole of Scotland co-existing happily with a local authority which itself covered half the population. The local-government lobby was thus firmly in the anti-devolution camp in the 1960s.

Labour's narrow electoral victory of 1964 could not have been achieved without its disproportionately large share of Scottish seats, a fact of which the Labour leadership was acutely aware. It was therefore vital for the party to be seen to be delivering on its promises. Under the energetic leadership of Willie Ross, it set about doing so, and by the mid 1960s Labour's Scottish strategy seemed to be crowned with success. A Highlands and Islands Development Board had been established, Fairfields Shipyard on the Clyde had been rescued, and the *Plan for Expansion* for the Scottish economy, published in January 1966 to complement the National Plan, promised lavish public investment and development-area status for the whole of Scotland, excepting Edinburgh and Leith.

II. LABOUR UNDER ATTACK, 1967–74

Labour's Scottish fortunes reached their peak in 1966, when the party, in what was seen as a triumphant vindication of the politics of Willie Ross and his school, won forty-six of the seventy-one Scottish seats. Of course, the electoral system grossly exaggerated Labour's advantage. It had gained 65 per cent of the Scottish seats for slightly under half the Scottish vote. Even in terms of votes, however, it marked Labour's Scottish high-water mark and a divergence from the pattern in England, where Labour has never bettered its 1951 vote. Few noticed the Scottish National Party's respectable 5 per cent of the poll (representing an average of 14·5 per cent in seats contested) or were aware of the decline of partisanship beginning to set in amongst the electorate. Nor was much attention given to the shaky state of Labour organisation in Scotland, particularly in Glasgow, where success was taken so much for granted that the party machine had been allowed to atrophy. However, the shock to Labour's complacency was not long in coming. The victory of March 1966 was followed by the drastic deflation of July, which effectively killed the National Plan stone dead. As unemployment mounted, the reverberations were soon felt in Scotland. At a by-election in the Labour constituency of Glasgow Pollok in March

1967, the SNP polled 28 per cent and, by splitting the Labour vote, handed the seat to the Conservatives. At the municipal elections in May, the SNP polled 16 per cent of the total vote and won twenty-three seats.[8] But the worst was yet to come. In November 1967 Mrs Winifred Ewing captured the safest Labour seat in Scotland, at Hamilton, with 46 per cent of the vote. By the following May, Labour was facing a rout in the local elections, when the SNP outpolled all the other parties with 34 per cent of the vote. Labour was even dislodged in Glasgow, where the Progressives and Conservatives formed a minority administration dependent on SNP support.

Scottish politics were never the same after Hamilton, and the shock to Labour's confidence cannot be overestimated. Immediately, demands were made for a fresh examination of the devolution question. A flurry of resolutions on the subject appeared on the agenda at the Scottish conference in 1967 and 1968, but Labour was not ready to change its tack. The 1968 resolutions were met by Willie Ross with a vehement attack on nationalism and delegates got the clear impression that the Government intended no concession at all. In 1968, after a meeting with ministers, at which very cautious schemes for expanding the work of the Scottish committee of Parliament were discussed, the Scottish Executive appointed a sub-committee on Scottish government. This met over a period of two years, producing an interim report in 1969 and a final report in 1970. The final report, presented to the full Executive in March 1970, firmly rejected a Scottish assembly and was accepted by the Executive with only two dissenting votes (W. Fräser and T. Fulton). This document, after consultation with the National Executive and ratification by the Scottish conference, formed the basis of the Scottish Council's evidence to the Commission on the Constitution.

The Commission had been appointed in 1969 following wrangles within the Government over what to do about the nationalist threat to Labour's position. Richard Crossman, as Lord President of the Council, was a believer in devolution, which he was further convinced was essential if Labour was not to suffer severe losses at the next election.[9] He was also convinced that Scottish nationalism needed to be taken seriously, that it was not simply a manifestation of discontent at the economic situation. Ross, however, was as adamant as ever in his opposition to devolution and stuck to the traditional Labour line that all would be well given the right economic policies.[10] Nor was the rest of the Cabinet any more amenable. In 1968 Ross was able to sway Harold Wilson to his own interpretation, following the Prime Minister's visit to the Scottish conference, at which the devolutionists were routed. At this time, too, with the replacement of Cledwyn Hughes by George Thomas, the Welsh Office moved into the anti-devolution camp. Crossman was able to get an interdepartmental devolution committee established and pursued the subject with considerable enthusiasm, even retaining the chairmanship of the committee when he moved to the Department of Health and Social Security, but he failed to get his own radical proposals through it. Instead there emerged a scheme for limited administrative changes and reforms in Parliamentary procedure, which Crossman by now regarded as too little and too late. In May 1968 he sent the report to the Prime Minister, adding his own rider that he favoured setting up a Royal Commission on Devolution, in order to out-manoeuvre the Conservative leader, Edward Heath, who had set up his own committee under Sir Alec Douglas Home. However, Wilson accepted the committee's limited recommendations and the main outcome of the exercise was that a Select Committee on Scottish Affairs was established in the session 1968–9.

The argument for a royal commission went on, with Ross and Thomas coming round to the view that it would be a useful means of delaying action, while Crossman now moved against the idea. At last, in October 1968, after some opposition from Peter Shore at the Department of Economic Affairs and Anthony Greenwood at the Ministry of Housing and Local Government, who were worried about the effects on their departments, the Cabinet agreed to appoint a Royal Commission on the Constitution. The evidence presented to the Commission by the Labour Party's Scottish Council was a restatement of the unionist case. As expounded in 1970 by their witnesses before the Commission, the arguments against an assembly were based on the divisive effect on the UK Parliament, the threat to the new local authorities proposed by Wheatley, the dangers of economic separation, and satisfaction with the performance of the current system, under Labour, in promoting economic development, while allowing such pioneering Scottish measures as the Social Work (Scotland) Act of 1968. 'Any form of assembly with substantial legislative devolution' would, it was feared, be a 'slippery slope towards total separation, or at least a form of separation which would set up divisions within the United

Kingdom'.[11] Greater responsiveness and democratic scrutiny in Scottish administration could be achieved through an expansion of the work of the Scottish committees of Parliament. The council concluded that the only way to solve the Scottish problem was to have a Labour government at Westminster, but it declared that even a UK Conservative government would be preferable to any sort of devolved assembly.[12] After 1968, the nationalist challenge subsided and so did Labour's interest in devolution. Most people in the party were thankful to have weathered the storm without making any concession on the constitutional issue. However, things were never to be the same. The constitutional debate, once started, continued, and Labour became even more conscious of the need for a distinctively Scottish electoral strategy.

The STUC, too, following the Nationalist successes, returned to the subject of devolution, which was tackled in a major set-piece debate in 1968.[13] The devolutionist view was put by the Communist Mick McGahey, of the Scottish miners, who reminded Congress that Scotland was a nation, not merely a region, and had a right to determine its own future. He himself favoured a federal system. This was in accordance with the Communist Party line since the policy shift of 1964, when the party had come out in support of the right of self-determination. He was opposed by R. Garland of the Amalgamated Union of Engineering and Foundry Workers, who attacked nationalism and declared that an economically viable and secure Scotland could be achieved only within the economic framework of Great Britain, with the pay and conditions of Scottish workers kept in parity with those of England and Wales through national joint negotiating machinery. After support for both sides had been expressed by various speakers, both the miners' resolution and the engineers' resolution were referred to the General Council, which was thus left with a free hand. It produced an interim report for the 1969 congress, backing a legislative assembly. Perhaps surprisingly, in view of the passions which this issue was arousing elsewhere, this document was unanimously accepted and formed the basis of the STUC's evidence to the Commission on the Constitution. By the time it came to give oral evidence to the Commission, however, the General Council had changed its membership and its opinion and no longer favoured a legislative assembly. Instead it supported the creation of an assembly without legislative powers. Later, after the Commission's report, it reverted to its support for a legislative assembly.

These changes and ambiguities in the STUC's attitude, puzzling at first sight, stemmed from a genuine dilemma – how to reconcile its support for the economic unity of the United Kingdom with its desire to democratise the structure of Scottish administration – and from the relatively pragmatic attitude it was prepared to take to the latter where its economic interests were not at stake. While Congress's pronouncements on political and constitutional matters were often hasty and ill thought-out, its support for economic unity, the theme which ran through all the deliberations and the evidence to the Commission, was firmly rooted in the unions' economic self-interest and had been thoroughly researched. Even the fact that the argument could potentially cut both ways had not escaped the leadership. In a revealing passage of evidence before the Royal Commission, James Jack, the general secretary, asked by Lord Crowther whether 'our starting assumption is that the essential unity of the United Kingdom should not be disturbed', replied:

> For the time being, at any, rate because it is also explicit in our evidence that the basic argument which we advance is one which when it is met does imply there might well be a time when we were well off, generating our own new resources, standing on our own two legs and no longer appearing to be on public relief or 'on the parish'. This would be a different thing and we could, I might say personally, and perhaps indiscreetly, at that particular point be hoist with our own petard.[14]

However, for the time being at least, the STUC considered that the health of the Scottish economy required unity and an effective regional policy, steering development away from the prosperous regions of England and towards Scotland.

Within the assumptions of economic unity, the STUC was prepared to consider a variety of political arrangements for rendering Scottish administration more accountable, but it must be said that here its schemes were much less convincing. The proposal for a legislative assembly was dropped on the ground that it would pose a threat to the UK Parliament, and thereafter the General Council sought to grapple with the difficulties of reconciling the maintenance of the Scottish Office machinery and the Secretary of State's membership of the Cabinet, which it regarded as vital, with accountability of the bureaucracy and the Minister to an elected assembly. This sort of problem was one of the factors in the Labour Party's opposition to an assembly, but, as the STUC admitted, it did not have great expertise in drafting constitutional machinery and was only concerned with pointing out the general direction in which development should proceed. Political thinking amongst the STUC leadership was also influenced by the Communist Party. The STUC continued to permit the affiliation of trades councils, which were often, as in the case of Glasgow, Communist-dominated. The Communist Party, for its part, lacking an effective electoral platform, sought influence within the Scottish trade union movement and, in particular, took the trades councils and the STUC more seriously than did a great many Labour Party members. In addition, its position in many unions, particularly the miners', was stronger in Scotland than south of the border. On the other hand, Communist advocacy of a proposal was often enough to damn it in the eyes of some Labour loyalists, so that the devolution issue was often caught up in the wider divisions of the movement. Further, although the Communists advocated Home Rule for Scotland after 1964, they, like the rest of the movement, had great difficulty in reconciling this with the need for economic unity.

At the 1970 General Election the Nationalist challenge seemed to fade, as the SNP lost Hamilton and gained only the Western Isles. Following the election, the Scottish question was submerged, certainly as far as the Labour Party was concerned, in the heightened political and industrial conflict over issues such as the new Conservative Government's Housing Finance Acts and the Industrial Relations Act. The latter was a matter of general UK concern and raised no distinctively Scottish questions. On the contrary, the renewal of industrial class conflict reinforced the belief of many in the irrelevance of national distinctions, while the disputes over the Industrial Relations Act were typically large-scale, UK-wide actions. The Housing (Financial Provisions) (Scotland) Act did raise distinctive questions, as the whole tradition of Scottish housing had been different from that of housing in England and Wales, with a greater legacy of slums, a much larger public sector and a pattern of low rents. For England and Wales, the Conservatives proposed that local authorities should move towards market rents, but, because in Scotland this would have led to very large increases, the Scottish Act retained the historic cost basis of rents and merely proposed that local authorities should balance their housing accounts. Then, not later than the financial year

1974–5, the Secretary of State was to consider the possibility of moving on to a 'fair rents' system for Scotland.

This allowed the Labour Party to resume its poise as defender of Scottish interests. In the House of Commons, Willie Ross lambasted the Conservative Secretary of State, Gordon Campbell:

> One of the great responsibilities of a Secretary of State for Scotland is to convince his Cabinet colleagues that the Scottish housing position is very much worse than the English one and that the whole position is different.[15]
>
> The whole tradition of Scottish housing finance which it should have been the right Hon. Gentleman's responsibility to safeguard, has gone.[16]

However, Labour avoided taking too 'nationalist' a stance on this, partly for fear of giving credibility to the SNP, now a permanent threatening presence, and partly because many Labour MPs were privately relieved that the Conservatives had grasped the nettle of Scottish housing finance, which they were unable, politically, to touch, and were indeed horrified at the thought of the low levels of rents which a Labour Scottish assembly might set. In the event, the battles which took place in places such as Dunbarton after the passage of the Act lacked any specifically nationalist dimension and the SNP largely failed to exploit the issue. Had it done so, Scottish Labour could have been placed in a most embarrassing and difficult position.

The other piece of Scottish legislation in this Parliament was the Local Government (Scotland) Act, based on the Wheatley proposals. In spite of later claims by the SNP, this reform was not forced through by English votes and had the support of the great majority of Scottish MPs, including Labour MPs.[17] Indeed, Labour support for Wheatley is an indication of how far the party was at this time from thinking seriously about a Scottish assembly. Only a few isolated figures, such as John Mackintosh and Jim Sillars, complained that, if the Commission on the Constitution was a serious exercise, its report should be awaited before the Government implemented Wheatley's regional scheme.

However, despite the other preoccupations of politicians, and Labour's apparent success in opposition in resuming its traditional strategy, there were many signs that the national issue was far from dead. In 1971, concerned about mounting unemployment in

Scotland, the STUC announced plans for a 'Scottish Assembly' to be held the following year, with representatives from local authorities, political parties, employers' associations, religious bodies, trades unions, trades councils, students' unions, the CBI, the Scottish Council (Development and Industry), chambers of commerce and Scottish MPs, to discuss the state of the Scottish economy. At the assembly, held in February 1972, devolutionist feeling came through strongly. According to Hamish Grant, secretary of the Confederation of British Industry (Scotland): 'The intensity of the feeling for further devolution came through in a way which I have never heard before. It was obvious that there is a call for greater devolution and responsibility through the institutions of Scotland.'[18] John Boyd of the Amalgamated Union of Engineers and Foundry Workers, a former chairman of the Labour Party, caused some surprise when he said, 'I am slowly and painfully coming to the conclusion that the only answer to Scotland's economic problems is a Scottish Government.'[19] A second assembly was held the following year, but the Scottish Council of the Labour Party was unimpressed. It had raised the 'Scottish issue' in the very way the party wanted to avoid and, in the view of the Scottish Executive, merely gave publicity to the Nationalists.[20]

Two factors in particular were serving to keep alive the Scottish constitutional question in the early 1970s. These were the discovery of North Sea oil and entry into the European Economic Community. Oil discoveries brought James Jack's predictions of 1969 a stage nearer, and by the early 1970s were undermining Labour's traditional arguments about the economic necessity of the union and its own efficacy in securing the maximum economic benefit for Scotland. EEC entry posed the question whether Brussels would not, at some future date, come to rival London as a decision-making centre for economic matters. In that event, Scotland's interests might better be promoted by direct representation in the EEC than by continuing to send Labour MPs to Westminster. This argument was developed by Jim Sillars, MP for South Ayrshire, who in 1973 founded a Scottish Labour EEC 'watch-dog committee', a group of MPs who monitored developments in the Common Market as they affected Scotland to see that Scottish interests were not neglected. In July 1973 a *Scotsman* editorial commented that support for devolution was building up among influential bodies and individuals in Scotland as a result of EEC entry.[21]

These developments occurred at a time when Labour's confidence in its electoral hegemony was at a low ebb. That it could no longer afford to take for granted its former strongholds was demonstrated by the shock of the Dundee East by-election in March 1973, when the seat almost fell to the SNP. All were agreed that the party needed to take the Scottish question seriously. On the appropriate response to adopt, two schools of thought developed: one holding, either from conviction or for electoral reasons, that concessions would have to be made on the constitutional issue; the other holding that the problem was still primarily an economic one and that the right economic policies at the UK level, together with special measures for Scotland, would stem the tide. In July 1973 John Warden reported in the *Glasgow Herald* that the Labour Party was about to split on the Home Rule issue.[22] Since 1970, when the party had submitted its evidence to Kilbrandon, opinion had shifted substantially, Warden claimed. At that time John Mackintosh and Willie Baxter had been alone in calling for Home Rule. Now they were joined by Messrs Sillars, Lambie, Robertson and Ewing. Ronald King Murray was said to be another convert and even William Ross was reported to be less determined in his opposition. In fact, Ross, though still opposed to an assembly, now believed that, once the issue was seriously raised, it would be very difficult for the Labour Party, in its exposed position in the Scottish political structure, to resist it. In October 1973 Warden reported that ten Labour MPs were in favour of an assembly of some sort, ten were against and the rest were undecided, except for some anti-Marketeers, who tended towards Scottish sovereignty with direct representation in the EEC. The argument within the party was beginning to heat up.

In January 1973 the Scottish Executive had decided to review its position on Scottish government, because of the imminent publication of the report of the Royal Commission on the Constitution. A sub-committee was appointed to consult with interested parties and draft a report. By October, with the long-delayed Kilbrandon Report imminent and a by-election pending at Glasgow Govan, the report was ready. It flatly rejected the idea of an assembly. Pro-devolution members of the Executive tried first to get it amended, then to delay publication, but they were overruled and the document[23] appeared one day before the Kilbrandon Report and just a few days before the SNP victory at Govan. *Scotland and the UK* was a firm restatement of Labour's position as developed since the 1940s. It ruled out 'any new-fangled Assembly', on the grounds that

Scottish influence at Westminster would be reduced and that an assembly would be tied by financial restrictions, pose a threat to the new local authorities, threaten the economic unity of the UK and fail to bring any real benefits to the Scottish people. Instead, the new local authorities should gradually be given more powers and the work of the Select Committee on Scottish Affairs[24] and the Scottish Grand Committee should be expanded. Another document[25] issued at the same time proposed a Scottish National Enterprise Board to work in conjunction with the proposed UK National Enterprise Board. (In due course this proposal bore fruit in the shape of the Scottish Development Agency.) Together, it was hoped, these measures, described as 'a major increase in administrative and economic devolution', would stem devolutionist demands, help to revive the Scottish economy and demonstrate Labour's concern for Scotland's problems.

However, in the aftermath of Govan, where the SNP had again overturned a massive Labour majority – but this time while the party was in opposition – this was widely considered to be too little and too late, and the Kilbrandon Report gave ammunition to both sides in the argument, which now began in earnest. The Commission had failed to reach a unanimous conclusion, but the majority recommended a legislative assembly for Scotland, to take over the work of the Scottish Office. It would be financed from UK revenues, through an independent Exchequer Board. A minority of the Commission rejected the idea of legislative powers and favoured an assembly with more limited functions. Two members submitted a memorandum of dissent, arguing for a scheme of executive devolution throughout the United Kingdom, on the principle that no part of the UK should be given privileges which were not enjoyed by other parts. All agreed that the establishment of a Scottish assembly should entail the abolition of the office of Secretary of State, and the majority also recommended a reduction in the number of Scottish MPs. The devolutionist wing of the Labour Party seized on the proposal for a legislative assembly, while Ross and the anti-devolutionists pointed to the recommendation for the abolition of the Secretaryship of State and the reduction in the number of Scottish MPs. The secretary of the Scottish Council said that the party would particularly oppose the latter, and a recommendation that the assembly should be elected by proportional representation, while Ross christened Kilbrandon the 'kill-devolution' report.

Kilbrandon crystallised the debate on devolution. Now that a specific and authoritative proposal for a legislative assembly had been published, individuals' positions on devolution had to be measured by reference to it. It was no longer enough to claim that the proposals of *Scotland and the UK* represented an advance towards devolution. By falling far short of Kilbrandon's recommendations, they now had to be regarded as centralist. As a failed compromise, they thus fell by the wayside, and resolutions began to flow from constituency parties and other organisations calling for endorsement or rejection of Kilbrandon, with the tide clearly flowing in favour of acceptance.

III.   1974: THE MOVE TO DEVOLUTION

At the end of 1973 and the beginning of 1974, the devolution question was submerged by the Conservative Government's confrontation with the miners and the consequent General Election, but the result of the February Election, with the return of seven Scottish and two Welsh Nationalist MPs and a minority Labour Government dependent on their goodwill pushed it to the forefront again. Willie Ross, back in office as Secretary of State, took a noticeably less hard line on the subject, and it was reported in the *Glasgow Herald* of 7 March that, among Scottish Labour MPs, 'soundings indicated that far more than the 14 committed devolutionists would support an Assembly'. In the same month, in advance of the Labour Party Scottish Conference, four MPs, Sillars, Robertson, Ewing and Eadie, produced a pamphlet urging devolution to an assembly on the lines of the majority Kilbrandon recommendation, but with greater economic powers. On 10 March 1974 the Scottish Labour Executive met and approved the report of a sub-committee, which, in very carefully chosen words, said,

> There is a real need to ensure that decisions affecting
> Scotland are taken in Scotland, wherever possible. A measure
> of devolution could perhaps give to the people a feeling of
> involvement in the process of decision making. We believe
> this *might* best be done by the setting up of an elected Scottish
> Assembly. Any such Assembly would have to have defined
> and relevant powers which would contribute to the economic
> growth and good government of the country.

Newspaper headlines such as 'Ross backs call for Scottish Assembly',[26] however, were premature. The crucial word was 'might', and the Executive statement was aimed principally at keeping some sort of unity at the impending Scottish conference. Later that month, the conference adopted the Executive statement against three other motions, demanding, respectively, no change; a commitment to an assembly; and separation. The Executive was thus given, apparently, a free hand in interpreting its ambiguous statement, and the Government and the national party leadership, who were moving towards a devolutionist position, were saved embarrassment. However, this attempt to paper over the cracks could not survive long in view of the deepening division.

The SNP had won two Labour seats in February, while taking four from the Conservatives. There now developed an acute fear among the national leadership that, with Labour in government, it could become the main victim in the next election, which was inevitable within the year. Something therefore needed to be done to stem the tide, but what that should be depended on one's perception of the causes of the discontent. Of course, the traditional remedies of giving special consideration to Scotland could be and were adopted, and a further phase of 'pork-barrel' politics opened. Scotland was to have its development agency, Edinburgh and Leith received development-area status, and a whole range of lesser measures was brought in.[27] However, this, it was widely thought, would not be enough. Polls in Scotland showed strong support for devolution, and one well leaked poll conducted for the party in the summer by Bob Worcester of MORI claimed that, if it did not change its policy, Labour would lose up to thirteen seats.[28]

The national leadership acted quickly in response to these alarming signals. Lord Crowther-Hunt, who had written the memorandum of dissent to the Kilbrandon Report, was brought into the Government as constitutional adviser. Clearly, Harold Wilson was moving towards acceptance of devolution. A hint of this had been given as early as 1973, when, in a speech at Edinburgh, he had called for regional government in England and implied that this should be part of a general scheme of devolution. Now, in 1974, he clearly indicated his intentions. In the debate on the Queen's Speech he told Winifred Ewing, newly elected as SNP member for Moray and Nairn: 'Of course we shall publish a White Paper and a Bill.'[29] The pledge was repeated the following week by Robert Sheldon, Minister of State at the Civil Service Department.

In June 1974 the Government published a discussion paper. This listed five possible schemes of devolution, derived from Kilbrandon, and asked for comments by the end of the month. In Scotland, Ross himself was to take charge of the consultation exercise. The next step was for the Government to bring its Scottish supporters into line behind a policy of devolution. The party in Scotland was by now seriously split on the issue, with substantial pro- and anti-devolution factions and a large group waiting for a lead. It seems likely that, had a vote been taken at the March 1974 conference, it would have gone in favour of devolution but with a considerable strength of opposition. By June the tide was still flowing in favour, and the principal obstacle to the Government's plans was the Scottish Executive. On 23 June it met to consider its position. Eleven of the twenty-nine members attended, and, contrary to all predictions, voted by six to five to reject all the alternatives in the Government discussion paper. The decision caused a storm in Scotland and alarm at Transport House, and the Scottish Executive became the subject of intense pressure. The National Executive Committee, like Wilson and his advisers, was concerned primarily with the electoral position and was easily convinced that a more positive response was needed. It therefore agreed to instruct the general secretary to write to the Scottish Executive saying that its attitude could damage the party and asking it to recall the Scottish conference. This the Scottish Executive agreed to do. Further pressure was applied when, on 24 July, the NEC without a vote, towards the end of a meeting attended by fifteen of its twenty-eight members, called for the establishment of a legislative assembly in Scotland. The motion, which was moved by Alex Kitson, Scottish leader of the TGWU, read:

That the NEC recognise the desire of the Scottish people for the establishment of an elected legislative Assembly within the context of the political and economic unity of the United Kingdom. The NEC calls on the Labour Government to declare its support in principle for such an Assembly with a view to introducing legislation on the matter.

Ron Hayward, general secretary of the Labour Party, explained that it would be 'rather silly for the NEC to have a regional conference precisely on this, at our request, and not express a point of view'. In fact, as the policy-making body of the party between national conferences, the NEC's view prevailed, whatever the special conference should say. Ross and Allan Maclean, the chairman of the Scottish Council, protested that this made the party look ridiculous, but they were placed in an ironical position, as anti-devolutionists, in demanding more autonomy for the Scottish organs of the party and protesting at the NEC intervention in Scottish affairs.

In August 1974 the recalled Scottish conference met at the Co-operative Halls in Dalintober Street, Glasgow. By now the big unions had been lined up to support the Government's view, so that, had the issue come to a card vote, the outcome would not have been in doubt. This, however, was not necessary, as it rapidly became apparent that devolution commanded a majority among both union and constituency delegates. The conference was presented with five propositions. The first two, declaring opposition to separation and support for the return of a Labour government, were carried unanimously. The third opposed 'the setting up of a Scottish Assembly as being irrelevant to the needs and aspirations of the people of Scotland'. It was defeated overwhelmingly. The fourth proposal was 'That this conference, recognising the desire of the Scottish people for a greater say in the running of their own affairs, calls for the setting up of a directly elected Assembly with legislative powers within the context of the political and economic unity of the UK.' This was carried overwhelmingly, as was the next proposition, calling for the retention of the office of Secretary of State and all seventy-one MPs.

As this had proved to be one of the most controversial decisions in modern Scottish politics, it is worth analysing in some detail. First, we must look at what was decided. Here it is important to note that the decision was a compromise. Many of the difficulties over which devolutionists had agonised for years were solved at a stroke by incorporating in the successful propositions the principal demands of both devolutionist and unionist factions. Thus, after devolution, Scotland was to retain the Secretary of State, the seventy-one MPs and the economic union, with the assembly simply inserted into the old structure. The decision could thus be regarded as incremen-talist, the incorporation of new demands into an existing policy programme without upsetting the other elements of the programme. Certainly, if devolution had been presented as a radical alternative to the constitutional *status quo*, it would not have been accepted so readily and the Scottish MPs in particular would not have come round so soon. The decision should not, therefore, be represented as a radical departure from Labour's centralist beliefs. Such a departure would not be typical of the party which customarily takes many years to abandon deeply held beliefs, as the battles over the dropping of the old Home Rule policy show.

On the other hand, despite the later complaints of Tam Dalyell,[30] there can be no doubt that the conference did commit itself to a legislative assembly. In July the NEC had approved Alex Kitson's resolution calling for 'an elected legislative Assembly within the context of the political and economic unity of the United Kingdom'. It was this proposal which was repeated in the fourth proposition put to the conference, and which was carried. Delegates thus realised that they were voting for legislative devolution, and Alex Donnet, who swung the General and Municipal Workers' Union block vote behind the proposal, specifically stated that 'his union considered the time had come to devolve power to a legislative assembly'.[31] Devolution had been the subject of the most intense debate in constituency parties and among Scottish MPs, and there is no doubt that the conference approved an assembly which would take over much of the work of the Scottish Office and the Scottish committees of Parliament.

However, legislative devolution was the only option open to the conference short of total opposition to the setting up of an assembly, as favoured by the Scottish Executive. The conference had been called at short notice, and affiliated organisations were, on these grounds, refused the right to submit amendments. It was a straight either–or choice, with the NEC policy and that of the Scottish Executive at either end of the spectrum of views on devolution. Thus, as we go on to examine below, principled support for legislative devolution was by no means the main reason for the decision.

The second question to examine is why the party changed its policy. Here there are factors which permitted it to change and factors which impelled it to do so. The decision has often been presented as simple electoral expediency in the face of opinion polls. Such an explanation is too simple and ignores the nature of the policy-making process in the Labour Party, which has often insisted on doing the least expedient thing, to the despair of revisionist leaders. So, in 1974, Bob Worcester was telling the party that nationalisation was very unpopular and that the party must backtrack on it.[32] Instead, the party moved to propose further measures of nationalisation.

Policy change in the Labour Party is rendered much easier where there is a sound ideological rationale for the new policy in terms of Labour's traditional tenets. Then it can be presented as a logical development in Labour's march to a better society. Home Rule for Scotland had a respectable ideological pedigree. It had been Labour Party policy for the whole of the party's history, apart from the period 1958–74, and had been endorsed by Keir Hardie, John Maclean, Jimmy Maxton and Tom Johnston. Thus, a return to a Home Rule policy was not ruled out ideologically – though, ironically, from this point of view, the Nationalist pressure made it more difficult to adopt Home Rule, as it could then be presented by anti-devolutionists as a concession to forces antagonistic to Labour. After 1974 there was a great effort by Labour leaders to present the decision as a logical development and to claim continuity in policy. Even the 1958 decision was reinterpreted as a move towards devolution,[33] while the shade of Keir Hardie was constantly evoked. Labour's support for administrative and Parliamentary devolution was reinterpreted as leading logically to an assembly rather than as a means of heading off demands for an assembly. These efforts were basically unconvincing but played an important part in rallying the party around the new policy.

The second ideological factor which allowed the party to change its mind on this issue is that devolution, unlike most controversial issues within the party, failed to follow the traditional right–left line of cleavage. One of Labour's weaknesses as a party has been that the lines of cleavage on various party issues have tended to reinforce each other, rather than being cross-cutting. Thus, the EEC issue, once it was seriously raised in the party, rapidly developed into a right–left issue, with right-wing anti-marketeers and left-wing pro-marketeers shifting positions. Issues such as nationalisation or Clause Four, of course, raise the right–left issue very directly. However, on the devolution issue there were right- and left-wingers in both camps. Thus, although the issue did divide the party and from time to time has raised considerable passions, it did not tap any of the permanent divisions in the party and the split was soon healed. Further, no group in the party regarded the issue as vital in the continuing battle for the Party's soul, so that a policy change could fairly easily be accommodated. An illustration of the danger of the issue's slipping into the traditional ideological mould came in 1975, when John Mackintosh, supporting the pro-devolution motion at the Scottish conference, was thought to have lost some votes by associating it with his own pro-EEC position.[34]

The third permissive factor was the assurance, which we have discussed, that the essentials of the unionist settlement would not be disturbed. This factor led many to withdraw their opposition to devolution, if not to give it their wholehearted support.

There were four major factors which impelled the party to adopt a policy of devolution. These were conviction, pressure from the national leadership, the support of loyalist trade union leaders, and electoral worries. The number of those convinced of the correctness of devolution was, as we have seen, growing in the early 1970s and formed an increasingly vocal lobby in the party. However, by 1974 they were far from being in the majority and were probably almost matched in number by the committed 'antis'. For most people in the party, it was not until the SNP advances made them take it seriously that they saw the issue as of great significance.

Pressure from the national leadership, which was more worried about the electoral consequences than was the Scottish leadership, was certainly intense and caused considerable bitterness. Transport House regarded the Scottish Executive, in the light of Govan, the February election and opinion polls, as obstinate and bent on suicide. For their part, most members of the Scottish Executive considered Transport House out of touch with the realities of the Scottish situation and were sure that they knew bes how to deal with SNP. There are limits, however, to the extent to which the London leadership can push its followers in the country. It could, and did, lean on the Scottish Executive to recall the conference, but was unable to persuade the Executive to change its line on devolution. It could not directly lean on the activitists in the constituencies or the constituency Labour Party delegates to the conference, and any attempt to do so might have backfired seriously. On the other hand, the behaviour of the Scottish Executive and its alleged mishandling of the issue caused consider-able resentment among activists, who began to feel that the party, by vacillating on the issue, was maximising its own disadvantage. Many people were looking for a clear lead either way, and, failing to get this from the Scottish Executive, were prepared to look to the national leadership. The Executive's notorious six–five vote, in particular, gave a very bad impression in the party and the country and deprived it of much of its moral authority.

One way in which the leadership could influence the conference, however, was by lining up the union leadership behind it. This was the period of the first 'social contract', in which, in the wake of the debacles over the 1969 White Paper *In Place of Strife* and the Heath Government's confrontations with organised labour, concessions were being traded between Government and the major unions, so as to build up a new relationship. Devolution was not an issue about which most union leaders felt strongly. The concessions which the Government wished to make to Scottish nationalism were purely in the 'political' field, with the unified, centralised economy remaining the centre-piece of its plans. It was not, therefore, difficult to swing the major union leaders round to supporting devolution, particularly when it was pointed out to them that the Government's survival, and therefore their own gains in other fields, might depend on it. Thus, unions such as the General and Municipal Workers, who had opposed Kilbrandon at both the 1974 STUC and the March annual conference of the Scottish Council in 1974, had swung round by August to supporting devolution. The TGWU was brought into the devolution camp by Alex Kitson, whose views on Scottish matters had been generally accepted by the national union leadership since he had brought the Scottish Commercial Motormen's Union (formerly the Scottish Horse and Motormen's Association) into the TGWU in the 1960s. The Scottish leadership of the Amalgamated Union of Engineering Workers was, and remains, divided on the issue, but was brought into line for the 1974 conference. The National Union of Mineworkers (Scottish Section), of course, had long favoured devolution and continued to do so. In the event of serious opposition, therefore, the big unions could have swamped constituency delegates in a card vote, though this would have caused serious divisions and bitterness in the party.

While the unions certainly provided fairly solid backing for devolution at Dalintober Street, they could not on their own have been responsible for the overwhelming majority on the show of hands. They provided only 183 of the 354 delegates, a bare majority. The full attendance was as follows:

Trade unions	183	Women's councils	9
Constituency parties	94	Young Socialists	7
City parties	7	MPs	29
County federations	2	Parliamentary Prospec-	
Socialist societies	10	tive candidates	13

The Young Socialists, controlled by the 'Militant' group, were opposed to devolution. The MPs and candidates do not have a vote unless they have been appointed as delegates by affiliated bodies. This would suggest that there was considerable support amongst Constituency Labour Parties. In part, this reflected genuine commitment to devolution, but it was mainly owing to a belief that they had no choice if the Labour Party were to remain the dominant force in Scottish politics and stem the nationalist tide before the impending election. They were convinced that Labour had to make some drastic, immediate gesture to re-establish itself as the party with Scotland's interest at heart. One can ask whether this judgement was correct or whether some other strategy could have been adopted, but to have done nothing at all could have been to commit electoral suicide, because the foundations of Labour's position in Scotland were beginning to crumble. These foundations were the electoral dominance based on solid working-class support, which in the past had allowed the party to suppress the national dimension in Scottish politics; and the economic argument, that the UK link was economically vital to Scotland and that Labour was the best party to exploit it. Having defended its position in terms of the economic benefits which it was able to bring to Scotland, Labour was now outflanked by a party which, with oil, could promise more. In Jimmy Jack's words of 1969, they were hoist with their own petard.

Labour could in these circumstances adopt one of three strategies: it could concede the constitutional issue and establish an assembly; it could make no constitutional concession but dip further into the pork barrel; or it could try to suppress the Scottish question altogether by stressing UK-wide issues on which it possessed an advantage. All three courses were fraught with danger. The pork-barrel approach was tried during 1974, turning Scottish politics for a time into a Dutch auction. Thus, the 1974 Scottish manifesto contained long lists of the special measures which the Government had taken for Scotland, but Labour was constantly being outbid. As far as UK issues were concerned, there were very few at this time working in Labour's favour as far as Scotland was concerned, now that the economic card was being played against it with a vengeance. Of course, it may be that Labour did possess the best economic politics, but there was not a great deal of time in 1974 to demonstrate this in practical terms. In any case, Scottish Labour was not in a position to fight on the importance of UK issues, having itself for so long insisted on the importance of the Scottish question, while it was working in Labour's favour. Reluctantly, therefore, the party adopted the first strategy and aligned itself with the national dimension in Scottish politics. This it did by adopting the policy of an assembly with limited powers, combined with continued economic unity and the presence of the Secretary of State and the seventy-one MPs in London. This had the dual advantage of corresponding to what the Scottish people, according to the opinion polls, wanted, in preference to the status quo or independence, and of allowing a concession to nationalism which was not damaging to Labour's fundamental concerns and could be presented in terms compatible with Labour ideology.

The Scottish Parliamentary leadership's rapid policy switch must be seen in tactical terms. The vigorous attacks of Willie Ross and his colleagues on nationalism and devolution had failed to kill the public demand or halt the nationalist advance. Their old method of handling the Scottish question was failing. A new one therefore had to be found. Life might have been easier for them had they simply been the centralisers and integrators which their opponents alleged them to be. Then they could have denied the existence of any distinctively Scottish questions. However, they had conceded the devolutionists' case by their own advocacy of administrative devolution and had positively revelled in the argument that Scottish problems, being distinct, merited special treatment. Ross himself had believed for some time that, once the issue of an assembly was seriously mooted, it would be difficult to resist it. 1974 proved him right. Once the devolution battle lines were drawn on the issue of an assembly, parties had to declare themselves for it or against it. It was no longer possible to cloud the issue, as both major parties had done since 1968. Having decided that its 'anti-assembly but special treatment for Scotland' position was untenable, therefore, the Labour leadership was faced with the clear choice of an assembly or a decisive move *away* from its traditional Scottish-oriented position, towards new issues. On the Scottish issue, there were no further compromise steps short of an assembly. Thus, what appeared as a dramatic policy U-turn was in fact one of a very few options available.

After August 1974, then, the party in Scotland was committed to a legislative assembly and the way was open for the Government to draw up definite plans in advance of the election. In September 1974 these appeared in the shape of a White Paper, *Democracy and*

Devolution: Proposals for Scotland and Wales (Cmnd. 5732). This proposed a Scottish legislative assembly with an executive, possessing powers over a wide range of functions at present administered by the Scottish Office but with no power to raise revenue, no substantial economic functions and subject to a veto power by the Secretary of State, subject, in turn, to affirmative resolution in Parliament. For the October 1974 General Election, the Labour Party for the first time issued a separate Scottish Manifesto. This contained the essence of Labour's Scottish strategy. Special measures already taken to help Scotland, especially in the field of employment, were listed, and separate sections dealt with North Sea oil and the promise of a legislative assembly. At the same time, the unity of the UK was strongly defended and the continued existence of the Secretary of State and the seventy-one Scottish Parliamentary seats was promised. It was a programme on which Labour could face the country apparently united. Not one Labour MP publicly denounced the assembly commitment in the campaign, though Tam Dalyell later caused some surprise by claiming that, not having read the Manifesto, he was not aware that the party was committed to a legislative assembly.[35]

The assembly commitment certainly appeared to perform the task required of it. At the October 1974 election, Labour avoided any further losses, though four more Conservative seats fell to the SNP. Whether it was the assembly pledge which saved Labour's position is, of course, by no means clear. William Miller of Strathclyde University considers that, once devolution had become an issue in 1974, Labour was obliged to move towards the SNP position in order to retain the middle ground, or else suffer an electoral setback which might have left it with no more than twenty-six seats.[36] Miller suggests that, before October 1974, Labour might just have been able to suppress the issue of Scottish government and avoid losses to the SNP in that way. As we have seen, this was precisely the leadership's strategy before February 1974, but the way in which it suppressed it was not by denying that there was a 'Scottish issue' and projecting UK issues, but by denying that there was a *Scottish government* issue and projecting other Scottish issues. This was a dangerous strategy. It was a strategy which the leadership felt unable to maintain after February, as the devolution issue had become salient. Whether the issue could have been suppressed in 1974 and other issues projected is one of the points of contention between pro- and anti-devolutionists in the party. After the October election, the general feeling in the party reflected Miller's comment, 'Before October 1974, it might have been difficult to suppress the issue of Scottish government, and success could not be guaranteed. But after [Labour's] own behaviour in 1974, failure can now be guaranteed. The issue can no longer be ignored.'[37]

IV. THE POLITICS OF DEVOLUTION, 1974–8

A great number of people were thus brought round to an acceptance of devolution, albeit an unenthusiastic one, after October 1974. Now that the party was committed to devolution, had fought an election on the issue and had a manifesto commitment, the general feeling was that it had better go ahead and implement it as soon as possible. The Parliamentary situation provided another incentive. With a majority of only three, and that soon to disappear, the Government was dependent on the goodwill of Scottish and Welsh nationalists for its survival. While some leading figures in the SNP shared the official Labour analysis that, with devolution, Labour's position in Scotland would be secured and the Nationalist challenge fade, the official SNP view was that devolution was to be supported as the first stage of independence. A devolution Bill thus became one of the new Government's priorities. However, opposition in Cabinet soon developed as English ministers came to realise what had been promised, and it was not until November 1975 that a further White Paper appeared.

The 1975 White Paper was widely criticised in Scotland for its 'negative' tone. It was indeed a fairly dry, Civil Service document, dealing in minute detail with some minor points – for instance, it revealed that Welsh civil servants would have the right to sit in the Scottish Assembly and *vice versa* – but skimming over some of the major issues, such as the economic role of the assembly. On the vital issue of revenue-raising powers, it made the half-serious proposal that the assembly should be allowed to make a surcharge on local taxation – which effectively meant the rates, as the Government had no intention of introducing new forms of local taxation. The other feature causing most offence was the provision for the Secretary of State to veto a bill which he judged to be *ultra vires* and to propose to Parliament the rejection of bills adjudged to be unacceptable 'on general policy grounds'. Such was the reception of the White Paper that after further discussion the Government was obliged to issue a *Supplementary Statement*, virtually another White Paper, in August 1976. This reduced the Secretary of State's 'governor-general' role and proposed the complete devolution of the Scottish Development Agency, but made no concession on the issue of revenue-raising powers. At last, in November 1976, the Scotland and Wales Bill appeared, only to be blocked by the failure, in February 1977, of the guillotine motion to restrict the timetable for its committee stage. The famous guillotine defeat was made possible by the combined opposition of Conservatives, Liberals and twenty-two Labour MPs. Of the Labour rebels, only two, Tam Dalyell and Willie Hamilton, represented Scottish constituencies. Apart from two Welshmen, the remainder represented the 'English backlash' which developed once the Government's intentions on devolution had become apparent to English MPs. This backlash should not have taken the Government by surprise. It had been trying to conduct two debates at once. Unconvinced of the merits of devolution, it failed to adopt a general policy stance on the matter, based on a philosophy of decentralisation. Equally, it had failed to adopt a firmly centralist approach. Instead, it made a series of concessions to Scottish opinion, which it described for the benefit of the Scots as a 'massive handover of responsibility for Scotland's affairs',[38] while insisting that the unity of the United Kingdom was uninfringed and assuring the English that the changes would not give Scotland any special advantages. On the part of the English rebels, the main grievance seemed to be less that an autonomous Scottish administration was being set up – after all, they had showed little interest in Scottish policy in the past – than a vague feeling that the Scots were now going to gain economic advantages and that concessions had been made to the Scots which would not be made to them, despite their loyalty to the party. The irony of this is that, as we have seen, Scotland had for many years been enjoying special treatment in the allocation of public resources and that Scottish Labour had long opposed devolution precisely because it might prejudice this special treatment. Perhaps, then, the English MPs would have done better to have looked at the pork-barrel tactics which the party had used to try and stave off the demand for an assembly and which continued to be used to fight the nationalists. In any case, the Government, in seeking to regain their support, in the absence of any demand for an English assembly or assemblies, started looking at economic concessions which might be made to them, with consequences which we examine later. For its part, the Government should have realised that to reopen one part of the Scottish constitutional settlement would necessarily entail a look at other elements of it, and that the questions of Scotland's constitutional and economic links with the UK could not be so neatly be separated.

The failure of the guillotine presented the Government with a strong temptation to drop the whole devolution business, but a salutory reminder of its importance was delivered to it and the rebellious backbenchers the following month when the Government, now deprived, because of the devolution failure, of the support of the SNP members, was saved from defeat on a vote of confidence only by the 'Lib–Lab' pact. A new Bill could also regain the tacit Parliamentary support of the SNP and shore up Labour's still delicate electoral position in Scotland. In November 1977 the new Bill duly appeared. This time there were separate Bills for Scotland and Wales, with the Scotland Bill incorporating several changes from its predecessor. In particular, the role of the Secretary of State was further reduced, with provision for disputes over the *vires* of the assembly to be referred to the judicial committee of the Privy Council. On the other hand, the Treasury had prevented any concession on revenue-raising powers and the assembly was still to be without major economic or industrial functions. Shortly afterwards the Government conceded the demand for a referendum, in order to try and persuade reluctant Labour MPs to help get the measure through the House and reserve their opposition for the referendum campaign. This effectively shifted the focus of the battle to the referendum, and indeed the only really serious defeat which the Government suffered in the Bill's passage was on the amendment providing that a 'Yes' vote in the referendum, to be effective, must be backed by 40 per cent of the Scottish electorate.

Meanwhile, the Scottish Council of the Labour Party, thrown into confusion by the events of 1974, painfully sought its way to a new consensus on the constitutional question. The Dalintober Street decision had left unanswered as many questions as it had solved. Despite the claims of anti-devolutionists such as Tam Dalyell, there was no doubt about the commitment to a legislative assembly to assume many of the functions of the Scottish Office. Where doubt remained was on the scope and powers of the assembly, particularly in the economic field and on whether the Government's package would be sufficient to stem the nationalist tide. The fact that a commitment had been made and embodied in a manifesto commitment largely ended the argument on principle. Any remaining doubts were largely stilled in 1976 by the adoption of devolution as official policy by the Labour Party's annual conference and the TUC, both anxious to shore up the Government's electoral and Parliamentary position. In particular, this disarmed those left-wing opponents of devolution who had been accustomed to upholding the sanctity of conference decisions. Opposition to devolution remained, but until the referendum concession in 1977 it was expressed largely in efforts to limit the powers of the assembly. It was behind this 'minimalist' position that the majority of the Executive and the Constituency Labour Parties initially lined up.

On the other hand, there had now developed in the party a 'neonationalist' element, comprising the remaining Home Rulers of long-standing, such as David Lambie, MP for Central Ayrshire, together with the group around Jim Sillars, who had been moving in an increasingly nationalist direction since his election in 1970. The change of mood in Scotland, developing since the mid 1960s, was further hastened by the breakthrough of the SNP and reflected in an increased national consciousness in all areas of Scottish life, but particularly in the media. Members of the Labour Party were not entirely immune from this change of mood and, though only a minority gave it political expression, it created a favourable climate for those pushing for a more radical measure of devolution. The latter, and in particular the neo-nationalist group around Sillars, now seized the initiative and started to push for a more far-reaching commitment, to include economic powers for the assembly. They were joined by several trades unionists, such as Alex Kitson of the TGWU. A third group in the devolution camp consisted of those who had been unhappy about the decision of 1974 but believed that, now the commitment had been made, the assembly must be given sufficient powers to make it viable, so that a stable constitutional settlement could be secured. At the 1975 Scottish conference, the division between the devolutionists and the minimalists came out into the open. A composite motion from the TGWU calling for economic and revenue-raising powers for the assembly was opposed by the Executive, whose spokesman George Robertson put the traditional case against devolving economic powers. It would lead to a perpetual auction sale for advance factories, Industrial Development Certificates and development grants, in which Scotland could lose out. Despite support from other unions, including the Amalgamated Union of Engineering Workers, whose delegation decided the issue by only two votes out of thirty, the resolution was lost by 353,000 votes to 341,000. The defeat was attributed in some quarters to the mysterious disappearance of the boilermakers' 15,000 votes, but it is clear that the constituencies were overwhelmingly behind the Executive. It was a defeat for the devolutionists, including those within the Government who were fighting for a radical measure, and for the Sillars group, which now began its decisive move out of the party.[39]

From 1975, mainstream opinion within the party began to shift and to adjust to the new political situation in Scotland. The background to this shift was the continued disastrous decline in the party's fortunes in opinion polls and local elections throughout 1975-7. In the district council elections of 1977, Labour suffered massive losses to the SNP and even surrendered control of Glasgow. The defection of the Sillas group early in 1976 reflected a belief on the part of the group that Labour was on the verge of collapse and that only a completely new mix of socialism and nationalism could meet the needs of the time. Sections of the press were ready to write the Labour Party off completely, and, while the predictions of a Labour collapse in industrial Clydeside can, in retrospect, be seen to have been seriously misplaced, there is no doubt that the movement was seriously demoralised. As the challenges by both the SNP and the new Scottish Labour Party (SLP) came from the nationalist-devolutionist quarter, any backtracking on the devolution commitment was more than the bravest Labour souls dared contemplate. Instead, the belief grew that a credible and realistic devolution policy was needed. From 1975, the initiative was taken by the 'moderate' pro-devolution group.

Publication of the 1975 White Paper was important in crystallising this feeling. The grudging, unenthusiastic and negative tone of this document won it few friends in Scotland. Sillars and his neo-nationalist group saw it as the final straw, an indication that Labour was not prepared to take devolution seriously. Even the Scottish Executive now saw it as inadequate and proposed a resolution to the 1976 Scottish conference calling for revenue-raising powers for the assembly, the devolution of the Scottish Development Agency and the removal of the Secretary of State's veto. The mood of the party in accepting the Executive report was summed up by Geoffrey Smith in *The Times*:

There remain the convinced anti-devolutionists. But among
the rest there is a general movement to a compromise
position where the majority can stand and fight. There is a
widespread recognition that something more than the White
Paper will be needed to satisfy Scottish opinion. In some
cases, that recognition is enthusiastic. More often, it is the
reluctant acceptance of political necessity. But one also
encounters a feeling that, while there must be more
devolution than the Government have yet proposed, there
must none the less be strict limits as to how far it would be
safe to go without jeopardising the integrity of the United
Kingdom.[40]

Now it was the Scottish Council, with a dissenting but scarcely vocal
minority in its own ranks, which was pushing the Government for
more devolution, a reversal of the 1974 position. The Government
was pressed throughout 1976 to hurry ahead with the production of
a Bill and, after the failure of the guillotine, to try again next session.
Opinion was moving in Scotland towards acceptance of devolution
as a fact, and the debate was increasingly about the form which it
should take and the opportunities which it might present to
socialists. By 1977, even the 'Militant' group on the Trotskyist left
had abandoned opposition to devolution and begun to explore ways
of exploiting it.

In part, this was a recognition that the fight had really been won
and lost in 1974; in part, it stemmed from straightforward electoral
fears; but there was also a growing belief in devolution as an
important aspect of the politics of the future. The failures of the
1960s had shaken faith in the prescriptions of economic planning.
Now, in the 1970s, the oil crisis and recession further undermined
the old belief in the power of centralised government and led to a
general lowering of expectations. In the recession, the old tools of
regional policy, based on inducements to private industry to
relocate intended investments, proved ineffective when industry
was hardly investing at all. In any case, regional policy was rapidly
run down once the effects of the recession began to hit the formerly
prosperous areas in London and the Midlands. Industrial
Development Certificate policy had been relaxed and Regional
Employment Premium abolished. In Scotland, as a consequence,
Labour has sought alternative means of mobilising resources for
economic development. The National Enterprise Board was part of

the party's answer to the failure of purely indicative planning in the 1960s. The Scottish Development Agency was proposed by the Scottish Council as an indigenous Scottish element of the strategy of direct industrial intervention, though it was conceded by the Government as part of the pork-barrel politics of the early 1970s. Its devolution to the assembly is seen as providing the necessary political impetus for its interventionist strategy. At the same time, the party favours the unified economy, a principle it places above all others. By 1976 it had, to the satisfaction of most of its members, produced a strategy which combined central control over macro-economic policy and UK-wide resource allocation with continued opportunity for Scotland to lobby for extra resources and to mobilise its own resources for development. Anti-devolutionists were still not satisfied. They pointed to the paucity of economic powers at the disposal of the assembly even after the Government's concessions of the Scottish Development Agency and the Highlands and Islands Development Board and continued to argue that the assembly would merely raise economic expectations without providing the means to meet them. The SLP, starting from the same premiss, argued that major economic powers must be devolved. Majority opinion, however, had by 1977 come to the view that the proposals embodied in the Scotland Bill were the most and the least that could be devolved, and the arguments on the powers of the assembly had effectively come to an end.

Among the Scottish Parliamentary contingent, for whom questions of electoral security were paramount, the decision of 1974 had been accepted without dissent, though in general without enthusiasm. After the October election, the anti-devolutionists began to re-emerge, along with a vigorous pro-devolution lobby. The most vocal opponent of devolution was Tam Dalyell, who was joined in his opposition by Willie Hamilton and Peter Doig. Other MPs were known to be uneasy, but went along with the majority feeling, which was that the issue should be disposed of as quickly as possible and that it was impossible in any case to escape from such a public and painfully adopted commitment. The radical devolutionists were represented by Jim Sillars and John Robertson who were to defect with the SLP, and David Lambie, who had long favoured Scottish independence but whose influence on the party was reduced on this account. Two strong devolutionists were taken into the Government, Alex Eadie as Parliamentary Under-Secretary for Energy, and Harry Ewing, in 1975, as Parliamentary Under-

Secretary at the Scottish Office, with responsibility for devolution. Day-to-day charge of the devolution bills was later given to another Scottish MP, but a late convert to devolution, John Smith. The other notable advocate of the policy among the Scottish MPs was John Mackintosh, who had for many years believed in devolution as a contribution to the reform of British government, but the absence of any nationalist dimension to Mackintosh's thinking as well as his increasing alienation from the Labour Party after 1974 tended to distance him from the other devolutionists. At a meeting in November 1975, at the time of the publication of the second White Paper, the Scottish group of Labour MPs voted to support devolution. The vote was unanimous but nine members of the group were absent, including the leading 'antis', such as Dalyell. Despite the unanimity of the meeting, however, the division between the enthusiastic devolutionists and the rest was apparent when Jim Sillars, a left-winger and former chairman of the Tribune Group, put his support behind the right-winger Dickson Mabon in the election of the group chairman, against the left-winger Norman Buchan, on the grounds that Mabon was a firmer supporter of devolution.

For the most part, the argument in the Parliamentary Party, like that in the Scottish Council, concerned the scope and powers of the assembly, rather than the principle. In early 1976, for example, a row blew up over a document drawn up by John Mackintosh and Maurice Miller, MP for the backbench devolution committee. This called for increased powers for the assembly, particularly in the economic and taxation fields. After complaints from Robin Cook, it was made clear that this was simply a discussion document. Tam Dalyell also argued on the nature of the assembly rather than the principle and began to deploy the argument that, not having read the October 1974 Scottish Election Manifesto, he had believed that the party was committed only to a super local authority. However, by late 1976, with the Government's further concessions, disquiet was spreading. Six MPs warned Michael Foot against imposing a guillotine on the Bill. Bob Hughes and Alex Wilson declared that, while they would support the forthcoming Bill, they would not accept any further concessions.

In the event, the attitude of most of the MPs to the Scotland and Wales Bill was one of resigned acceptance, and only two Scottish members, Dalyell and Willie Hamilton, voted against the guillotine motion. On the other hand, few MPs seriously regretted the Bill's demise, except on purely electoral grounds. The Scotland Bill of 1977–8, regarded as a great improvement, aroused a little more enthusiasm and a genuine commitment on the part of several members to make it into a workable piece of legislation which the party could defend. This followed the trend in the Scottish Council which we have examined. Thus, MPs, such as Norman Buchan, who had been unhappy about the original devolution commitment now applied themselves to forging a devolution settlement which would survive. The referendum concession disarmed most of the opponents of devolution, and only Dalyell voted against a second reading and the guillotine. From the devolution side, an amendment to give the assembly revenue-raising powers was supported by nine Scottish members. Although this crucial amendment failed, the consensus of opinion in the Parliamentary Party was, by 1978, lined up, albeit for the most part reluctantly, behind the view of the party in Scotland that at last a position had been found where it could stand and fight.

In the trades unions, there was also a move after 1974 to come to terms with the new political situation. As we have seen, the STUC, with its traditional concern for matters of Scottish government, had been thinking about devolution since 1968, though it had not worked out a comprehensive strategy. The change of policy by several unions in 1974 was faciliated by their lack of concern with purely political matters, which allowed them to give unequivocal backing to the Government. The loyalty factor served to sustain the unions' support for devolution in the difficult days of 1974–7. Their attitude was usually determined by this and by the views of their Scottish officials, who were often given a free hand in determining the line on Scottish political issues. For instance, the Amalgamated Union of Engineering Workers, whose decisions to back devolution in 1974 had been taken by their delegates to the Dalintober Street conference, at the urging of the leadership, did not discuss devolution at its policy-making National Committee until 1976, when it endorsed the leadership's action in backing the TUC commitment to devolution. The TGWU left Scottish political matters largely in the hands of Alex Kitson and the Scottish Section, which, as the descendant of Hugh Lyon's Scottish Horse and Motormen's Association, had a traditional commitment to devolution. The policy of the General and Municipal Workers' Union, which had reversed its line to back devolution at Dalintober Street, was set largely by its Scottish organiser, Alec Donnet, and endorsed by its National Executive Committee. In 1976 it was Donnet who wrote the document expressing the union's attitude to the 1975 White Paper. This barely concealed his lack of enthusiasm and concentrated largely on the centralist aspects of the White Paper, but it backed the paper none the less.

However, from an early stage in the debate, some trade-union leaders had begun to think about the uses to which an assembly could be put and, in particular, as might be expected, about the economic consequences of devolution. The danger of economic separation was a concern of many of them and led to some argument within the AUEW which has been split on the issue since 1974. Thus, in 1976, Alex Ferry, its Scottish organiser, was quoted as saying that the commitment had been assumed too hurriedly and that more thought was required on the specifics of devolution.[41] Dissent was also heard from the Edinburgh divisional officer, who complained at the union's intention of backing the motion for economic powers at the Scottish Labour conference. On the other hand, a movement to give the assembly economic powers did gather pace in the unions after 1974 and was particularly associated with Alex Kitson of the TGWU, who had played such a major part in the events of 1974. Given that an assembly was apparently going to be established, it is not surprising that the unions started thinking of ways in which it could be used to advance their own material interests and act as a lobbyist for Scotland. Their thinking was influenced, too, by the factors which affected the Labour Party – the failure of centralised indicative planning, the run-down of regional policy, and the potential of the Scottish Development Agency. As in the Labour Party, so in the trade union movement, there was an English backlash, which may have convinced some Scottish union leaders that, if Scotland was going to come under attack for being unfairly favoured, it was important to have a political institution capable of defending her interests. Now that the quiet, 'behind closed doors' system of Scottish office lobbying had broken down, a vocal assembly might be the best safeguard of those interests. So in 1976 the TGWU resolution calling for economic powers for the assembly was strongly backed by the unions.

These attitudes were reflected in the STUC, which was one of the other major forces pushing the Government to deliver on its devolution commitments. A Scottish assembly with economic powers, besides providing a means of economic lobbying, could give enhanced status to the STUC itself, and the full-time officers are all advocates of devolution. Within the STUC, the role of the Communist Party continues to be strong, finding expression in the Secretariat and through the miners and the trades councils. The policy of the Communist Party has been to push for the devolution of greater economic powers, including powers over trade, industry and labour, in line with its evidence to the Commission on the Constitution – a policy similar in many respects to that of the SLP but without the European dimension. The Communist Party line was based on three elements:

(1) the Scottish people, like any other nation, have the right to self-determination and this must be recognised by the labour movement;
(2) the SNP is a petty-bourgeois and reactionary party whose policies do not reflect the interests of the Scottish working class; and
(3) the Scottish working class must retain economic unity and class solidarity with the rest of the British working class.

The political strategy drawn from this was that the Scottish working class should not leave the leadership of the national aspirations of the Scottish people in the hands of the SNP. Instead, the organised labour movement should place itself at the head of these aspirations and give them a working class and democratic character. This allowed the Communist Party great flexibility in responding to nationalism and forging its own policy on devolution. It enabled it to pour scorn on the SNP while at the same time pushing for an advanced programme of devolution and guarding against the charge of putting national before class interests. Thus, the Communists were able to push hard within the STUC for devolution. However, they were no more successful than the Labour devolutionists in coping with the economic contradictions of their position.

The STUC's response to the 1975 White Paper was to welcome the commitment to devolution and reaffirm its commitment to the economic unity of the UK, but to regret the absence of economic or revenue-raising powers for the assembly and to criticise the scope of the Secretary of State's proposed veto powers. It also wanted a special 'oil fund' to be used for the benefit of all the depressed regions of the UK. When the 'economic powers' were spelled out, however, it became clear that these were only those powers which could be conceded without prejudice to economic unity. Specifically, they boiled down to control of the Scottish Development Agency, the Highlands and Islands Development Board and the Secretary of State's functions in Agriculture and Fisheries. The STUC also wanted Scottish committees of the Manpower Services Commission and the Health and Safety Commission, but, in line with its longstanding policy of supporting unified labour legislation, did not want to see these devolved to the assembly. Outside the economic field, it wanted the assembly to assume responsibility for law and order, police, prosecutions and the universities. In essence, the STUC had adopted the same line as the Scottish Council of the Labour Party. Its proposals were designed to retain the unified economy, to stave off the threat of separatism and to ensure the maximum advantage for Scotland in the promotion of economic development.

Labour's convinced anti-devolutionists were distinctly subdued in this period. They had been placed at a tremendous disadvantage after 1974, opposed to a manifesto commitment which, after 1976, had become an official party policy and which formed a major item of the Labour Government's legislative programme. Little was heard of the argument against the whole idea of an assembly until 1976, when a 'scrap the assembly' group of Labour Party members briefly appeared, led by Alex Cameron, a Glasgow district councillor, and Willie Hannan, the former MP for Maryhill. In the summer of 1976, an all-party 'Scotland is British' campaign was launched. This attracted some figures mainly on the right of the Labour Party, such as George Lawson, the former MP for Motherwell, Tam Dalyell and Danny Crawford of the Union of Construction, Allied Trades and Technicians, but it was financed by industrialists and, for many of the anti-devolutionists on the left of the party, it smacked too much of the Scottish Conservative establishment and, indeed, looked uncomfortably like the pro-EEC umbrella group which had out-campaigned and out-spent them in 1975. The anti-devolution forces were thus split between those who were prepared to collaborate with political opponents and those who were not.

It was the failure of the guillotine on the Scotland and Wales Bill in February 1977 which brought the anti-devolution case out into the open again. The lack of any marked popular reaction confirmed the views of those who had argued against the necessity of 'appeasing' nationalism, though, in turn, the SNP successes at the local elections in May reinforced the tactical case for devolution. A fringe rally of anti-devolutionists was organised at the Scottish conference in March by Tam Dalyell, Brian Wilson, a radical journalist, and Allan Campbell Maclean, who as chairman of the Scottish Council had fought against the decision of 1974. However, the meeting, like a pro-devolution gathering at the same conference, failed to attract much support and the distribution of 'Scotland is British' literature led some delegates to walk out.

What really galvanised the anti-devolution forces into action and provided a precise focus for their campaign was the Government's decision to allow a referendum, a move originally designed to permit anti-devolution MPs to support the new bill. It now allowed the anti-devolutionists to campaign openly against Government and party policy. After the Scottish Executive had voted, by a majority, to give official backing to the Yes campaign, a Labour No campaign was formed, in January 1978. Besides such predictable figures as Tam Dalyell and Peter Doig, MP, this included the MPs Robert Hughes, Richard Buchanan and Robin Cook, who had previously expressed their unease over devolution. Dalyell, Cook, Doig, Hughes and Willie Hamilton went on to vote for the '40 per cent amendment' to the Bill. The first real test of the No group was an amendment to ban the use of party funds in the referendum campaign, put to the 1978 Scottish conference. This was heavily defeated and the party remained firmly committed to the devolution line. The Garscadden and Hamilton by-elections and the regional elections showed a dramatic improvement in Labour's fortunes at the expense of the SNP. The reasons for this improvement may have been various, but within the party the devolution policy was seen as a vital element. It may not in itself have won votes, so the argument went, but it had deprived the SNP of a vital issue and allowed Labour to attack it on the issue which now marked the nationalists off from the Labour: separatism. Devolution was thus taken out of the political battle by ceasing to be an issue between the two parties and was replaced by the issue of separatism *versus* the United Kingdom. This also enabled Labour to play up other issues on which it possessed an advantage, notably the fear of unemployment and the fall in the rate of inflation.

Thus, ironically, support for devolution, which had previously been sustained by Labour's weakness, was now sustained by its reviving strength. However, the fall in Nationalist support was accompanied by a cooling of public enthusiasm for devolution as the referendum campaign opened. The campaign itself caught the Labour movement unprepared. Most party members had come by now to accept devolution as a necessity, a more or less desirable necessity, depending on the point of view of the individual. It had been conceded in response to perceived public demand rather than, as other policies, fought for. Few realised that it would have to be fought for now in the face of a No campaign able to capitalise on the voters' fear of change once it was presented to them in concrete terms and on the sudden fail in popularity of the Government in 1979. Labour's devolution campaign was thus lack-lustre and lacking in conviction, while the No campaign hammered away very effectively at fears of more government, more bureaucracy, higher taxation and separatism. So the indecisive result of the referendum could be put down ultimately to a lack of conviction within the Labour Party.

Before the referendum, it was difficult to assess the depth of genuine support for devolution in the Labour Party. In the immediate aftermath of the marginal victory for the Yes side, this became much easier. Had there been solid and enthusiastic support for devolution, the party in Scotland would have demanded immediate implementation of the Act and condemned those party members who had campaigned against party policy. Instead, the keynote of the Scottish conference of March 1979 was unity, with delegates determined to do nothing to embarrass the Government, for whom Scottish devolution was by now little more than one of the counters in the game of parliamentary survival. The opportunity to thrash out the party's genuine differences on the issue and to take a principled stand was lost and instead a compromise resolution merely reaffirmed support for devolution, giving little indication of how it was to be achieved.

So the issue of devolution, far from being resolved by the Scotland Act and the referendum, was in many respects back where it was in 1974. Scottish nationalism is unlikely to disappear altogether and the future of Scottish government is an unresolved issue. The party and the wider Labour movement will thus once again have to face the issue of centralisation *versus* decentralisation and ask itself how far concessions to Scottish demands for constitutional change can be reconciled with its overall strategy. Issues which might have been resolved, or at least postponed, by the compromise of devolution, now face the movement with even greater urgency and it is with a consideration of these that we conclude the book.

6 Conclusion

1. TOWARDS A TERRITORIAL POLITICS?

We have traced the way in which the labour movement in Scotland has treated the 'national' issue from the formation of an independent labour movement to the present day.

Its attitude has depended on factors external to *and* internal to the movement itself. So, in the early days, unable to build a solid electoral base solely on the organised working class, it was forced to accommodate other interests, such as that of Scottish nationalism. Later, with a secure electoral base, it was able to ride out nationalist storms, while still accommodating Scottish demands within a centralised framework. In recent years, as its working-class electoral base has eroded, it has returned to the earlier strategy. The internal requirements of the Scottish labour movement have led, at one time, to support for Home Rule and, at others, to support for the centralised state to plan the economy and to divert resources to Scotland.

In the first period of our study, Labour found itself subject to conflicting pressures, for centralisation and decentralisation. In the middle period, nearly all pressures pointed to centralisation and integration. Now, once again, Labour finds itself torn. Its response to the new demands made upon it has been vacillating and uncertain. Yet, if it is to remain a party of government, it will have to learn how to handle territorial politics and to formulate a consistent and coherent view on the issues which they raise. The Government's handling of the Parliamentary passage of the devolution legislation shows how far the party is from such a view. We have seen how the legislation was described in different terms for Scottish and English audiences. The press as well as the Government played its part here. For instance, the *Daily Mirror* commented on the 1975 White Paper, 'It's the least that could be offered and also the most', while its Scottish sister paper, the *Daily Record*, roared, 'We were PROMISED more, now. WE WANT MORE because, Harold, your deal is just not good enough.'[1] When the first devolution bill failed, because of English alarm that the Scots were getting *too* good a deal, the Government's response was to try and bribe the north of England into support for devolution by pork-barrel measures such as the order for the Drax B power station – the equipment for which was to be built in Newcastle – and special committees of the National Enterprise Board. These, in turn, merely confirmed the importance of territorial issues and fanned resentment elsewhere.

How, then, can the labour movement come to terms with the territorial element in UK politics? In particular, can it reconcile concessions to territorial demands with its other policy objectives? The debate on this has suffered from a number of confusions. In particular, the issue of the territorial distribution of resources – which is the principal concern of regional politicians in England – has been confused with the issue of regional autonomy. Demands for a greater share of national resources for a region are, as we have seen in the case of Scotland, a centralising influence, as it is only the centre which can redistribute resources. Demands for autonomy are decentralist and may run counter to the demand that the centre should redistribute resources. Labour must, therefore, formulate a strategy on both these issues. The debate has hardly yet begun, but, to show the directions in which it is likely to develop, we shall state the 'devolutionist' and the 'anti-devolutionist' views.

II. THE DEVOLUTIONIST VIEW

On the one hand, the devolutionists maintain that people do not exist solely as members of social classes, that they have demands and aspirations to which politicians must respond. These other aspirations should be catered for and encouraged by Labour as long as they are healthy and progressive. The literature on nationalism has long distinguished between the liberal conception of nationalism, which, starting from individualist premisses, represents an urge on the part of the individuals to control their own destinies and participate more fully in politics, and, on the other hand, the 'German' or 'continental' conception of nationalism, in which the organic nation is placed above the individual, and in which, instead of the nation's growing out from the individual, the individual is subject to the exclusive claims of the nation. The former type of

nationalism, to which Scottish nationalism has, with some exceptions, traditionally belonged, is compatible with progressive and
socialist politics and with international solidarity. In so far as
nationalism represents a desire for a more responsible and partici-
pative form of government, it should be catered for, though its
chauvinist and divisive tendencies should be resisted.

The evidence shows clearly that most people in Scotland have
long demanded a greater degree of self-government and that this
demand is a crucial element in support for the SNP.[2] Were the
SNP's support simply a reflection of economic adversity, we should
expect nationalism to be strongest (a) at times of economic gloom in
Scotland, and (b) amongst the most deprived sectors of the
population. Neither has been shown to be the case. Even attitudes to
North Sea oil fail to distinguish nationalist voters from non-
nationalists in the way which the issue of self-government does.
Therefore, in conceding devolution, Labour is responding to a
legitimate and genuine demand, a demand not for independence
but for a degree of Home Rule which, while Labour was wedded to
a policy of rigid centralisation, could find expression only through
the SNP. Further, as the by-elections of 1978 showed, it was only by
taking its stand on the centre ground of devolution that Labour
could effectively assail the separatist policy of the SNP.

The referendum result by no means disproves this argument. The
partial success of the No campaign was achieved largely by
exploiting people's fear of change and by converting the issue of
devolution as embodied in the Scotland Act from an association
with 'more democracy' to one of 'more government'. The Labour
movement cannot and should not rely for success on appeals to the
electorate's most conservative instincts but should seek to guide the
movement for change into constructive channels. Labour would not
be prudent to imagine that devolution is now dead. After all, the
Yes side did win a clear majority of the votes cast and, were it not for
the unfair 40 per cent provision, the issue would not be in dispute.
An opinion poll during the campaign showed that 60 per cent of
Scots thought that, if the Scotland Act failed, the Government
should come up with another devolution scheme and the
Conservative Party's hints, however insincere, that they, if returned
to power, would oblige, certainly led many voters, who disliked the
specific provisions of the Scotland Act, to vote No. This provides a
firm basis on which the SNP can regroup and present a fresh
challenge to the political system in the years to come. If devolution

were to die, there would be no constitutional middle ground and room only for a stark confrontation between the forces of centralisation and those of separatism.

Further arguments for devolution arise from the nature of modern British government. The growth of bureaucracy and the centralisation of the state has seriously eroded control and accountability in the public sector. These are still based on the same principle as a hundred years ago: that of ministerial responsibility to Parliament. In the modern world, ministers are unable to know what is going on in their departments, let alone control it. Meanwhile, major decisions are taken in secret by ministers and civil servants, in consultation with the powerful interest groups. Devolution, by breaking open the nexus of decision-making and introducing another layer of accountable politicians, could make government both more open and accountable. It is no accident, therefore, that devolution has been opposed by powerful business interests, while the Civil Service has been insistent on retaining an unified structure. Of course, certain key decisions on resource allocation will need to be taken centrally, in the interests of efficiency and equity, but there are many important decisions in government which do not fall into this category and which can thus be decentralised, and within a system of centralised resource allocation there is considerable scope for local variation in the pattern of service provision.

Among devolutionists, there are still differences on the precise degree of autonomy which is desirable and on the direction in which Scottish politics might develop. There is, however, a general rejection of the scenario-building found on the anti-devolutionist side, in which confident assertions are made about the inevitability of various patterns of development. Devolutionists point out that most countries in the world have subordinate tiers of government and that the disintegration of states is usually based on serious underlying cultural, ethnic or economic differences and not on purely institutional mechanics. If the UK is headed for disintegration because of the divergence of English and Scottish demands, then devolution will at most influence the pace and form of the process.

While the devolution process has started in Scotland, few devolutionists would wish to see it end there. Tam Dalyell has posed devolutionists the 'West Lothian question', asking why he, as a Scottish MP, should be able to vote on English matters, while

CONCLUSION193

English MPs cannot vote on Scottish affairs. For the devolutionist, this is a good question but addressed to the wrong people. Given that the Labour Party has conceded Scottish demand for devolution, English politicians must consider whether they would prefer to put up with an unbalanced constitution or to demand devolution for themselves. So the West Lothian question can become an argument in favour of English devolution. English politicians may reject this in favour of the centralised state, but their right to deny devolution to Scotland simply because they do not want it for themselves is questionable.

Devolutionists would tend to resolve the problem by advocating regional devolution for England. Here, however, is a problem. England has never had the same system of administration as Scotland. Both the pattern and the level of public service provision have differed historically. Further, public demands differ from those in Scotland, where national consciousness is a major factor. Therefore, it may not be possible to provide identical systems of government for England and Scotland in the future.

Nevertheless, the party must formulate a clear *attitude* to demands for regional autonomy, so that its reactions to them will be, if not identical, at least consistent. It must further address itself to the question of the territorial distribution of resources by formulating principles of territorial justice.[3] Devolution has not created the issue of territorial distribution. It has merely brought to public attention an issue which has been unjustifiably neglected in the past. Finally, the party must formulate principles of what constitute the rights of UK citizens *vis à vis* the public authorities. The Stormont experience shows that such overriding rights must accompany devolution, but, in this case too, devolution has merely brought into focus an issue which the party already ought to have considered.

The party cannot escape these questions simply by pretending that there are no distinctive territorial or national questions. It has already admitted their existence in relation to the EEC. In its reaction to UK entry into the EEC, the majority of the Labour Party took a British nationalist line, and, since entry, have argued that governments should strive to protect 'British oil' and 'British fish' instead of sharing them with other members of the Community. The relationship between the devolution issue and UK membership of the EEC has received little attention in the party since the defection of Jim Sillars, but is likely to become important in the future. In particular, the party will have to formulate a convincing view on the question of whether Scotland should become an independent member of the EEC. Given the similarities between the arguments of Scottish nationalists and many British anti-Marketeers, this question could be very embarrassing indeed.

So Scottish nationalism cannot be attacked simply on internationalist grounds. Indeed, if UK politics should be characterised by further bouts of chauvinism and racialism, it may be that it will be the Scottish nationalists who will have the more cosmopolitan outlook. There is, therefore, a clear duty on those who advocate a unitary British state outside the EEC to justify their support for that state in terms of their general ideology.

So the question of the territorial distribution of power must be approached free of the unionist shibboleths which have moulded the debate since the 1920s. Power should be located where it can most effectively be exercised, in order to attain Labour's objectives and render government more accountable. This is likely to point to further devolution upwards – although not necessarily to the EEC as at present constituted – and downwards, to the component parts of the UK.

III.   THE ANTI-DEVOLUTIONIST VIEW

The anti-devolutionists disagree about the nature of Scottish nationalism. They follow that tradition in the labour movement which sees nationalism in itself as a form the real content of which is provided by social movements radically differing in their objectives according to place and time. Modern Scottish nationalism, far from being an expression of profoundly held national aspirations of the Scottish people, is seen as a protest movement, based on economic grievances. The core of nationalist ideologues in the SNP has succeeded in providing an electoral focus for mass dissatisfaction with the way in which successive governments, including Labour governments, have failed to cope with worsening economic problems from the mid 1960s onwards. With the discovery of North Sea oil, nationalism has been boosted by the illusion that the benefits of the oil could be appropriated for Scotland without any concomitant loss of the benefits of economic unity in the UK.

From this premiss, anti-devolutionists argue that Labour must tackle the economic problems which are at the root of the decline in Labour electoral support and the growth of the SNP. Legislative devolution for Scotland has been presented as a measure to extend democracy and to satisfy legitimate national aspirations of the Scots people. In reality it is a concession to the nationalist argument that the social and economic problems of Scotland can be tackled by greater political independence. Whatever the rationalisations put forward by the Labour Government, the political movement which forced this concession was based on this argument, and Scottish devolutionists now expect a devolved assembly, if established, to come to grips with the problems of unemployment, bad housing and so forth.

Because it would inevitably be unable to control the underlying development of the economy, an assembly would fail to fulfil these hopes. But its failure would become the basis for assembly politicians – and not only those in the SNP – to blame central government and demand that the process of devolution be taken to its logical conclusion: full independence. Money, or the allocation of centrally raised resources through the block-grant, would be the main source of conflict. Every school or housing project turned down by the assembly would become an argument for a larger block grant or for control of the oil revenues. The English regional backlash would have a much clearer focus of opposition than at present, and Scotland would thus have *more* difficulty in getting a good deal from the Exchequer at the very time that pressure was building up within Scotland for an even better deal. The project of independence would thus be fuelled by the development of national antagonism between Scotland and England. Secondly, conflict between the Edinburgh and Westminster legislatures and govern- ments would arise whenever the same party could not control both bodies. In view of the SNP's likely place in a Scottish assembly, and the fact that elections would be held at different times for the two parliaments, there would more often than not be an inherent party conflict between Edinburgh and Westminster. Nationalism would become a weapon for the minority party at Westminster, whenever it managed to gain a majority in the Scottish assembly. The economic unity of the country would be placed under severe strain by the conflict of policies. Thirdly, Scottish representation at Westminster could not long survive the establishment of an assembly. Aside from the over-representation, which would become more intolerable to other regions, the very fact that Scottish MPs would be able to vote at Westminster on matters affecting England (housing, education, and so on), while for their own Scottish constituencies these matters would be the preserve of a purely Scottish assembly, would cause massive English resentment. This problem, the 'West Lothian question' raised by Tam Dalyell, has found no satisfactory answer from the proponents of devolution.

For all these reasons, anti-devolutionists agree with the view, shared by many nationalists, that, if a legislative assembly were to be established, the road to separation would be open. As Donald Stewart, Parliamentary leader of the SNP, put it, the process of getting a legislative assembly in Edinburgh is like heaving a huge boulder to the top of a hill. Once you have reached the top, it will run downhill under its own momentum – towards independence. Of course, a legislative assembly does not make independence any more viable as an option for a country which is economically an integral part of the United Kingdom. Therefore, to talk of the inevitability of independence is too pessimistic. However, anti-devolutionists would rather fight the battle against the economics of separation from the forward trenches of a unified political state, and not have to put up a last-ditch stand in a society split by national antagonism, territorial squabbling over resources, and against a legislative parliament bent on attaining full sovereignty in Scotland. The prospect of continued economic recession does not inspire confidence in the greater ability of the labour movement to preserve national wage bargaining and uniform regulation of the economy and the public sector in 1984 as compared with 1979.

The March 1979 referendum, with its slender majority for implementation of legislative devolution, and its failure to achieve the threshold of 40 per cent of the electorate in favour, re-opened the whole issue of devolution and provided an opportunity for the labour movement to review its commitment to devolution, at least in the form proposed in the legislation.

What then is the alternative? Anti-devolutionists have argued that they do not oppose devolution as such, but that it must be considered on its own merits and introduced all round in a uniform and equitable manner, if at all. However, they have been reluctant to argue the case for devolution in England purely as a way of preventing the Scots from getting an unfair advantage or of achieving constitutional balance. The prospects for devolution outside Scotland are poor. In Wales the project has been decisively rejected by a four to one vote in the 1979 referendum, while in most regions of England there is little sense of regional identity.

In 1978 the Labour Party conducted extensive consultations

throughout its English regions to ascertain the response to its proposed scheme of regional assemblies in England. Mostly the proposals were seen as an opportunity to return powers to the large urban councils, where Labour can hold control, and to ditch the Tory county councils. In the North East and North West there is a greater consciousness of the need to fight for the region's share of resources, to combat industrial and social decline, but little positive enthusiasm for an assembly, unless the Scots have one. With no consensus on the need for regional government, the plans were thus put into cold storage. The Stormont model, once used in Scotland as an argument *for* Home rule, is now seen as an argument against devolution, and, although the Government incessantly attempts to bring about some form of devolved power-sharing in Ulster, in practice direct rule is now well entrenched and the enlargement of Northern Ireland's representation at Westminster is likely to reinforce the trends towards integration. Labour has even begun to consider, albeit very tentatively, the possibility of organising directly in Ulster. Far from beginning a process of all-round devolution, a Scottish Assembly would therefore be an anomaly in a state otherwise tending towards greater unity.

Britain's entry into the EEC has been accompanied by severe political storms every time that the requirements of greater economic unity involve a measure of political integration. However, the trend is still towards a gradual political integration in the EEC, albeit largely unwilling, and the resurrection of a Scottish legislature is in a different order of narrow nationalism than the resistance of an established nation-state which is reluctantly sacrificing some of its sovereignty.

The anti-devolutionists therefore have to come up with a different strategy for Labour to retain and enlarge its electoral base in Scotland. No single policy has been put forward, because left and right of the movement may agree on the need to tackle the root economic causes of dissatisfaction, but cannot agree on the solution. The problem of bureaucracy in the public sector is a real one, but it has been argued on the left that democracy on an industrial basis, i.e. workers' control through the unions, is far more effective as a means of extending democratic control than is establishing elected regional authorities to which no corresponding organisation in the labour movement can relate. It would be pointless here to rehearse the arguments over broad economic strategy which must be fought out within the labour movement. However, a point with great insight made by William Elger, first full-time Secretary of the STUC, at the time of the election of the first minority Labour government in 1924, sums up the nature of the problem: a people would always judge a political administration by the extent to which it was effective in providing the goods and services they were entitled to expect; thus a Labour government could never be politically successful until such time as the labour movement was ready to assume responsibility for the running of industry, in order to reorganise the economy in a successful way.

It may seem that we are little closer to Elger's objective in 1979 than in 1924. Certainly the development of trade union power and responsibility has not yet enabled a Labour government to avoid suffering the electoral consequences of administering a capitalist system. Thus, in the short run, a confrontation with Scottish nationalism, as demanded by the anti-devolutionists, involved a defence of the status quo, however unappealing, as being preferable to the petty territorialism which nationalism would engender. Anti-devolutionists argue that Scots nationalism has gained most of its political credibility from the concessions made by Labour governments. The notion that oil off the Scottish coast entitles the Scots to a greater share of national resources without any corresponding loss of the benefits of economic union is in itself such a shaky illusion that the SNP bubble is always liable to burst at the first real clash. The status quo therefore *is* an option, and must be defended against nationalism, whereas a legislative assembly may tempt the Scots towards an action replay of the Darien disaster.

The economy of Britain is more than ever integrated, and this is a fact recognised both by capital, which has opposed devolution, and by labour, which has moved historically towards increasing unity. Scottish labour is part and parcel of British labour and wants to remain so, retaining national collective bargaining and fighting for common economic and social objectives. This existing unity is part of the status quo, which can become a powerful basis for defeating the illusory claims of nationalism. However, the Labour Government's failure to obtain convincing support in Scotland for its strategy of compromise with nationalism reflected the weakness of the Government and the division of the movement in general as much as the weakness of this particular strategy. The development of a stronger policy towards Scottish nationalism is therefore one aspect of the need for the labour movement to rebuild a united approach to Britain's economic crisis.

IV. AN OPEN QUESTION

The indecisive result of the March 1979 referendum and the result of the subsequent General Election, which saw the Labour Party slightly strengthen its hold in Scotland while the Conservatives gained a decisive victory in the UK as a whole, have left many questions unanswered. The decline of the SNP and Labour's success in winning 44 seats may seem, in some respects, to have put Scottish politics back to the pre-1974 position. However, its continued historically low share of the poll and the survival of the Nationalists as a political force leave it little room for manoeuvre. The measures of the Conservative Government, involving cutbacks in public spending – on which Scotland is particularly dependent – are likely to lead to mid-term unpopularity. Labour, as the leading party in Scotland, will be expected to take the lead in opposition to such measures. To attack the Conservative Government on the ground that it lacks a Scottish mandate may prove a strong temptation. Labour could use its strength in Scotland and, to a lesser extent, in the north of England, to become more of a party of territorial defence. This would carry two dangers. It would enhance the credibility of the nationalist case as, so we have suggested, happened in the 1960s and 1970s. It would also strain yet further the unity of the UK labour movement. On the other hand, not to adopt a strategy of territorial defence could be to allow the Nationalists the opportunity to make another comeback. Confronted with another revival of Scottish nationalism, Labour would once again face a choice between centralisation and decentralisation. If the policy of devolution is no longer available as a means of compromising the issue, the choice may be a stark one. Whichever road the movement takes, however, its policy, to be convincing, will have to be more clearly articulated and related to the movement's overall objectives and strategy. If Labour were to fail to link Scottish demands with that overall strategy, we could indeed witness the break-up of Britain.

Notes

BSSLH = *Bulletin of the Society for the Study of Labour History*; NLS = *National Library of Scotland*; SLHSJ = *Scottish Labour History Society Journal*.

CHAPTER 1

1. Quoted in E. Kedourie, *Nationalism* (London: Hutchinson, 1966) p. 108.
2. A. D. Smith (ed.), *Nationalist Movements* (London: Macmillan, 1976) p. 24.
3. E. Hobsbawm, *The Age of Revolution* (London: Weidenfeld and Nicolson, 1962) p. 73.
4. Ibid.
5. Hobsbawm, *The Age of Revolution*.
6. Ibid.
7. K. Marx and F. Engels, *The Revolutions of 1848*, in *Political Writings*, ed. O. Fernbach, vol. 1 (London: Allen Lane, 1973).
8. J. S. Mill, *Representative Government*; quoted in R. Coupland, *Welsh and Scottish Nationalism* (London: Collins, 1954) Introduction.
9. Quoted ibid.
10. S. M. Lipset and S. Rokkan, *Party Systems and Voter Alignments* (New York: Free Press, 1967) Introduction.
11. See M. Esman, *Ethnic Conflict in the Western World* (Ithaca, NY: Cornell University Press, 1978).
12. Lipset and Rokkan, *Party Systems*. Empirical evidence for this view came from studies such as D. Butler and D. Stokes, *Political Change in Britain* (London: Macmillan, 1969).
13. T. Nairn, *The Break-up of Britain* (London: New Left Books, 1977).
14. A. Mitchell, *Labour in Irish Politics, 1890–1930* (Dublin: Irish University Press, 1974) p. 107.
15. R. Kee, *The Bold Fenian Men*, vol. 2 of *The Green Flag*, (London: Quartet 1976) pt 2, ch. 2.
16. Mitchell, *Labour in Irish Politics*.
17. O. Bauer, *Die Nationalitatenfrage und die Sozialdemokratie* (Vienna, 1907) p. 302.
18. Ibid., p. 312.
19. H. Pelling, *A History of British Trade Unionism*, 2nd ed. (Harmondsworth: Penguin, 1976) p. 13.
20. S. and B. Webb, *The History of Trade Unionism*, 2nd ed. (London: Longman, 1920) p. 45.
21. Ibid., pp. 45–6.
22. S. Webb and B. Webb, *Industrial Democracy* (London: Kelly, Baker and Taylor, 1897) p. 77.

23. Ibid., p. 79.
24. Ibid., p. 82.
25. Ibid.
26. M. Hechter, *Internal Colonialism. The Celtic Fringe in British National Development, 1536–1966* (London: Routledge and Kegan Paul, 1975).
27. F. Bealey, *The Social and Political Thought of the British Labour Party* (London: Weidenfeld and Nicolson, 1970) Introduction.
28. Ibid.
29. Ibid.
30. G. Checkland, *The Upas Tree. Glasgow 1875–1975* (Glasgow: University of Glasgow Press, 1977) pp. 28–9.
31. This is a constant theme in the columns of the Labour paper *Forward*.
32. A. Sancton, 'British Socialist Theory, the Division of Power by Area', *Political Studies*, xxiv, no. 2 (1976).
33. V. I. Lenin, *Critical Remarks on the National Question and The Right of Nations to Self-Determination* (Moscow: Progress Publishers, 1971) p. 49.
34. Ibid., p. 83.

CHAPTER 2

1. Hechter, *Internal Colonialism*, pp. 93, 130.
2. J. Hunter, *The Making of the Crofting Community* (Edinburgh: John Donald, 1977) ch. 4.
3. Ibid., pp. 119–20.
4. W. Wolfe, *Scotland Lives* (Edinburgh: Reprographia, 1973), p. 150.
5. P. Beresford Ellis and S. MacA'Ghobhainn, *The Scottish Insurrection of 1820* (London: Gollancz, 1970).
6. P. Holt, Review of Ellis and MacA'Ghobhainn, *The Scottish Insurrection*, in *SLHSJ*, no. 3 (Nov 1970).
7. R. Coupland, *Welsh and Scottish Nationalism*.
8. W. H. Marwick, *Short History of Labour in Scotland* (Edinburgh: Chambers, 1967) pp. 16ff.
9. A. Wilson, *The Chartist Movement in Scotland* (Manchester: Manchester University Press, 1970).
10. W. H. Fraser, review of I. MacDougall (ed), *The Minutes of Edinburgh Trades Council, 1859–1873*, in *BSSLH*, no. 19 (1969) p. 37. and W. H. Fraser, 'Scottish Trades Councils in the Nineteenth Century', *BSSLH*, no. 14 (1967) p. 11.
11. H. J. Hanham, *Scottish Nationalism* (London: Faber, 1969) pp. 73, 77.
12. W. Ferguson, *Scotland: 1689 to the Present*, vol. iv of *The Edinburgh History of Scotland*, 2nd ed. (Edinburgh: Oliver and Boyd, 1975) pp. 326–7.
13. Hunter, *The Making of the Crofting Community*, p. 104.
14. J. G. Kellas, *Modern Scotland* (London: Pall Mall, 1968) p. 62.
15. F. Reid, 'Keir Hardie's Conversion to Socialism' in A. Briggs and J. Saville (eds), *Essays in Labour History*, vol. 2 (London: Macmillan, 1960) p. 31.
16. Hanham, *Scottish Nationalism*, p. 26.
17. Morrison Davidson, *Leaves from the Book of Scots* (Glasgow: Scottish Secretariat, n.d.) p. 42.
18. D. N. Mackay, in *Forward*, 23 Nov 1912.

19. *Forward*, 27 Oct 1906.
20. *Forward*, 8 July 1911.
21. Quoted in Coupland, *Welsh and Scottish Nationalism*, pt 6, ch. 7.
22. Hanham, *Scottish Nationalism*, p. 22.
23. *H C Deb.*, vol. 54 (1898), col. 1732.
24. D. J. Robertson, 'Wages', in A. K. Cairncross (ed.), *The Scottish Economy* (Cambridge: Cambridge University Press, 1951) pp. 150, 153.
25. D. H. Hunt, *Regional Wage Variations in Britain, 1850–1914* (Oxford: Clarendon Press, 1973) pp. 47–56.
26. Ibid., p. 358.
27. Ibid., p. 324.
28. Ibid., pp. 333, 335.
29. Marwick, *Labour in Scotland*, pp. 24ff.
30. Official Report, TUC, Edinburgh, 25–28 Apr 1900, pp. 24–6.
31. Hunt, *Regional Wage Variations*, pp. 345–7.
32. Marwick, *Labour in Scotland*, pp. 77–83.
33. Quoted in J. Kellas and P. Fotheringham, 'The Political Behaviour of the Working Class in Scotland', in A. Maclaren (ed.), *Social Class in Scotland* (Edinburgh: John Donald, 1976).
34. D. Harrison, 'STUC-Origins far from Nationalist', *Seven Days*, May 1978, p. 2.
35. STUC, Official Report, Mar 1897, p. 22; Apr 1898, pp. 19ff.
36. STUC, Official Report, Apr 1898, p. 31; Apr 1911, pp. 26, 41.
37. STUC, Official Report, Apr 1907, p. 20.
38. Harrison, in *Seven Days*, May 1978, p. 2.
39. STUC Parliamentary Committee Minute Book, 19 Dec 1908. Punctuation as original.
40. Glasgow Trades Council Minute Book, 11 and 18 Mar 1914.
41. Hunter, *The Making of the Crofting Community*.
42. *Highlander*, 24 June 1876; quoted in J. Hunter, 'The Gaelic Connection: Highlands, Ireland and Nationalism, 1873–1922', *Scottish Historical Review*, 59 (1975) 184.
43. Ibid.
44. Resolution adopted by the Glendale Branch of the Highland Land League: *Oban Times*, 19 Nov 1887; quoted by Hunter, in *Scottish Historical Review*, 59, 188.
45. *Forward*, 13 Aug 1910; Quoted in *Crann-tara*, no. 1 (Winter 1977) p. 13.
46. L. Thompson, *The Enthusiasts: A Biography of John and Katharine Bruce Glasier* (London: Gollancz, 1971) p. 35.
47. Reid, in Briggs and Saville, *Essays in Labour History*, vol. 2.
48. K. D. Buckley, *Trade Unionism in Aberdeen, 1878–1900* (Aberdeen: Aberdeen University Press, 1955) p. 93.
49. J. G. Kellas, 'Highland Migration to Glasgow and the origin of the Scottish Labour Movement', *BSSLH*, no. 12 (1966) p. 10.
50. A. Howkins, 'Edwardian Liberalism and Industrial Unrest: A Class View of the Decline of Liberalism', *History Workshop Journal*, no. 4 (Autumn 1977).
51. J. Saville, 'Trade Councils and the Labour Movement to 1900', *BSSLH*, no. 14 (1967) p. 29.
52. W. H. Fraser, 'Scottish Trades Councils in the Nineteenth Century', ibid., p. 11.

53. Buckley, *Trade Unionism in Aberdeen*, pp. 99ff.
54. Reid, in Briggs and Saville, *Essays in Labour History*, vol. 2.
55. *The Miner*, Apr 1887; quoted ibid.
56. H. Pelling, *The Origins of the Labour Party* (London: Macmillan, 1954) p. 65.
57. I. McLean, *Keir Hardie* (Harmondsworth: Penguin, 1975) p. 31.
58. Ibid., p. 30.
59. *The Miner*, Sep 1888; quoted in Pelling, *Origins of the Labour Party*, p. 71.
60. D. Lowe, *Souvenirs of Scottish Labour* (Glasgow: Holmes, 1919).
61. J. MacCormick, *The Flag in the Wind* (London: Gollancz, 1955) p. 15.
62. Buckley, *Trade Unionism in Aberdeen*, p. 93.
63. McLean, *Keir Hardie*, pp. 3–4.
64. *Forward*, 9 Sep 1911.
65. Buckley, *Trade Unionism in Aberdeen*, pp. 137–8.
66. Marwick, *Labour in Scotland*, pp. 70–1.
67. Aberdeen Trades Council Minutes, 28 Jan 1893; quoted in Buckley, *Trade Unionism in Aberdeen*, pp. 111, 162.
68. *Report of the First Annual Conference of the Scottish Workers' Parliamentary Elections Committee* (Glasgow, 5 Jan 1901).
69. F. Bealey and H. Pelling, *Labour and Politics, 1900–1906* (London: Macmillan, 1958) appendix B, pp. 293–7.
70. *Forward*, 4 Feb 1909.
71. STUC, Official Report, Apr 1912, p. 40.
72. Hunter, *The Making of the Crofting Community*, ch. 10.
73. Hunter, in *Scottish Historical Review*, 59.
74. *Forward*, 22 May 1908.
75. T. Johnston, *Memories* (London: Collins, 1952) p. 33.

CHAPTER 3

1. Labour Party Scottish Council, *Annual Report* 1919.
2. STUC Annual Reports.
3. This account is based on SHRA records, NLS.
4. Letter to *Glasgow Evening Citizen*, 29 Sep 1926; in Scottish Secretariat MSS., NLS.
5. *John O'Groats Journal*, 14 Feb 1922; in Scottish Secretariat MSS., NLS.
6. Labour Party Scottish Council, Executive Minutes, 13 Jan 1919.
7. SHRA records, NLS.
8. B. Lenman, *An Economic History of Modern Scotland* (London: Batsford, 1977) p. 211.
9. STUC, *Annual Report* 1919.
10. Hunter, in *Scottish Historical Review*, 59, 199.
11. For example, I. Maclean, 'Red Clydeside 1915–1919', in J. Stevenson and R. Quinault (eds), *Popular Protest and Public Order* (London: Allen and Unwin, 1974); W. Kendall, *The Revolutionary Movement in Britain, 1900–21* (London: Weidenfeld and Nicolson, 1969) p. 141.
12. J. Craigen, 'The Scottish Trade Union Congress (1897–1973) – A Study of a Pressure Group' (unpublished M Litt. thesis, Heriot-Watt University, Edinburgh, 1974).

13. STUC, *Annual Report* 1917.
14. STUC, *Annual Report* 1918.
15. Hechter, *Internal Colonialism*, pp. 283–4.
16. Hunter, in *Scottish Historical Review*, 59, 204.
17. *Forward*, 9 Oct 1909.
18. HLL, *Annual Report* 1916.
19. *Scottish Review*, Spring 1918, pp. 146–7.
20. Ibid., Autumn 1918, p. 321.
21. J. Lucas, 'Co-operation in Scotland' (unpublished MA thesis, Manchester, 1920) pp. 66, 73.
22. Labour Party Archives (Transport House), LP/SAC/14/285.
23. *Scottish Review*, Summer 1918, p. 190.
24. Lucas, 'Co-operation in Scotland', p. 72.
25. *Scottish Review*, Summer 1919, p. 158.
26. Lucas, 'Co-operation in Scotland'; SCWS, *Annual* 1896, p. 330.
27. STUC, *Annual Report* 1923.
28. *Glasgow Herald*, undated cutting in Scottish Secretariat MSS., NLS.
29. *Scotsman*, 27 Aug 1923.
30. *Glasgow Evening Citizen*, 27 Aug 1923; in Scottish Secretariat MSS., NLS.
31. Labour Party Scottish Council, *Annual Report* 1923.
32. Ibid.
33. Quoted in G. McAllister, *James Maxton: Portrait of a Rebel* (London: Murray, 1935) p. 152.
34. *HC Deb.*, vol. 173, 9 May 1924.
35. *Cabinet Conclusions*, 14 May 1924, CAB. 31 (24) 2; 30 May 1924, CAB. 35 (24) 7.
36. Ibid., 4 June 1924, CAB. 36 (24) 2.
37. Lenman, *Economic History of Modern Scotland*, pp. 212–13.
38. Ibid., p. 214.
39. Ferguson, *Scotland: 1689 to the Present*, p. 362.
40. Craigen, 'The STUC'.
41. J. Hinton and R. Hyman, *Trade Unions and Revolution: the Industrial Politics of the Early British Communist Party* (London: Pluto, 1975) p. 14.
42. William Diack, 'Scottish Trade Unionists and Industrial Unrest', *Scottish Review*, Autumn 1917. The details of wage levels and so on are also taken from this article.
43. Labour Party Scottish Advisory Council, *Annual Report* 1915.
44. Robertson, in Cairncross, *The Scottish Economy*.
45. STUC, *Annual Report* 1923.
46. Ibid.
47. STUC, *Annual Report* 1921.
48. R. Page Arnot, *A History of the Scottish Miners* (London: Allen and Unwin, 1955).
49. *Daily Record*, 11 Sep 1926; in Scottish Secretariat MSS., NLS.
50. *Glasgow Herald*, 17 Feb 1921.
51. *Bulletin*, 11 July 1924; in Scottish Secretariat MSS., NLS.
52. Railway Clerks' Association, Scottish Advisory Council records, NLS.
53. *Westminster Chronicle*, 13 Jan 1928; in Scottish Secretariat MSS., NLS.
54. *Scotsman*, 18 Apr 1931.

55. STUC, *Annual Report* 1921.
56. STUC, *Annual Report* 1925.
57. STUC, 1930.
58. TUC held in Glasgow, 1919.
59. STUC, *Annual Report* 1927, from which the rest of this account is drawn.
60. Hinton and Hyman, *Trade Unions and Revolution*, p. 47. The quotation is from NMM, *Is Trade Unionism Played Out* (Dec 1926).
61. *Daily Record*, 14 Jan 1929.
62. This account draws on National Convention records, in Scottish Secretariat MSS., NLS.
63. *HC Deb.*, vol. 206, cols 865–78, 13 May 1927.
64. Johnston, *Memories*, p. 66; *Sunday Times*, 10 Feb 1949.
65. STUC General Council Minutes :926–7, 1927–8.
66. *Scottish Home Rule*, vol. 3, no. 8 (Feb 1923).
67. Ibid., vol. 6, no. 4 (Oct 1925).
68. Ibid., vol. 8, no. 11 (May 1928). Thus, the SHRA did not, as suggested in some accounts (e.g. those of Hanham and of Webb), fuse with other nationalist organisations.
69. Labour Party Scottish Council, Executive Minutes, 21 May 1928.
70. *Scots Observer*, 15 Sep 1928; in Scottish Secretariat MSS., 14 Mar 1929, NLS.
71. *Aberdeen Press and Journal*, 14 Mar 1929; in Scottish Secretariat MSS., NLS.
72. *Daily Record*, 9 Jan 1929.
73. *Daily Record*, 11 July 1929.
74. *Glasgow Herald*, 11 July 1930.

CHAPTER 4

1. J. A. Bowie, *The Future of Scotland* (Edinburgh: Chambers, 1939).
2. G. M. Thomson, *Scotland that Distressed Area* (Edinburgh: Porpoise Press, 1935).
3. A. O. Campbell, 'Changes in Scottish Incomes, 1924–49', *Economic Journal*, June 1955, 226–40.
4. Ibid.
5. Thomson, *Scotland that Distressed Area*.
6. T. L. Johnston, *Structure and Growth of the Scottish Economy* (London and Glasgow: Collins, 1971).
7. Thomson, *Scotland that Distressed Area*.
8. C. A. Oakley, *Scottish Industry Today* (Edinburgh: Murray Press, 1937) p. 257.
9. Ibid., p. 244.
10. Craigen, 'The STUC'.
11. Bealey, *Social and Political Thought of the British Labour Party*.
12. C. L. Mowat, *Britain between the Wars, 1918–1940* (London: Methuen, 1968) pp. 462–3.
13. Johnston, *Memories*, p. 66.
14. Ibid.
15. *Scotsman*, 18 Apr 1931; in Scottish Secretariat MSS., NLS.
16. *Greenock Telegraph*, 16 Apr 1931; in Scottish Secretariat MSS., NLS.
17. For example, Ramsay MacDonald, *Labour and the Empire* (London: Allen, 1907).

206   LABOUR AND SCOTTISH NATIONALISM

18. R. McLaughlan, 'Aspects of Nationalism', in N. MacCormick (ed.), *The Scottish Debate* (London: Oxford University Press, 1970).
19. Nairn, *The Break-up of Britain.*
20. *New Leader*, 1 July 1932; in Scottish Secretariat MSS., NLS.
21. Ibid., 29 Aug 1942; in Scottish Secretariat MSS., NLS.
22. J. G. Kellas, *Modern Scotland. The Nation since 1870* (London: Pall Mall, 1968) p. 134.
23. Ferguson, *Scotland: 1689 to the Present*, p. 377.
24. McAllister, *James Maxton.*
25. *Daily Record*, 7 Apr 1931.
26. *Forward*, 27 July 1931.
27. Nairn, *The Break-up of Britain.*
28. Ferguson, *Scotland: 1689 to the Present.*
29. *Forward Scotland*, Sep 1964.
30. Nairn, *The Break-up of Britain*, p. 165.
31. Ibid., p. 95.
32. Mowat, *Britain between the Wars.*
33. F. W. S. Craig, *British Parliamentary Election Results 1918–1949* (Chichester: Political Reference Publications, 1969).
34. Ibid. The turnout was 46·8 per cent.
35. STUC, *Annual Report 1931.*
36. MacCormick, *Flag in the Wind.*
37. 'The present situation in Britain and the tasks of the Party', resolution of the Central Committee, CPGB, Mar 1930, in *Communist Review*, May 1930.
38. P. Kerrigan, 'The Scottish District's Immediate Tasks', ibid., Nov–Dec 1931.
39. W. Gallacher, 'The Dumbarton By-Election', ibid., May 1932.
40. Helen Crawfurd, 'The Scottish National Movement', ibid., Feb 1933.
41. Oliver Bell, 'The Scottish National Movement', ibid., Apr 1933.
42. Ted Bramley, 'Our Propaganda. The Problem as I See It', *Discussion*, Oct 1937, 8.
43. 'Problems of Propaganda in South Wales', *Discussion*, Dec 1937, 7.
44. CPGB, 14th Congress, 1937, p. 165.
45. H. McShane and J. Smith, *Harry McShane: No Mean Fighter* (London: Pluto, 1978).
46. Ibid.
47. Campbell, in *Economic Journal*, June 1955, 232.
48. Bowie, *The Future of Scotland.*
49. Oakley, *Scottish Industry Today*, pp. 244, 257.
50. Mowat, *Britain between the Wars*, p. 458.
51. For example, Bowie, *The Future of Scotland.*
52. *Glasgow Herald*, 9 Mar 1937.
53. Labour Council for Scottish Self-Government, *Scotland and Westminster: An Exposure of London Domination and a Plan for Scottish Socialist Government*, compiled by Oliver Brown (Glasgow, 1940).
54. C. Harvie, 'Scottish Nationalism and the Second World War', unpublished paper.
55. With exceptions such as Thomson, *Scotland that Distressed Area.*
56. Johnston, *Memories*, p. 167.
57. Harvie, 'Scottish Nationalism and the Second World War'.

58. Ibid.
59. Ibid.
60. Labour Party Scottish Council, Executive Minutes, 23 Aug 1941.
61. R. Muirhead papers, NLS.
62. *Forward*, 22 Oct 1949.
63. Convention papers, NLS.
64. *Report of Proceedings*, Scottish National Association, NLS.
65. Quoted in A. C. Turner, *Scottish Home Rule* (Glasgow 1952).
66. Note in Labour Party Scottish Council, Executive Minute Book, 1944.
67. *Scots Independent*, Sep 1940.
68. It did not endorse it either. After a brief debate, the previous question had been moved and carried.
69. *Forward*, 9 Oct 1948.
70. J. Gollan, *Scottish Prospect* (Glasgow: Caledonian, 1948).
71. *Scottish Affairs*, a memorandum presented by the Scottish Committee of the Communist Party to the Royal Commission, 1 Jan 1953.
72. *Daily Worker*, 14 Apr 1957; in Scottish Secretariat MSS., NLS.
73. *Weekly Scotsman*, 23 Nov 1957; in Scottish Secretariat MSS., NLS.
74. *Forward*, 23 Nov 1948.
75. G. McCrone, *Scotland's Economic Progress 1951–1960. A Study in Regional Accounting* (London: Allen and Unwin, 1965) pp. 48–9.
76. Ibid., pp. 48–9.
77. Ibid., pp. 28–9.

CHAPTER 5

1. M. J. Keating, 'The Role of the Scottish MP' (unpublished Ph.D thesis, Council for National Academic Awards, 1975).
2. J. G. Kellas, *The Scottish Political System* (London: Cambridge University Press, 1973) p. 61.
3. Scottish Office memorandum to the Select Committee on Scottish Affairs, Apr 1969.
4. M. J. Keating, 'Administrative Devolution in Practice: The Secretary of State for Scotland and the Scottish Office', *Public Administration*, 54, (1976) 133–45.
5. M. J. Keating, 'Parliamentary Behaviour as a Test of Scottish Integration into the UK', *Legislative Studies Quarterly*, 111, no. 3 (1978) 409–30.
6. M. J. Keating, *A Test of Political Integration into the UK*, Studies in Public Policy no. 6, University of Strathclyde (Glasgow, 1977).
7. R. Crossman, *Diaries of a Cabinet Minister*, vol. 3 (London: Hamish Hamilton, 1977). Crossman wrote, 'Willie Ross and his friends accuse the Scottish Nationalists of separatism but what Willie himself actually likes is to keep Scottish business absolutely privy from English business.'
8. Kellas, *The Scottish Political System*.
9. Crossman, *Diaries*, vol. 3, p. 82.
10. Ibid., p. 106.
11. Commission on the Constitution, *Minutes of Evidence, IV: Scotland* (London: HMSO, 1971) p. 29.
12. Ibid., p. 12.

13. STUC, *Annual Report* 1968.
14. Commission on the Constitution, *Minutes of Evidence, IV: Scotland*, p. 121.
15. HC Deb., vol. 827, col. 978, 6 Dec 1971.
16. Ibid.
17. M.J. Keating, 'The Scottish Local Government Bill', *Local Government Studies*, Jan 1975.
18. *Glasgow Herald*, Feb 1972.
19. Ibid.
20. Labour Party Scottish Council, Executive Minutes, 10 Feb 1973.
21. *Scotsman*, 10 July 1973.
22. *Glasgow Herald*, 10 July 1973.
23. *Scotland and the UK* (Glasgow: Labour Party Scottish Council, 1973).
24. The section on the select committee had originally been drafted by Michael Keating to show its inadequacy as a substitute for devolution!
25. *Scotland and the National Enterprises Board* (Glasgow: Labour Party Scottish Council, 1973).
26. *Glasgow Herald*, 11 Mar 1973.
27. See *Labour Party Manifesto for Scotland* (Glasgow: Labour Party Scottish Council, 1974).
28. Labour's pollsters even tried to gauge local feeling within the party. Their director, Bob Worcester of MORI, made a clandestine trip to Glasgow in the summer, posing as a visiting American sociologist. He was put in touch with Michael Keating, who was secretary of Kelvingrove Constituency Labour Party and, over copious supplies of beer and sandwiches, staged a recorded discussion with a sample of activists. Unfortunately, because of the short notice, the sample consisted of those members who were on the telephone, lacked prior engagements and were interested in talking to American sociologists, and was dominated by academics with English accents.
29. *HC Deb.*, vol. 958, col. 83, 12 Mar 1974. Sheldon's pledge was given on 20 Mar 1974: 'My rt. Hon friend the Prime Minister has stated clearly that we intend to publish a white paper on this subject and subsequently a Bill will be brought before the House' – *HC Deb.*, vol. 959, cols 1194–5.
30. T. Dalyell, *Devolution: The End of Britain?* (London: Jonathan Cape, 1977) p. 109.
31. *Glasgow Herald*, 19 Aug 1974.
32. *Public Opinion Digest*, 2 Aug 1974.
33. Dalyell, *Devolution*, p. 109.
34. H. Drucker, *Breakaway: The Scottish Labour Party* (Edinburgh: Edinburgh University Student Publications Board, 1978) p. 37.
35. Dalyell, *Devolution*, p. 110.
36. W. Miller, 'What Was the Profit in Following the Crowd?' (paper presented at Political Studies Association conference, University of Warwick, 1978) p. 29.
37. Ibid.
38. *Our Changing Democracy*, Cmnd. 6348 (London: HMSO, 1975) p. 24.
39. Drucker, *Breakaway*.
40. *The Times*, 4 Mar 1976.
41. Ibid.

CHAPTER 6

1. Quoted in D. Heald, *Making Devolution Work*, Young Fabian pamphlet no. 43 (London: Fabian Society, 1976) p. 5.
2. W. Miller, 'The Connection Between SNP Voting and the Demand for Scottish Self-Government', *European Journal of Political Research* 5 (1977) 83–102.
3. See D. Heald, *Why We Need a Concept of Territorial Justice*, Discussion Paper no. 3, Policy Analysis Research Unit, Glasgow College of Technology (Glasgow, 1977).

Index

Lightning Source UK Ltd.
Milton Keynes UK
UKOW01f2017281216
290939UK00001B/104/P

9 781349 046805